The French Quarter

New Orleans' Oldest Neighborhood

Jason Lykins

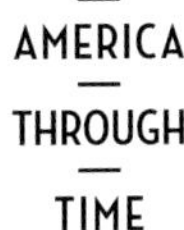

America Through Time®
An imprint of Sutton Publishing Inc
www.through-time.com

First published 2025

ISBN 978-1-63499-533-7

Typeset in Gotham Book
Printed and bound in England

Contents

Introduction

My story with New Orleans, particularly the French Quarter, is one of discovery, connection, and artistic inspiration. Born in Delaware to a Canadian mother, my early years were marked by a nomadic life, moving between Canada and the United States. This background, rich with cultural diversity, laid the foundation for my deep appreciation of places like New Orleans, where history and culture are not just preserved but lived.

Settling on the Mississippi Gulf Coast

Eventually, my family and I settled on the Mississippi Gulf Coast, a decision that placed us at the doorstep of New Orleans. This location was not chosen by chance but was drawn by the allure of the Gulf's natural beauty and its proximity to a city that pulses with life, history, and art. Living here provides a unique vantage point, where the rhythms of coastal life blend seamlessly with the vibrant heartbeat of New Orleans.

The French Quarter as a Canvas

For me, the French Quarter is more than a historic district; it is a canvas that changes with the light, the mood, and the moment. My journey into photography began under the tutelage of my father, a seasoned photographer for *The Tampa Tribune*. From him, I learned to see the world not just as it is, but as it feels. This skill became my passport to the soul of the French Quarter, a place I have grown to love for its vibrant tapestry of life.

With my Canon 6D Mark II, initially chosen for its prowess in low-light conditions during my daughter's cheerleading competitions, I have found a new purpose. It now helps me freeze the fleeting moments of the Quarter's daily life. Here, every corner tells a story. The musicians on the street corners, their fingers dancing over strings and keys, create symphonies that float through the air. The locals, with their easy smiles and rich histories, are as much a part of the architecture as the wrought-iron balconies and historic buildings.

I have always believed that the most authentic photographs are those taken when people are unaware, caught in their natural state. This philosophy guides me as I wander through the Quarter, camera in hand, capturing the candid expressions of joy, contemplation, and sometimes, sheer exuberance.

From the quirky signs that speak of the Quarter's unique character to the dogs that seem to embody the laid-back spirit of the place, each photograph in this book is a slice of life. The entertainers, with their flamboyant costumes and performances, add color to the monochrome history of the buildings. And the cyclists, weaving through the crowds, remind us of the city's pulse, always moving, always alive.

This book is not just a collection of images; it is my personal ode to the French Quarter. Through these pages, I invite you to see what I see: the beauty in the ordinary, the magic in the mundane. Join me in celebrating the people, the places, and the palpable atmosphere of New Orleans' oldest neighborhood, where every day is a festival of life.

1

The French Quarter

The Founding and Early Days

The French Quarter, or Vieux Carré, was established in 1718 by Jean-Baptiste Le Moyne de Bienville. This area was not just a settlement but a strategic military and commercial hub due to its location on the Mississippi River, making it vital for trade and defense.

The Original Forts

Five forts were constructed to safeguard New Orleans:

Fort St. Jean:	Named after Bienville's brother, located near Esplanade Avenue.
Fort Marigny:	Named after a French officer, near the French Market.
Fort St. Charles:	Named after Charles III of Spain, by the riverfront.
Fort de la Conception:	Also known as Fort St. Louis, near Jackson Square.
Fort Balise:	At the Mississippi's mouth, crucial for river defense.

The War of 1812 and the Battle of New Orleans

The Battle of New Orleans in 1815, led by Andrew Jackson with the aid of pirates like Jean Lafitte, free men of color, and Tennessee militia, was pivotal. This victory not only preserved New Orleans but also boosted American morale.

Jackson Square:	Originally Place d'Armes, renamed for Andrew Jackson, symbolizing his victory.

Spanish and French Influence

Despite its name, the Quarter was under Spanish rule from 1763 to 1801, then briefly French before the Louisiana Purchase in 1803. The Spanish influence is seen in architecture, while French culture remains dominant.

Survival Through Catastrophes

The Quarter has endured:

Fires: Major fires in 1788 and 1794 led to rebuilding with fire-resistant materials.

Hurricanes: Notably, Katrina in 2005, where the Quarter's elevated levees offered some protection.

Wars and Occupation: From the Civil War to World War II, experiencing economic and cultural shifts.

Notable Residents

The Quarter has housed:

Literary Figures: Like Tennessee Williams, who lived at 722 Toulouse Street, and William Faulkner, who wrote parts of *Absalom, Absalom!* here.

Musicians: Louis Armstrong, born in the nearby Tremé, often played in the Quarter. Jelly Roll Morton, a jazz pioneer, lived and performed here.

Politicians: Andrew Jackson, who practiced law here before his military fame.

Bourbon Street and Beyond

Bourbon Street, known for nightlife, is just one part of the Quarter. The neighborhood includes:

Residential Areas: Where locals maintain a vibrant community life, often in historic homes that have been passed down through generations or restored to their former glory.

Cultural Hubs: Preservation Hall, a bastion of traditional jazz, where musicians play in a setting that feels like stepping back in time. The Old Absinthe House, once a favorite haunt of famous figures like Mark Twain and Oscar Wilde, continues to serve its famous drink.

Art Galleries and Shops: Reflecting the Quarter's artistic heritage, these establishments range from high-end galleries to quirky boutiques, showcasing everything from local art to antiques.

The Mississippi River

The river provides:

Economic Vitality: Historically for trade, now for tourism with views of Algiers Point and ferry service. The riverfront has evolved from a working port to a tourist attraction, with riverboats offering jazz cruises.

Cultural Significance: The river's presence influences local culture, music, and literature. It is a muse for artists, a source of livelihood for fishermen, and a natural boundary that shapes the city's geography and identity.

Festivals and Events

French Quarter Festival: Celebrates local music and cuisine, filling the streets with stages for live performances and food stalls offering traditional dishes.

Mardi Gras: While city-wide, the Quarter is central with parades, balls, and the famous throwing of beads from balconies. It's a time when the city's spirit is at its most exuberant.

New Orleans Saint's: The New Orleans Saints, established in 1967, began as the NFL's laughingstock, often finishing last in their division. Their fortunes changed with the building of the Louisiana Superdome in 1975, providing them a permanent home. The team's only Super Bowl victory came in the 2009 season, defeating the Indianapolis Colts in Super Bowl XLIV, a triumph that symbolized New Orleans' resilience post-Hurricane Katrina. Despite fluctuating records, Saints fans, known as the "Who Dat" Nation, remain fiercely loyal, filling the Superdome with black and gold, their dedication unwavering, a testament to their love for the team and the city's indomitable spirit.

Jazz Fest: Although held in the Fair Grounds Race Course, its spirit permeates the Quarter, with many musicians performing in local venues before and after the main festival.

Music, Food, and Architecture

Music: From jazz's birth to modern genres, music permeates the Quarter's air. Clubs like Tipitina's and The Spotted Cat Music Club keep the tradition alive, with impromptu street performances adding to the soundtrack.

Cuisine: A fusion of Creole, Cajun, and influences from Africa, France, Spain, and the Caribbean. Iconic dishes like gumbo, jambalaya, and beignets from Café du Monde are staples, while restaurants like Commander's Palace offer fine dining with a local twist.

Architecture: A mix of French, Spanish, and American styles, with landmarks like St. Louis Cathedral, the Cabildo, and the Presbytère framing Jackson Square. The iron-lace balconies, courtyards, and shotgun houses are architectural features that define the Quarter.

The People

The Quarter's residents, from long-time locals to newcomers, contribute to its vibrant, diverse community life. This mix of people ensures that the French Quarter remains not just a tourist destination but a living, breathing neighborhood.

Local Characters: From street performers who've become local celebrities to shopkeepers who've run their businesses for decades, these individuals add to the Quarter's charm.

Artists and Writers: The Quarter has always attracted creatives. Modern artists and writers continue this tradition, often living in apartments above shops or in historic buildings, contributing to the cultural scene.

Activists and Advocates: The Quarter has been a hub for social and political activism, with residents often at the forefront of movements for preservation, civil rights, and cultural heritage.

Modern Challenges and Preservation

Preservation Efforts: The French Quarter has faced threats from modernization, gentrification, and natural disasters. Organizations like the Vieux Carré Property Owners, Residents & Associates work tirelessly to preserve its historic integrity.

Tourism *v.* Livability: Balancing the needs of residents with the demands of tourism is an ongoing challenge. Efforts are made to ensure that the Quarter remains a place where people live, not just visit.

Conclusion

The French Quarter's history is a tapestry woven from threads of resilience, cultural fusion, and continuous celebration of life. From its founding forts to its modern festivals, it remains a symbol of New Orleans' enduring spirit, where history is not just remembered but lived daily in its streets, music, food, and architecture. The Quarter's story is one of adaptation and survival, reflecting the broader narrative of New Orleans itself—a city that, against all odds, continues to thrive, celebrate, and inspire.

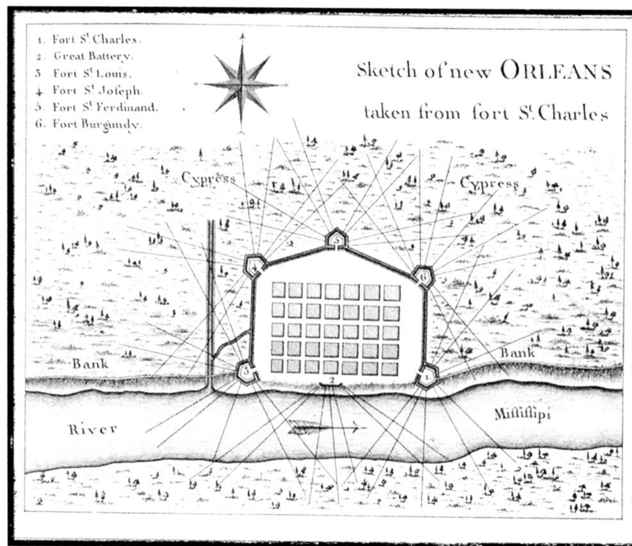

Five forts were constructed to safeguard New Orleans: Fort St. Jean; Fort Marigny; Fort St. Charles; Fort de la Conception; and Fort Balise. (*Photo Courtesy: neworleanshistorical.org/*)

2

The Heartbeat of the Quarter

In the French Quarter, every day is a parade of life, where the ordinary becomes extraordinary. This chapter is dedicated to the people who breathe life into this historic neighborhood, each contributing to the vibrant mosaic that is the Quarter.

The Residents and Workers: First, there are those who call the Quarter home. From the shopkeepers who open their doors to the world, sharing stories of the city's past and present, to the bartenders who mix not just drinks but memories. These are the people who live in the shadow of history, their lives intertwined with the streets they walk daily. They are the true custodians of the Quarter's spirit, preserving its authenticity amidst the tourist throngs.

The Entertainers: Then come the entertainers, the street performers who transform every corner into a stage. With their music, magic, and dance, they draw crowds, creating spontaneous moments of joy. From the jazz musicians whose notes echo through the night, to the living statues that challenge your perception of reality, these artists are the Quarter's heartbeat, pulsating with creativity and passion.

Wedding Parties and Clergy: The Quarter also witnesses the union of lives, where wedding parties spill out from historic churches, their laughter and cheers mingling with the hymns that float from within. Here, the clergy, in their solemn robes, add a touch of timelessness, reminding us of the sacred amid the secular.

The Visitors: And then there are the visitors, drawn like moths to the flame of the Quarter's allure. They come from every corner of the globe, seeking the magic that this place holds. Whether they're here for Mardi Gras, Jazz Fest, or just a random Tuesday, they are all part of the tapestry. Their cameras click, capturing moments, but it is their eyes, wide with wonder, that truly photograph the soul of the Quarter.

The Essence of the Quarter

When you strip away the architecture, the history, and the cuisine, it is the people who define the French Quarter. They are the living history, the ongoing story, the ever-evolving culture. From the locals who have seen it all to the tourists experiencing it for the first time, each person adds a note to the symphony of life here.

In this chapter, I aim to capture not just their faces but their essence, the way they interact with this place, how they contribute to its rhythm. Through these photographs, I invite you to meet the people of the French Quarter, to see them as I do: as the true architects of its enduring charm.

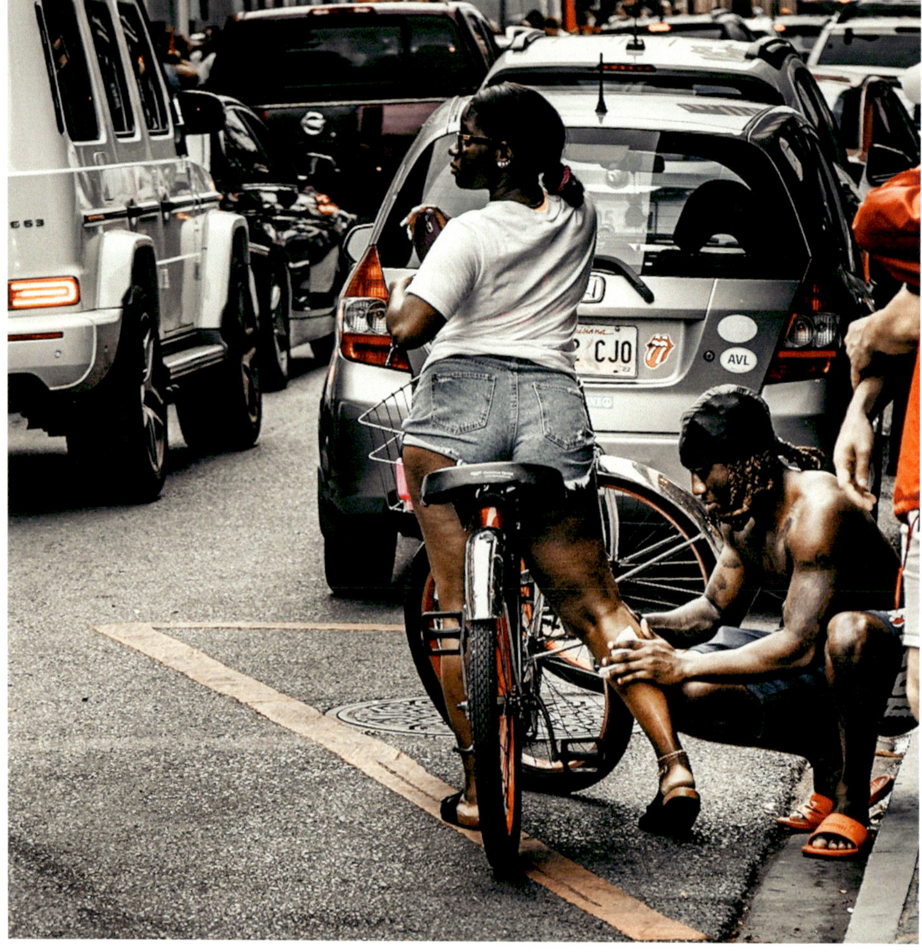

In the heart of the French Quarter, love finds its canvas in the simplest acts, like this tender moment where care and affection are as much a part of the scenery as the historic streets themselves.

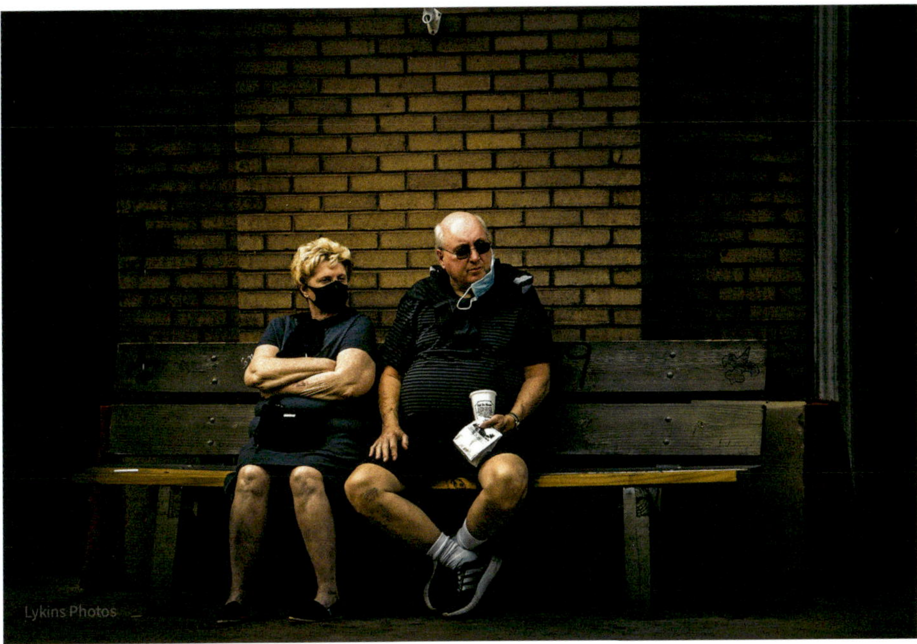

Amid the hustle of the French Quarter, this quiet bench outside the fire station becomes a sanctuary for love that has weathered the years, a testament to enduring companionship.

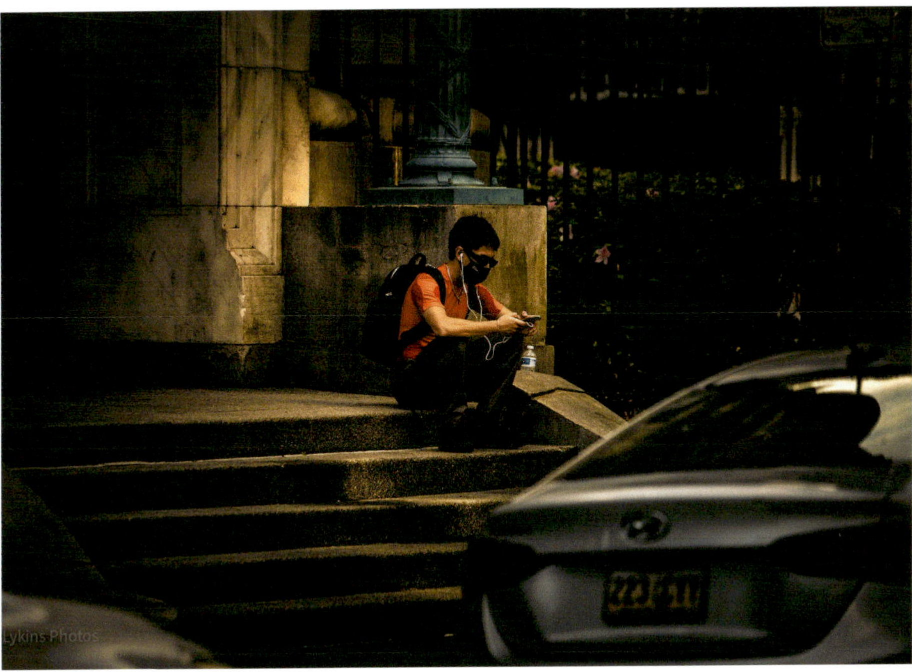

Lost in his world yet surrounded by history, he finds his own moment of peace on the steps of the French Quarter, where the past whispers and the present scrolls by.

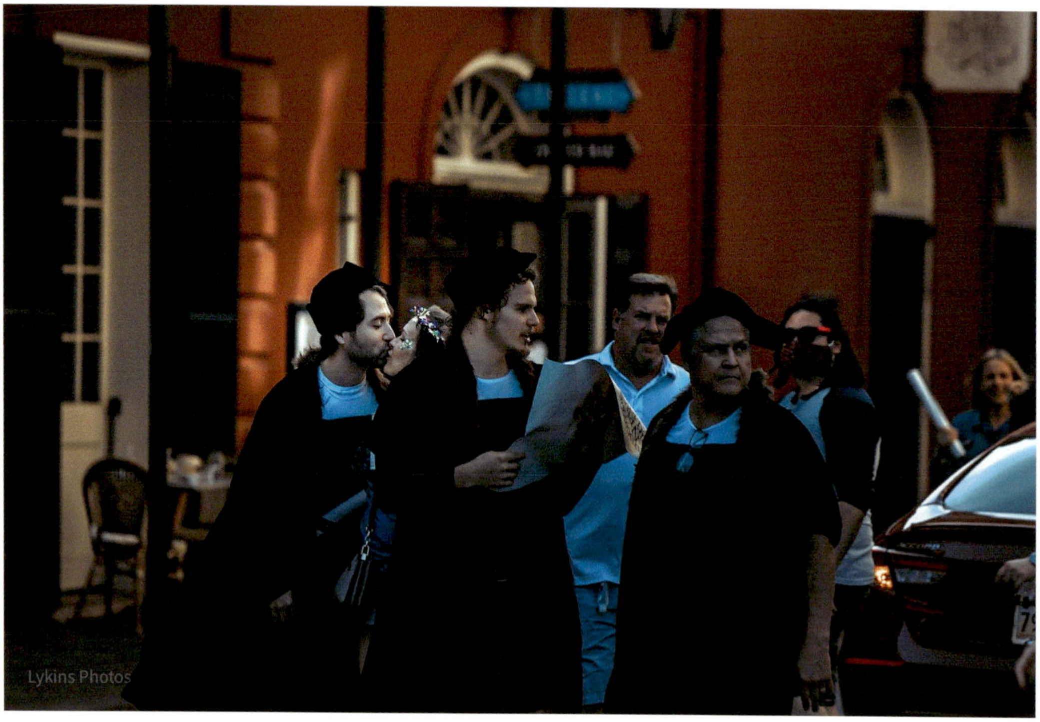

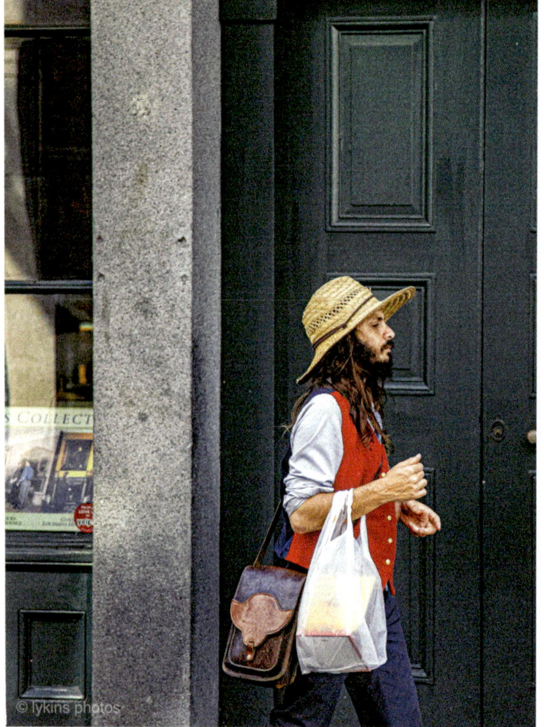

Above: Amid the reenactment of history in the French Quarter, a timeless kiss sneaks through, proving that love, like the spirit of New Orleans, transcends all eras.

Left: With a wide-brimmed hat and a cool leather satchel, this gentleman strides through the French Quarter, his groceries a testament to the day's simple joys, heading home with style.

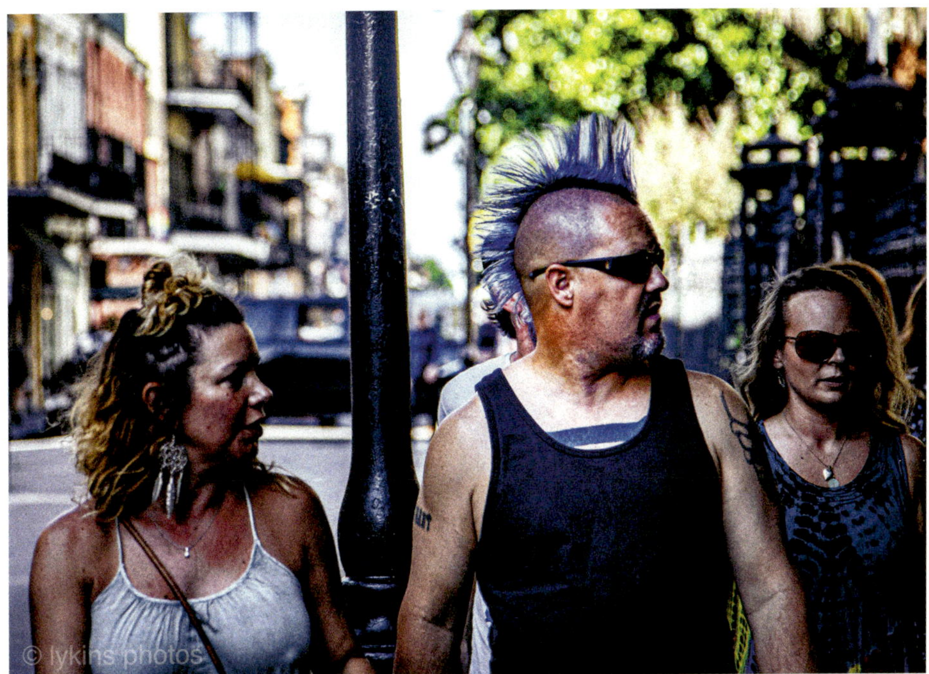

In the vibrant tapestry of the French Quarter, a couple pauses, his tall purple mohawk standing out like a beacon of individuality, as they soak in the historic charm together.

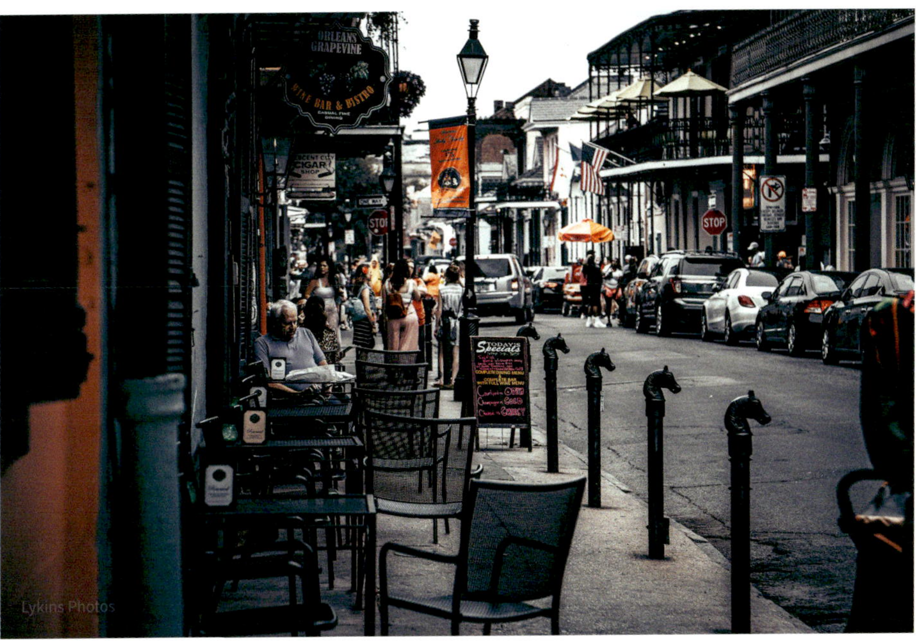

Savoring the morning's first light and the aroma of fresh coffee, he finds his perfect spot on the sidewalk, where the French Quarter serves up breakfast with a side of life.

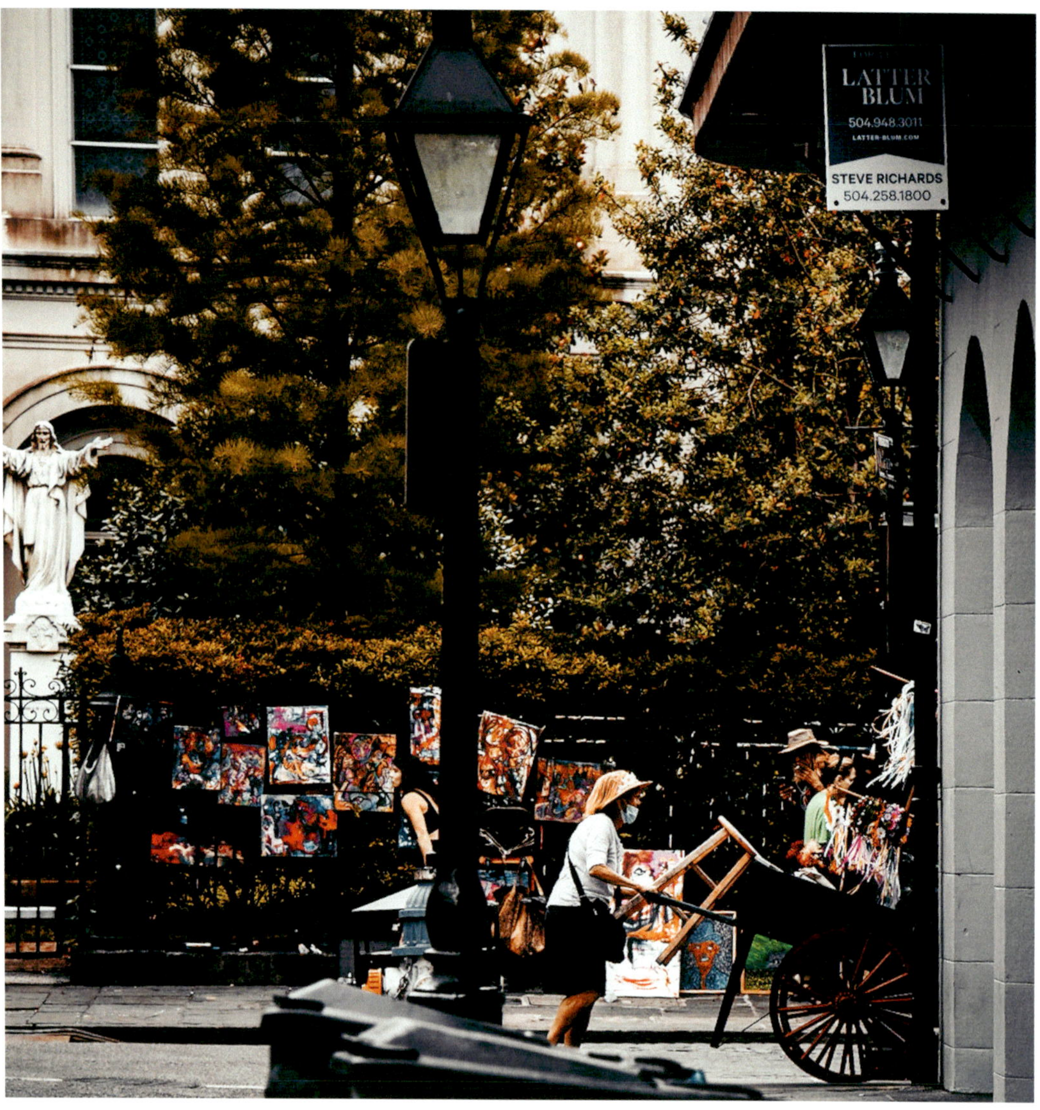

With the sun as his spotlight, he navigates the cobblestones, his cart a mobile gallery, seeking the perfect corner in the French Quarter to showcase his art.

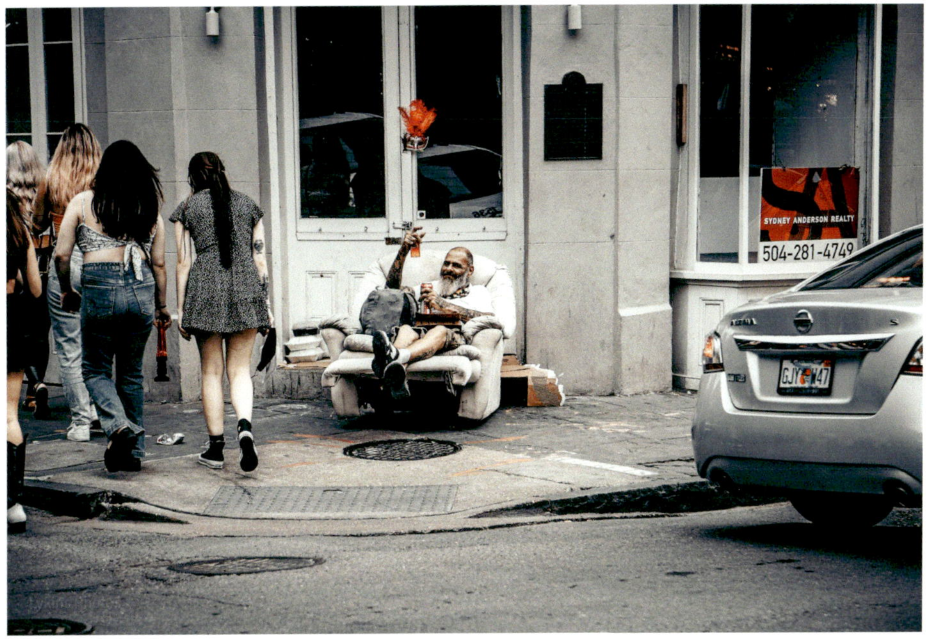

From his throne of humor, a recliner on the French Quarter's stage, he spins tales and jests, turning every passerby into an audience for his wit.

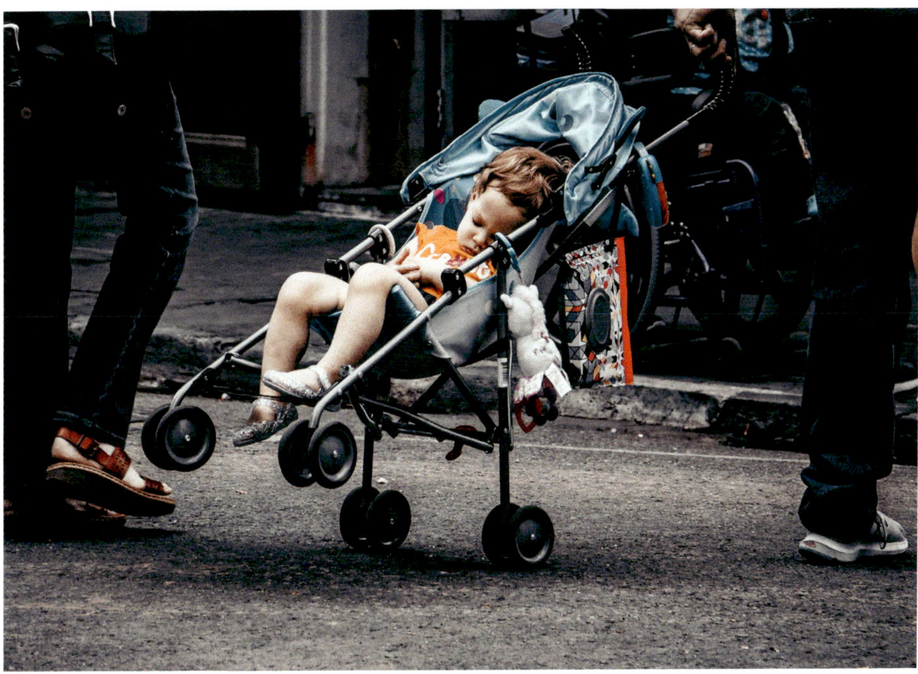

In the lull of a New Orleans' afternoon, a child dreams on, blissfully unaware, as his parents navigate the French Quarter's charm, their love a gentle pull through cobblestone dreams.

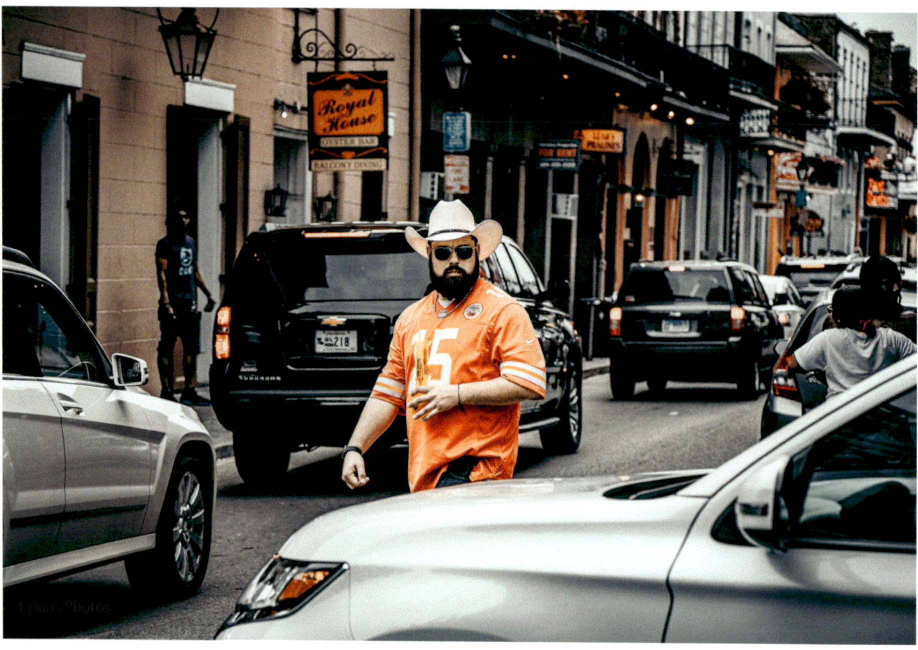

In a city where Saints jerseys reign, he stands out with a cowboy hat, confidently parading his unique spirit through the French Quarter, a testament to individuality.

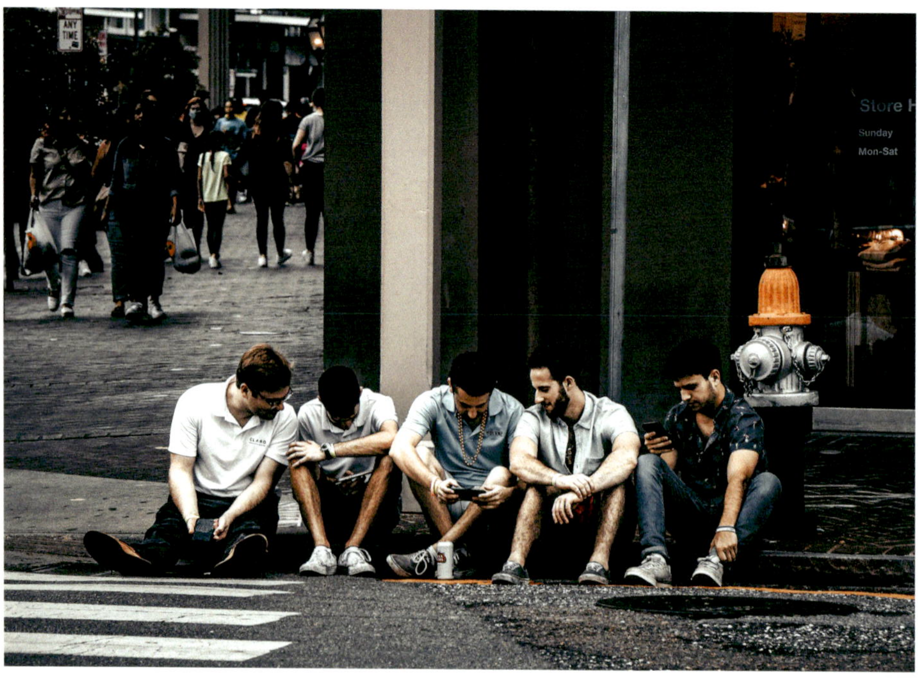

"The boys," gathered curbside in the French Quarter, erupt in laughter over a phone screen, their joy a spontaneous symphony amidst the historic backdrop.

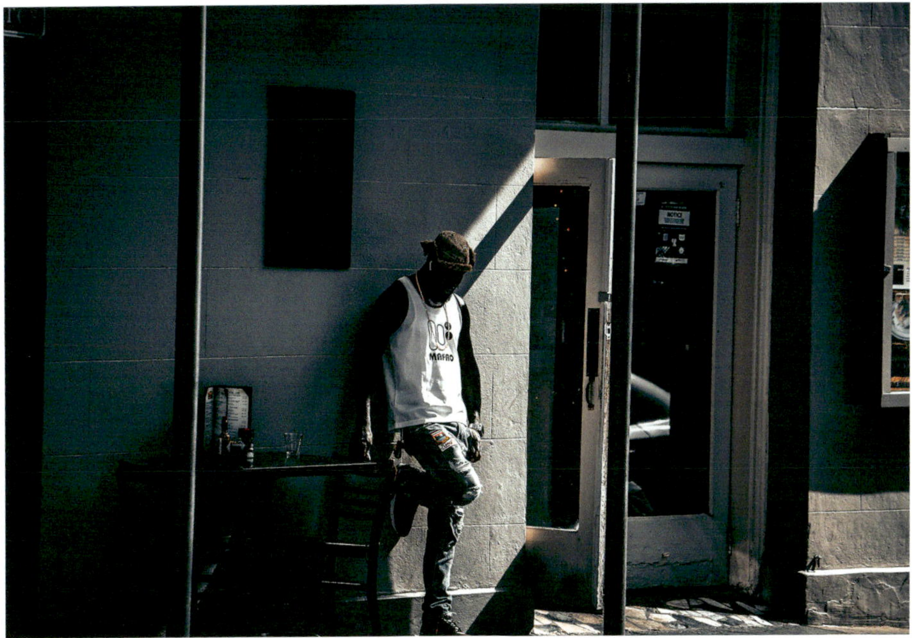

Channeling the spirit of an old west gunslinger, he leans against the café wall in the French Quarter, his pose a nod to bygone days of quick draws and quiet contemplation.

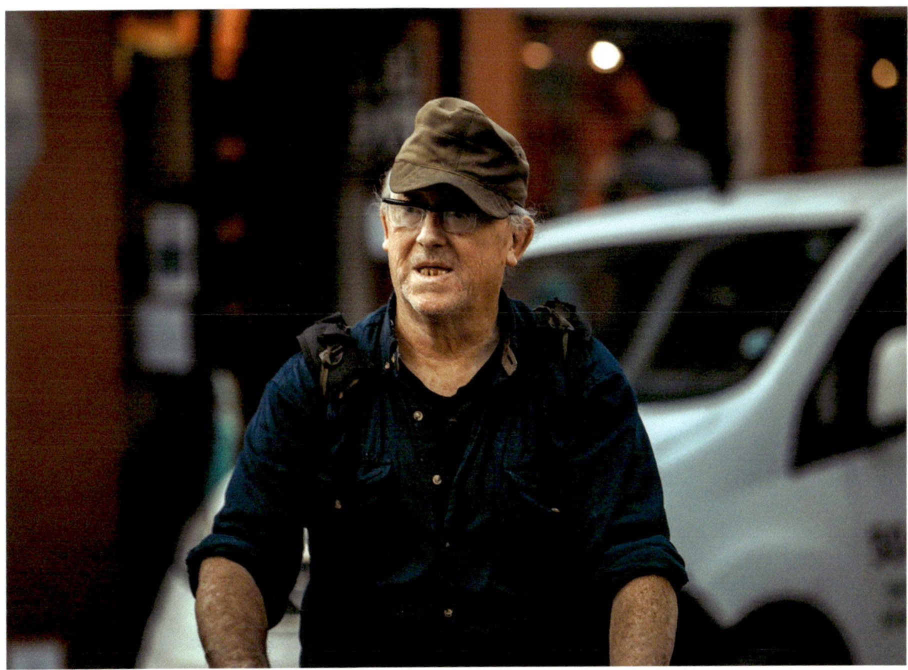

A mountain man reborn, he strolls through the French Quarter, his fresh shave contrasting with his rugged attire, a modern trapper navigating urban wilderness.

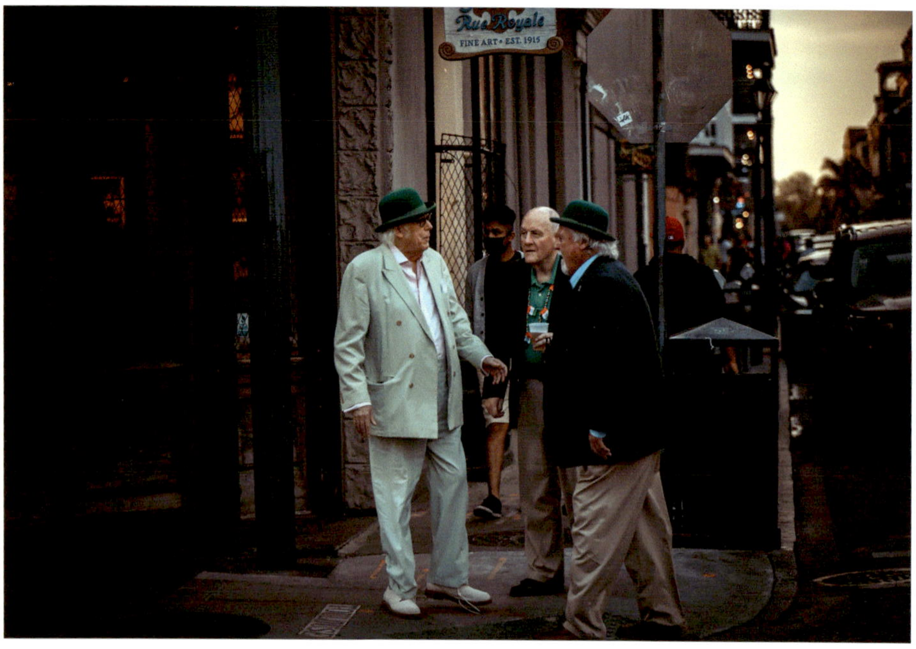

On St. Patrick's Day in the French Quarter, these three gents, adorned in green hats, raise their pints in camaraderie, proving age is but a number when it comes to festive spirits.

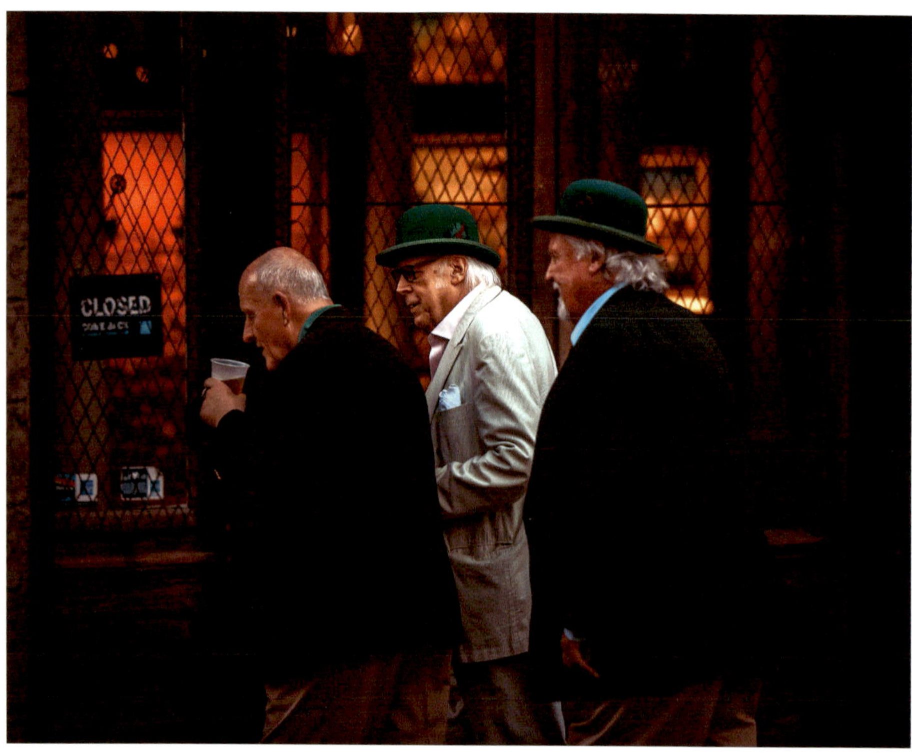

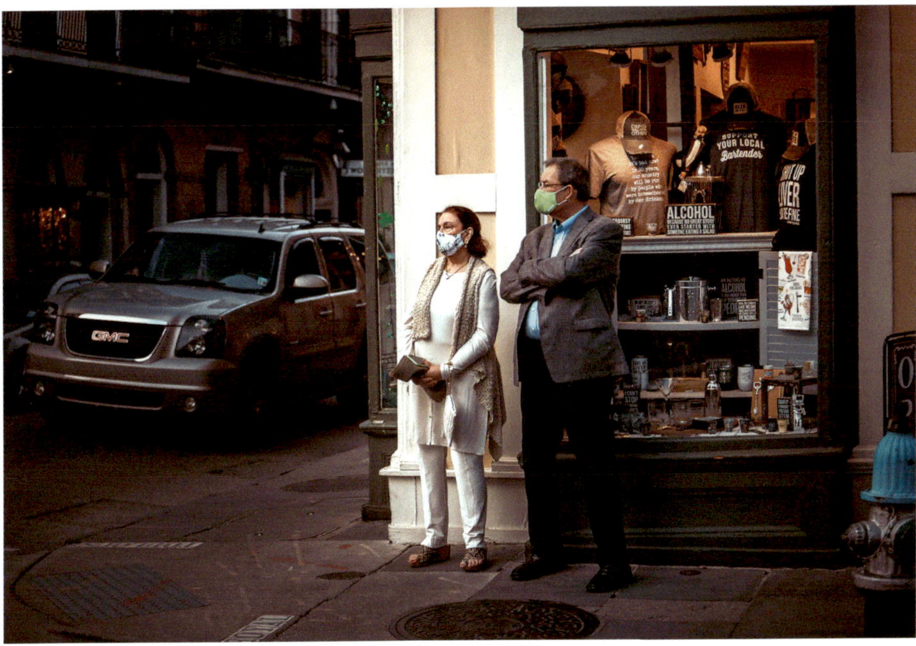

In the quiet anticipation of their Uber, this couple stands in the French Quarter, their silence speaking volumes of shared moments and the city's nocturnal whispers.

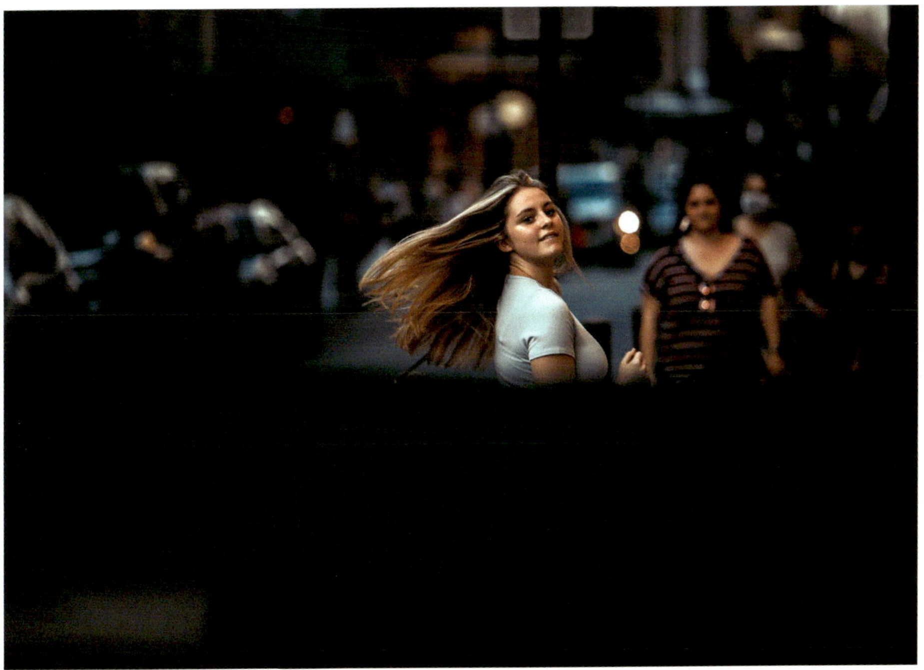

In a twirl of youth and beauty, she catches the lens, her hair a cascade of motion, turning the French Quarter into her personal runway of joy.

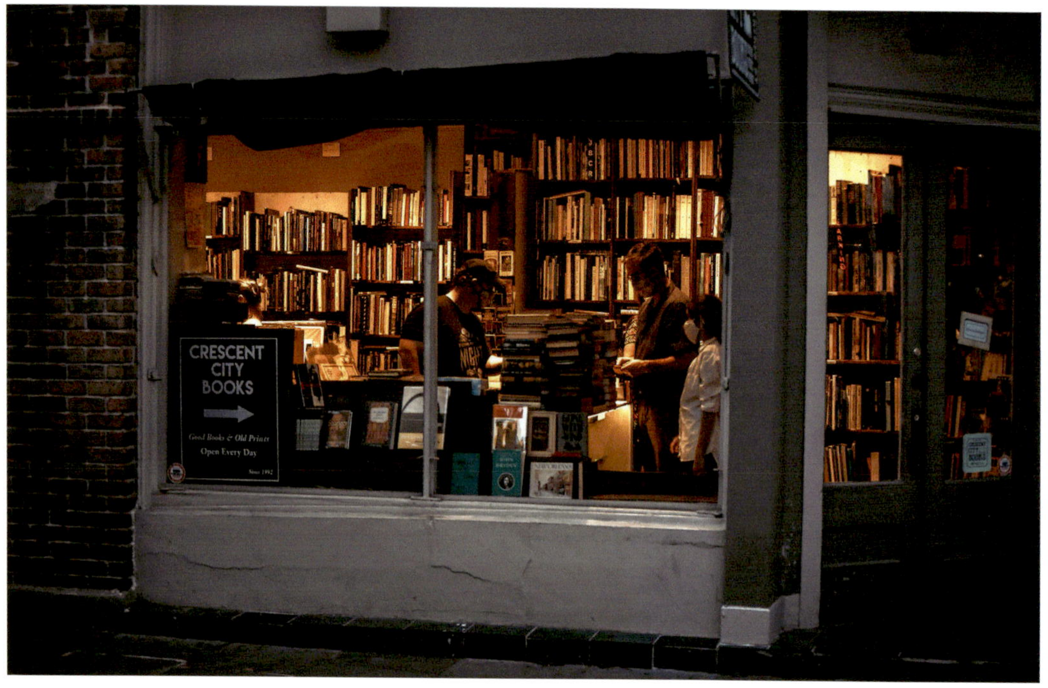

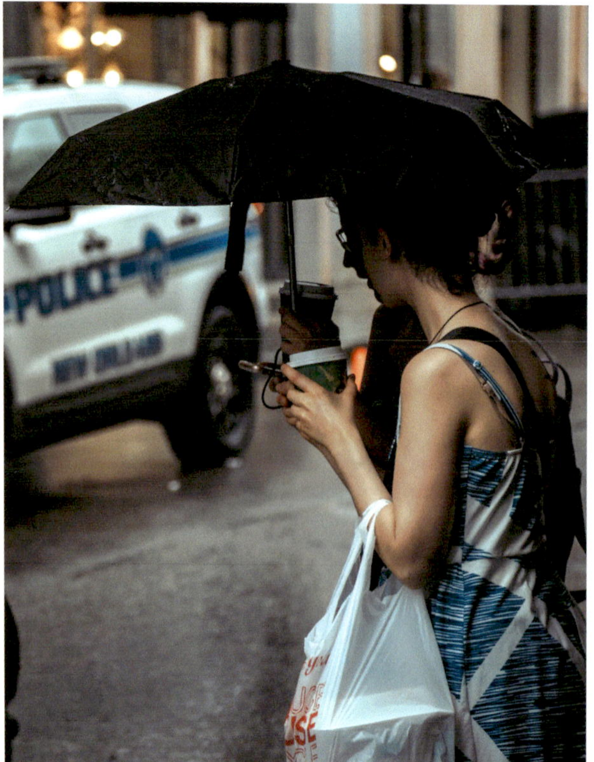

Above: Inside Crescent City Books, where stories come alive, patrons make their selections, each purchase a new chapter in their personal library of adventures.

Left: Under the shelter of an umbrella, this couple finds solace in their coffees, the rain's gentle patter a calming backdrop in the French Quarter's cozy embrace.

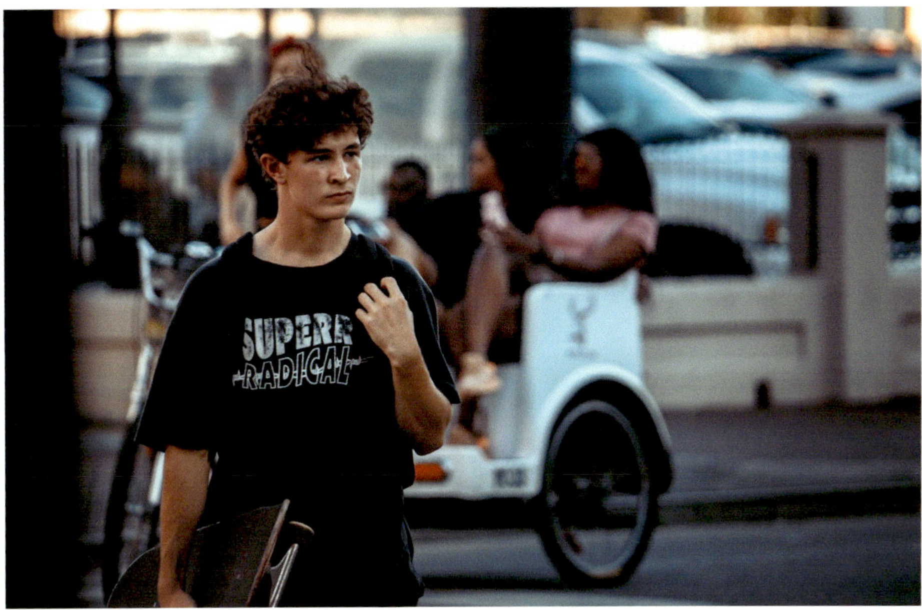

Rolling through time, this skater, board in hand, sports an '80s retro tee, blending the French Quarter's historic charm with a dash of vintage cool.

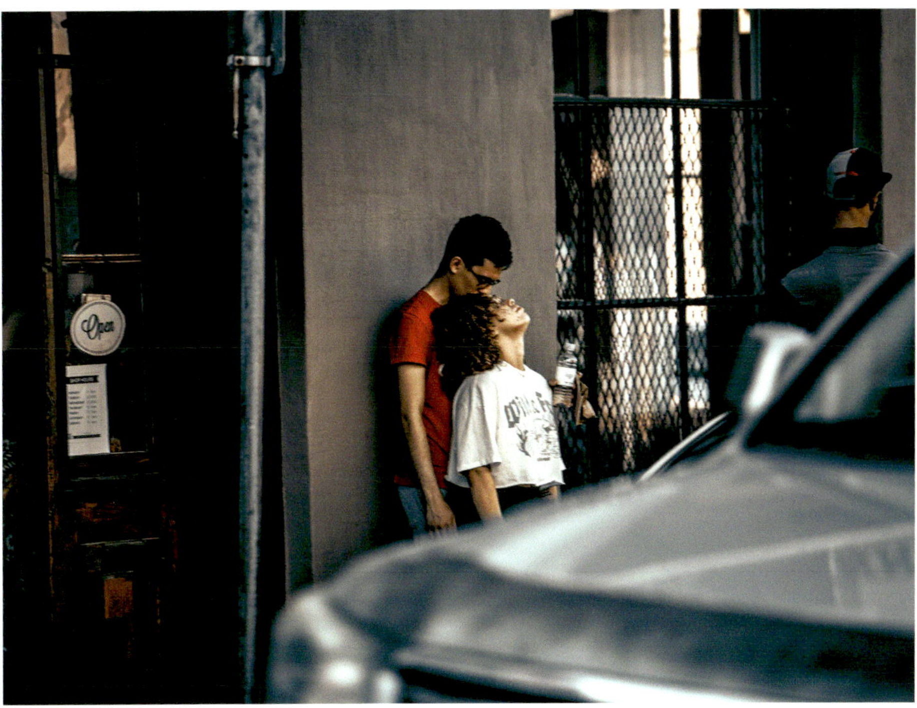

In the heart of the French Quarter, their love story writes itself; she leans, he kisses, and the world around them fades into a backdrop of timeless affection.

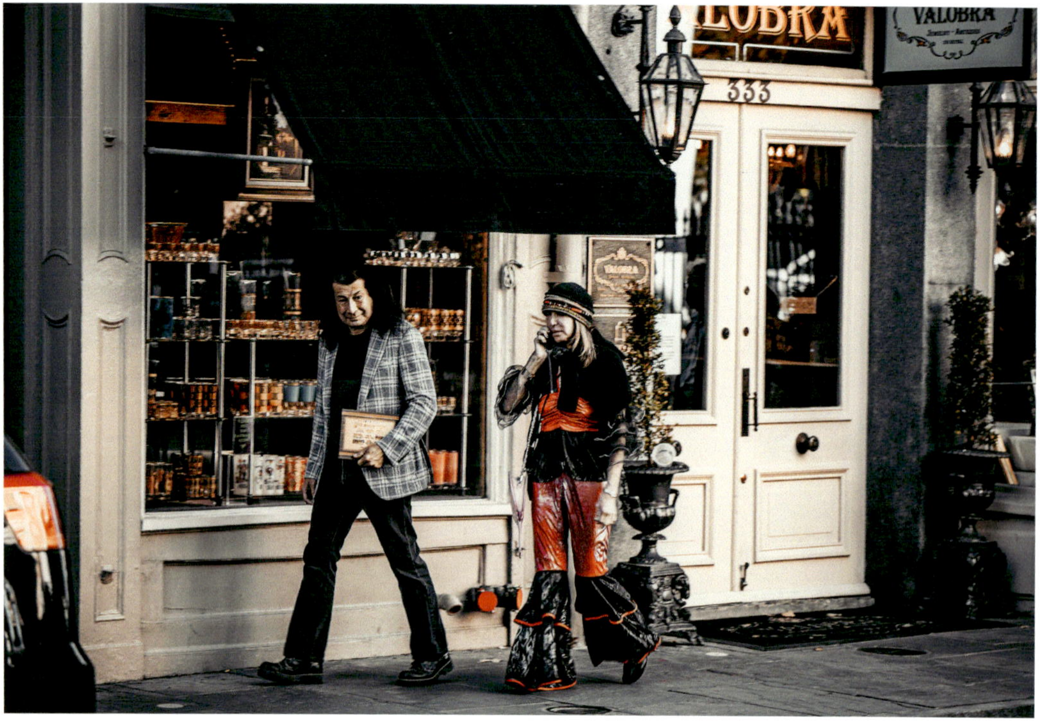

Strolling through the French Quarter, he in his timeless plaid, she in her Halloween splendor, they blend the everyday with the fantastical, a couple in perfect harmony with the city's eclectic spirit.

Opposite page: With the air of a spectral sage, he grips his staff, leading the way through the French Quarter's "Haunted History," his presence as eerie as the tales he tells.

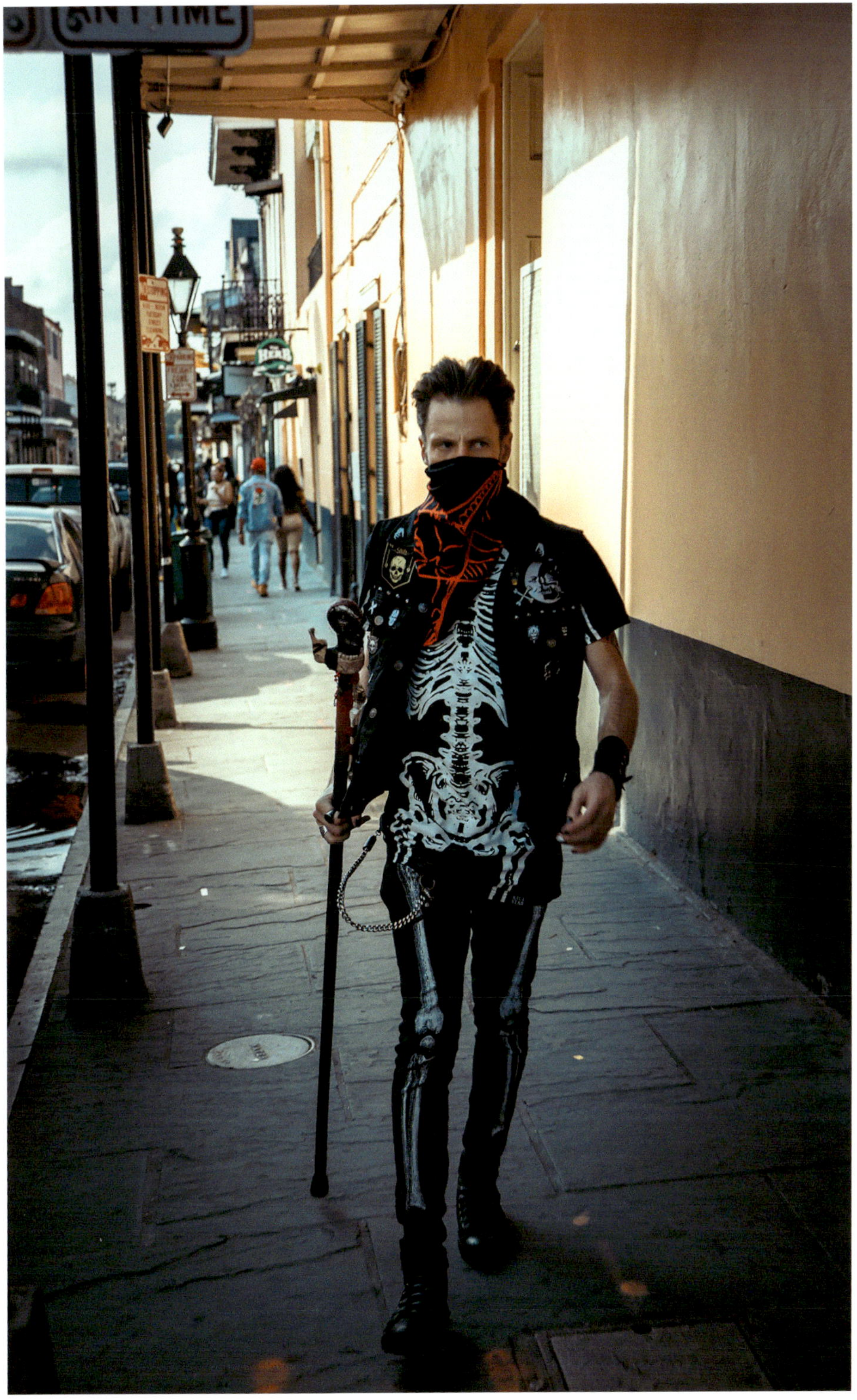

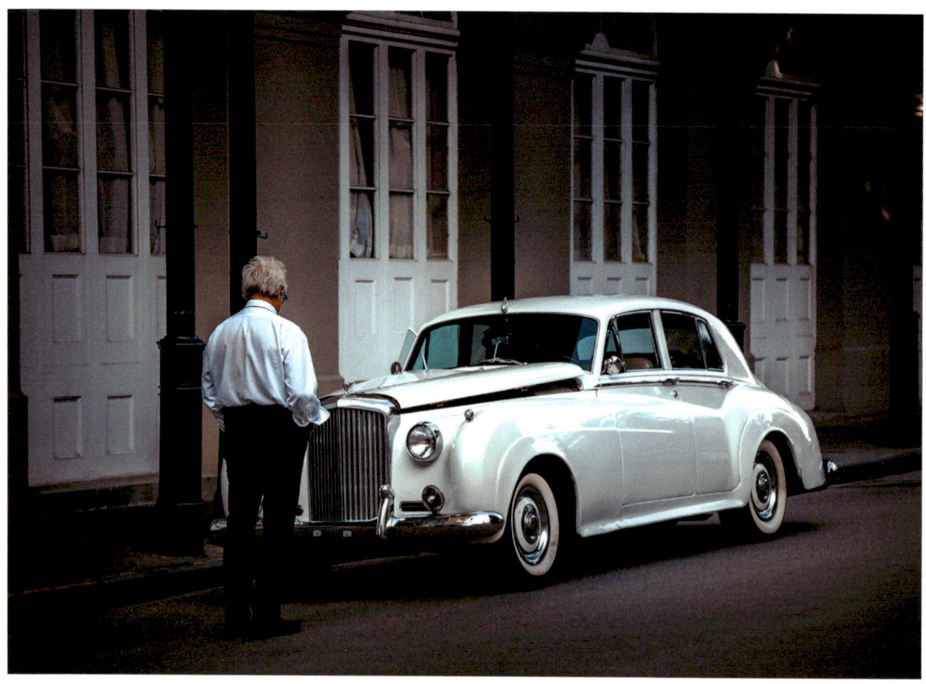

Is he the chauffeur or merely an admirer? In the French Quarter, he stands entranced by the sleek lines of a Rolls-Royce, where luxury meets mystery on every corner.

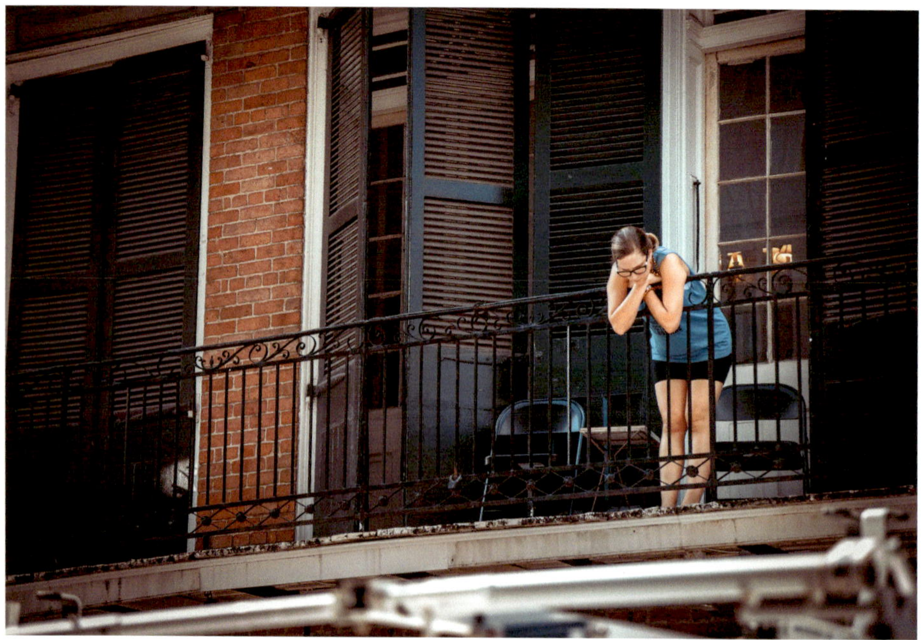

From her perch above the bustling streets, she leans, a silent observer of the French Quarter's theater below, where life plays out in vibrant scenes.

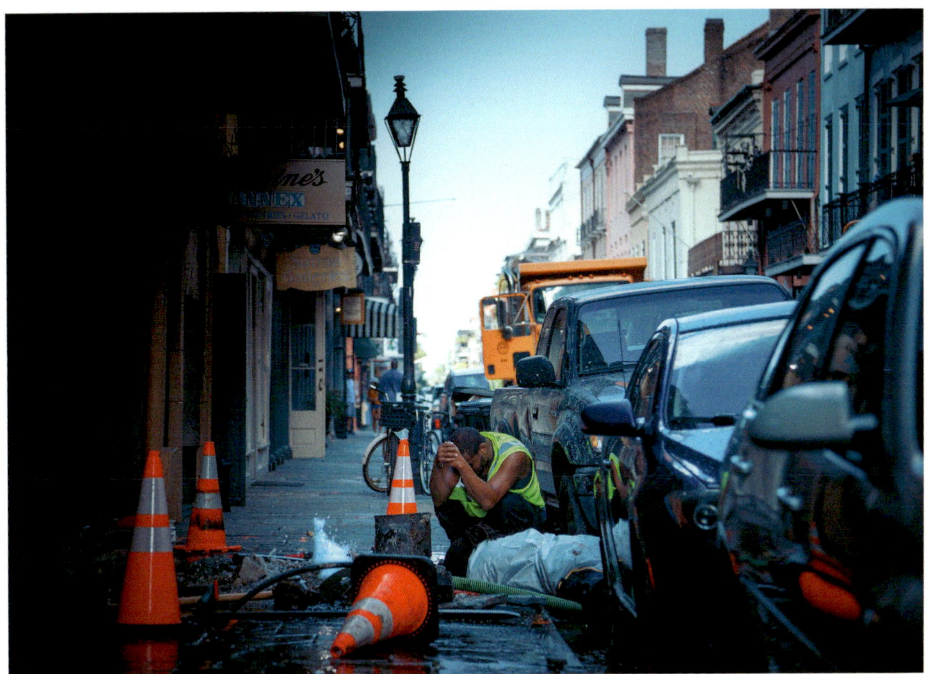

Amid the chaos of a busted pipe, one city worker seems to pray for a fix, their dedication to the French Quarter's infrastructure a quiet act of faith.

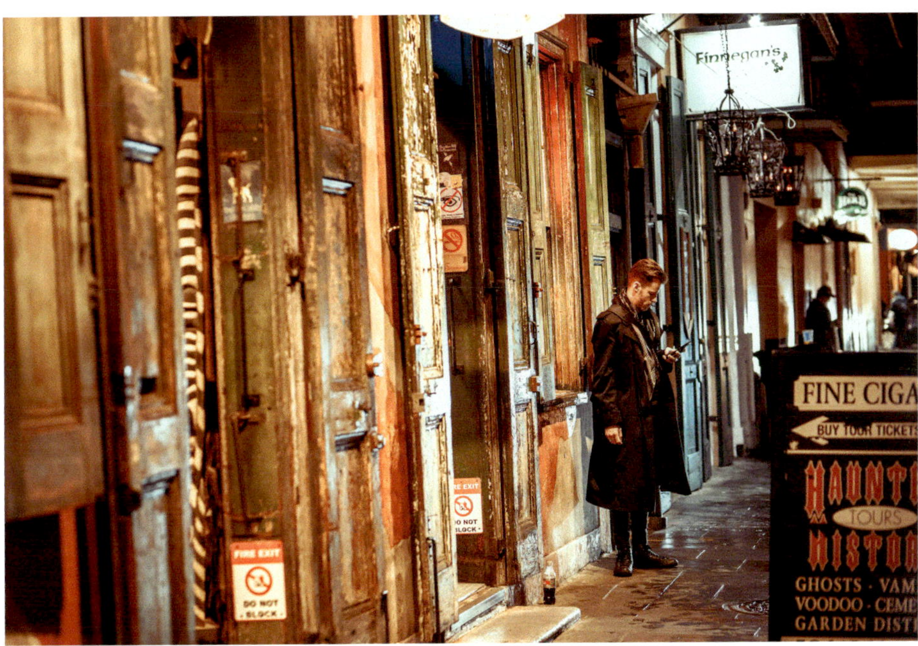

In the momentary lull, the "Haunted History" tour guide checks his phone, a modern pause in the ancient tales he's about to weave through the French Quarter's shadowy streets.

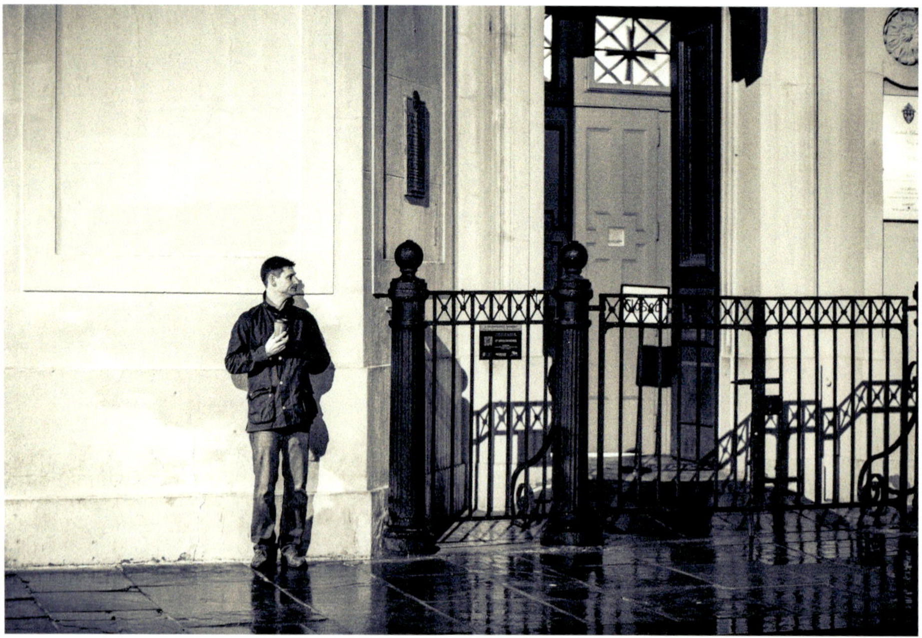

Leaning against the cathedral, coffee in hand, he absorbs the French Quarter's timeless beauty, where every sip and sight is a moment of pure New Orleans magic.

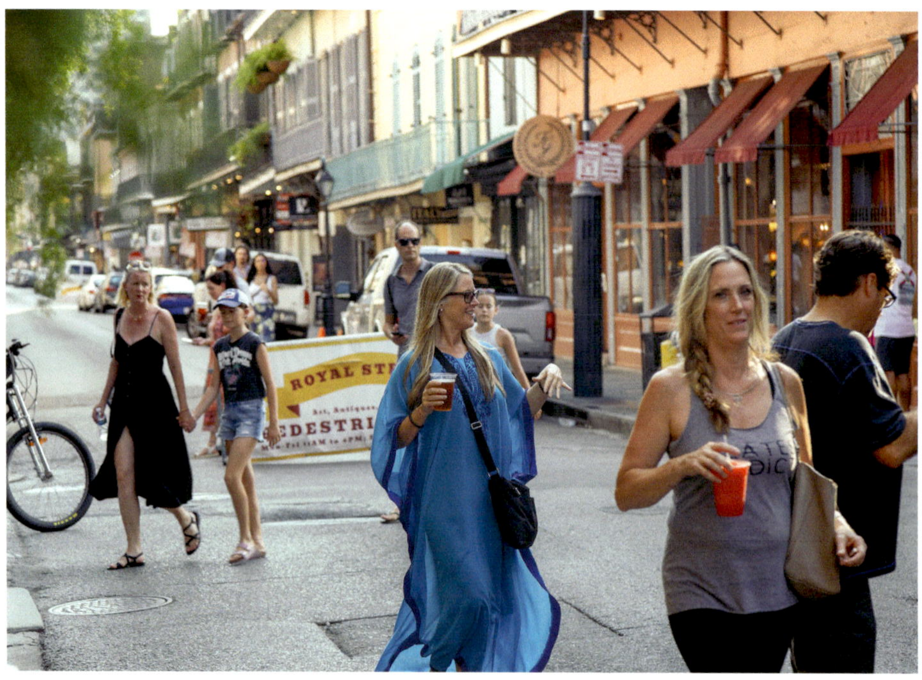

In the rhythm of the street, she dances, embodying the soul of New Orleans, where every step is a celebration of culture, music, and unbridled joy.

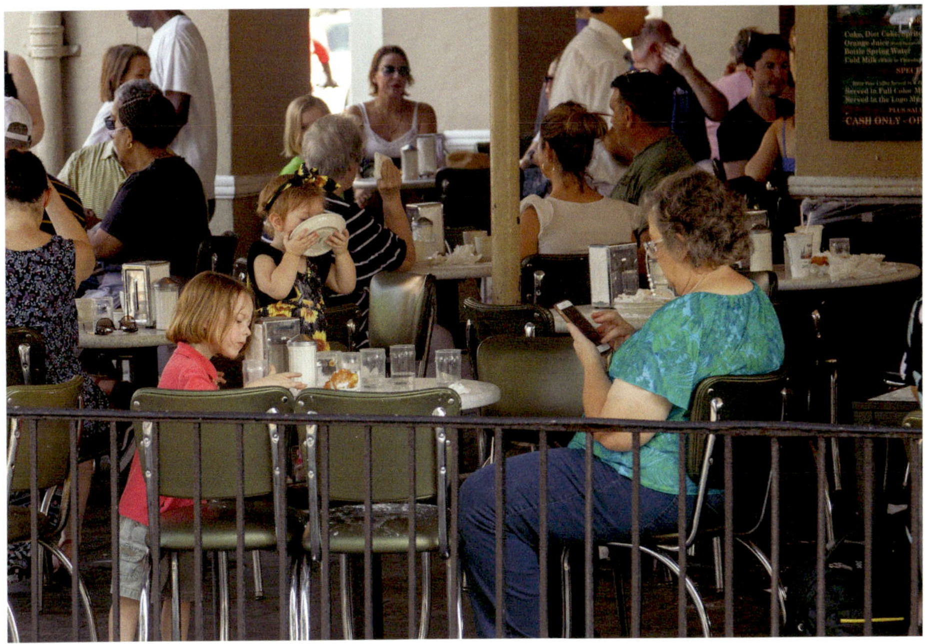

As grandma's eyes are on her phone, a little girl captures the sweetest moment at Café du Monde, her tongue reaching for the last of the powdered sugar, a scene of pure innocence amid the hustle.

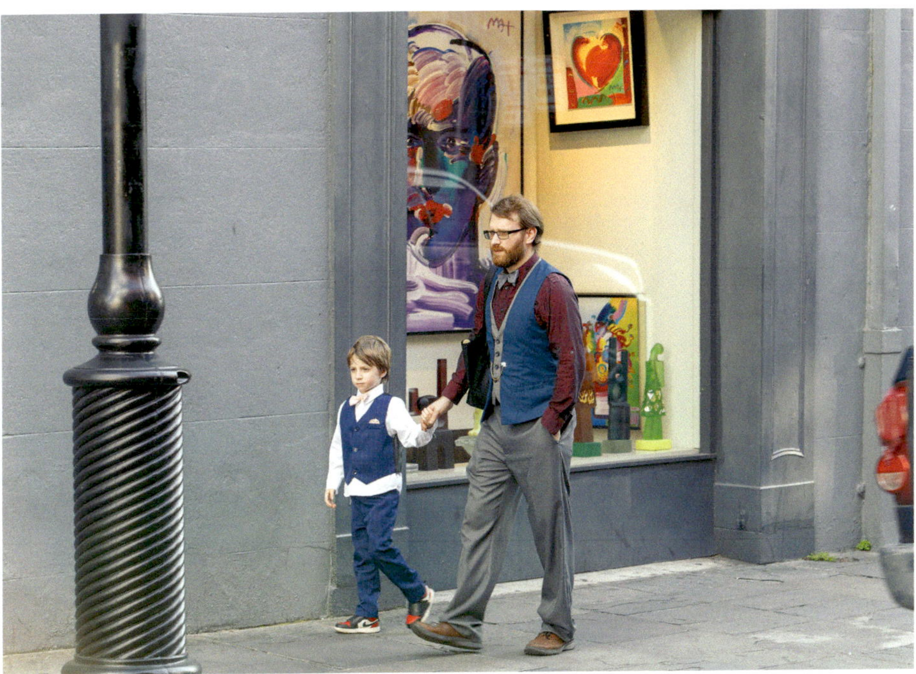

Matching in blue vests, a father and son stroll past an art gallery in the French Quarter, their journey through life's gallery just beginning.

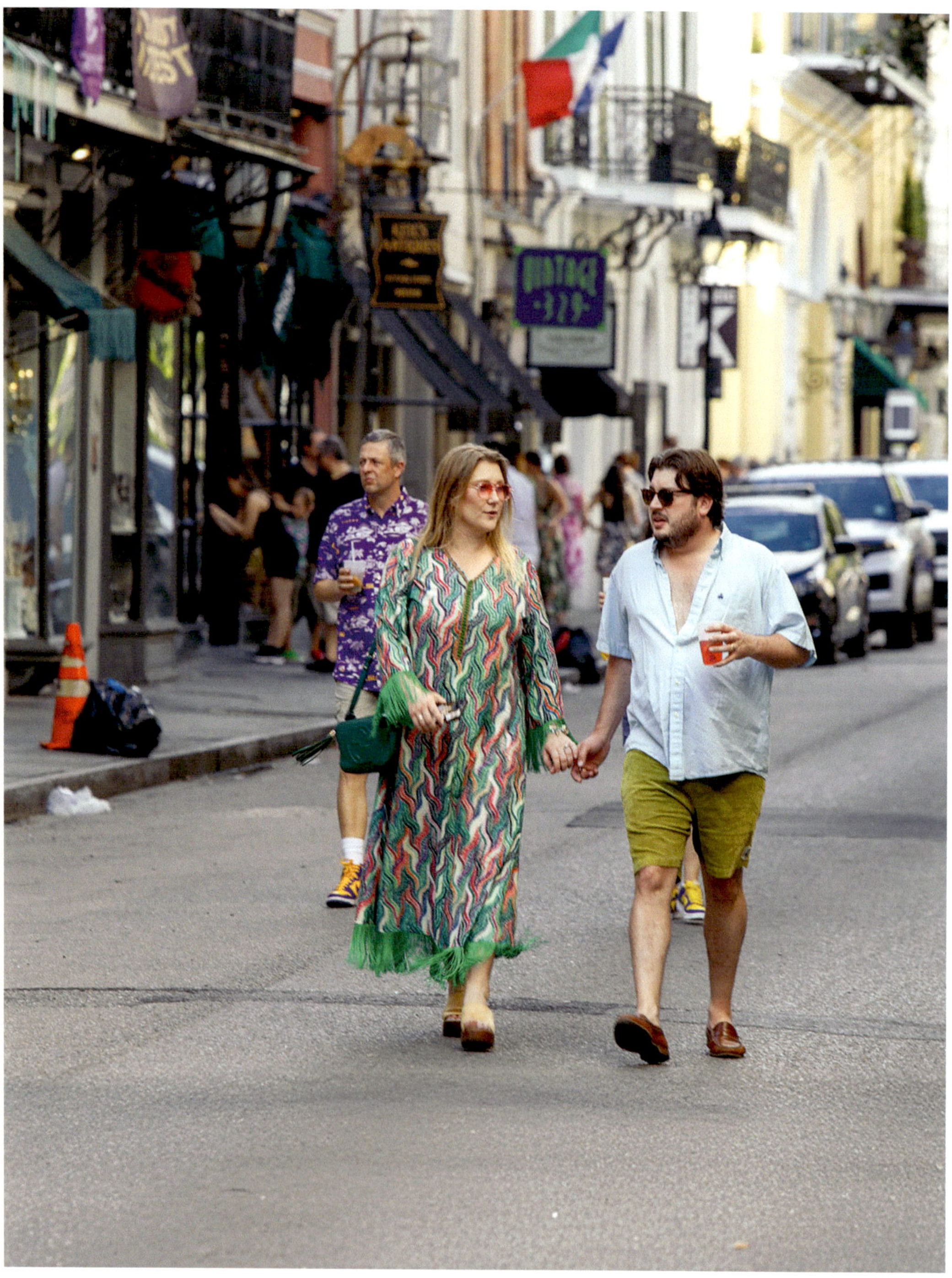

Hand in hand, they walk through time, she with the flair of the '70s, he with the vibe of the '80s, their love a timeless fusion in the French Quarter's ever-evolving scene.

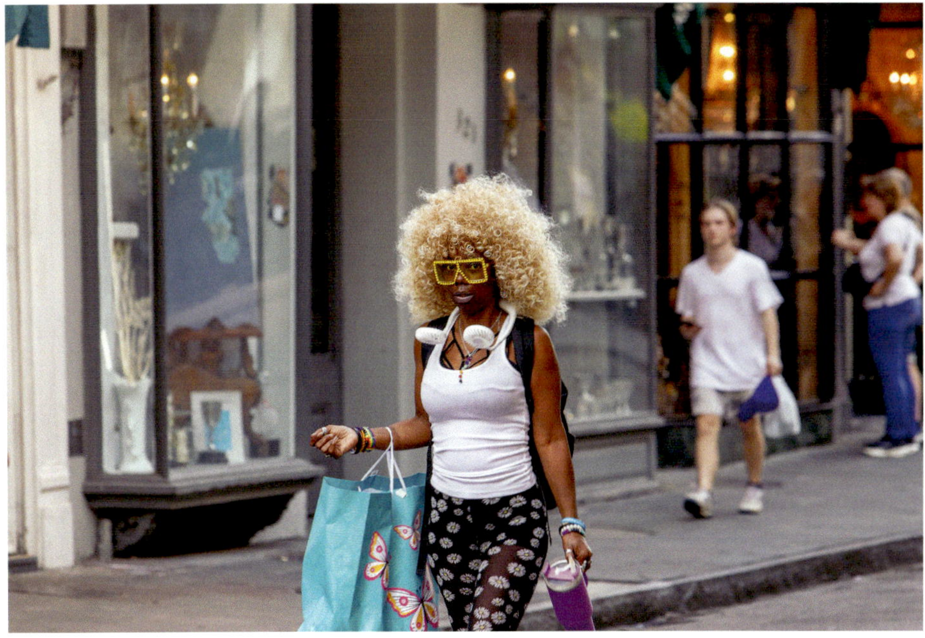

With a blonde wig and oversized yellow glasses, she is ready to take on the town, her shopping bags in tow, a walking testament to the French Quarter's vibrant character.

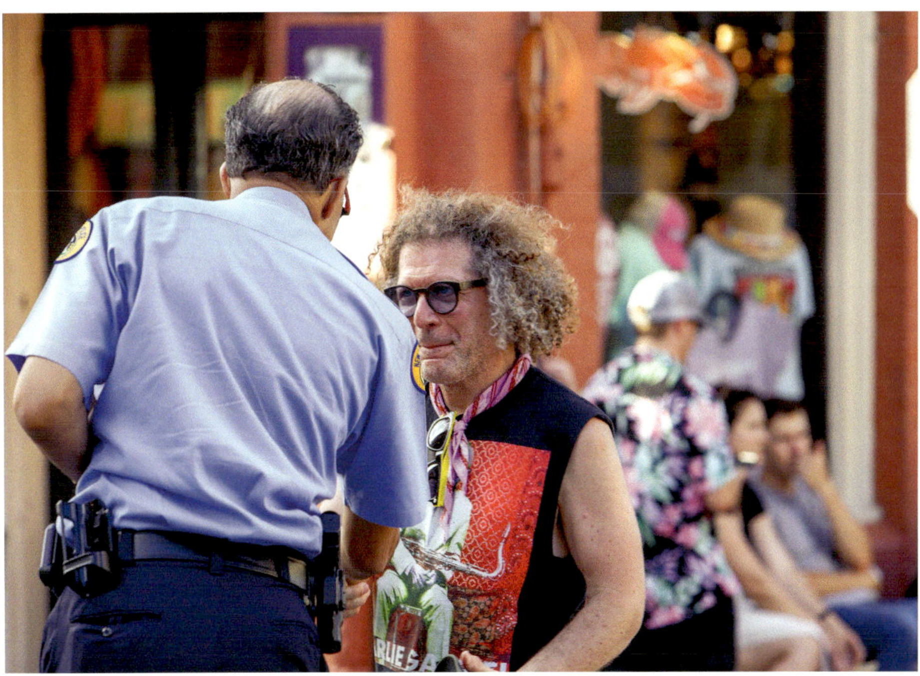

With a knowing smirk, he greets the officer, their friendship a nod to the tight-knit community spirit of the French Quarter, where even law enforcement feels like family.

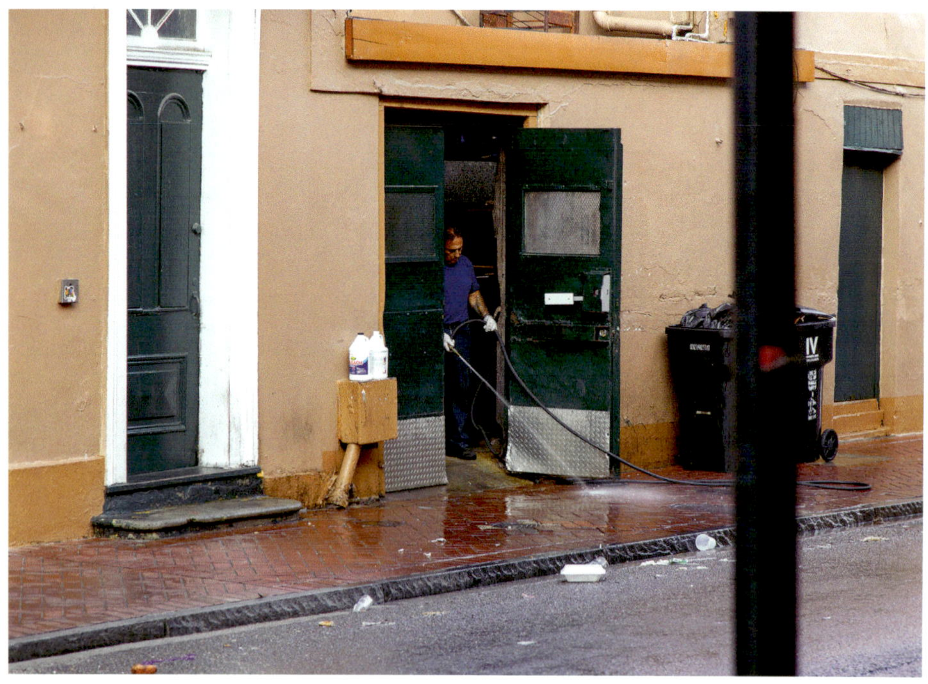

In the early morning light, he sprays down the sidewalk, washing away the remnants of last night's revelry, restoring the French Quarter to its daily charm.

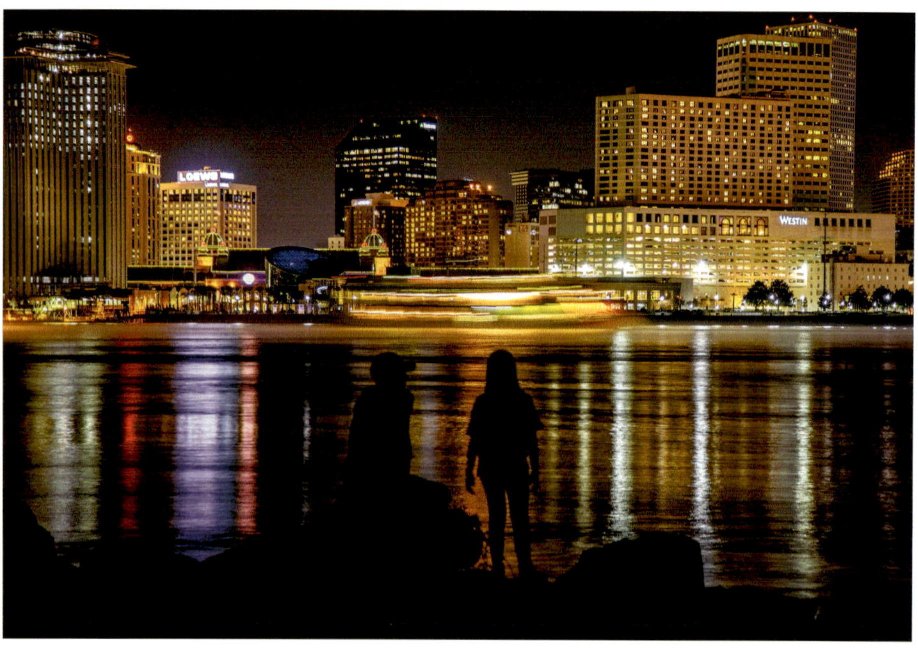

From Algiers Point, father and daughter gaze upon the French Quarter, its lights dancing on the Mississippi, a shared moment of beauty across the river's divide.

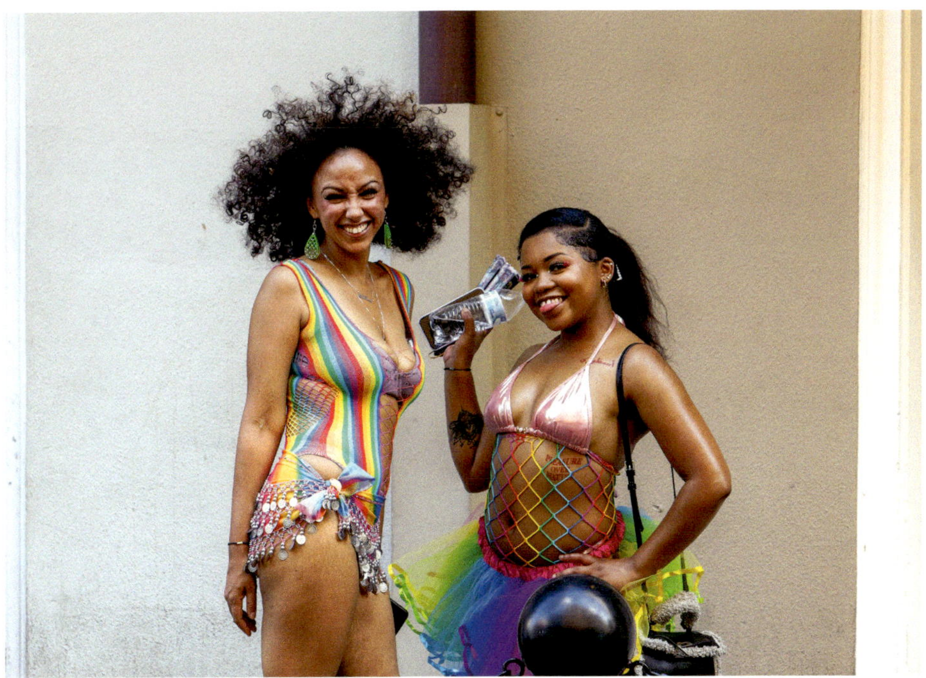

In a burst of rainbow hues, they pose, their scantily clad figures a vibrant splash against the French Quarter's historic backdrop, celebrating youth and freedom.

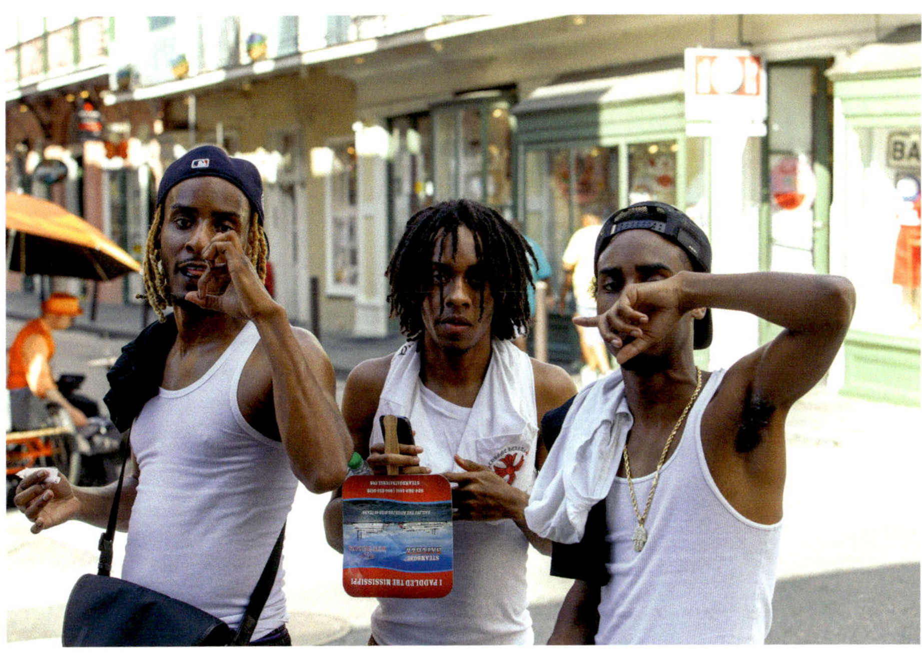

With a playful nod to the camera, they throw gang signs, asking for a photo, their youthful energy adding a modern twist to the French Quarter's timeless streets.

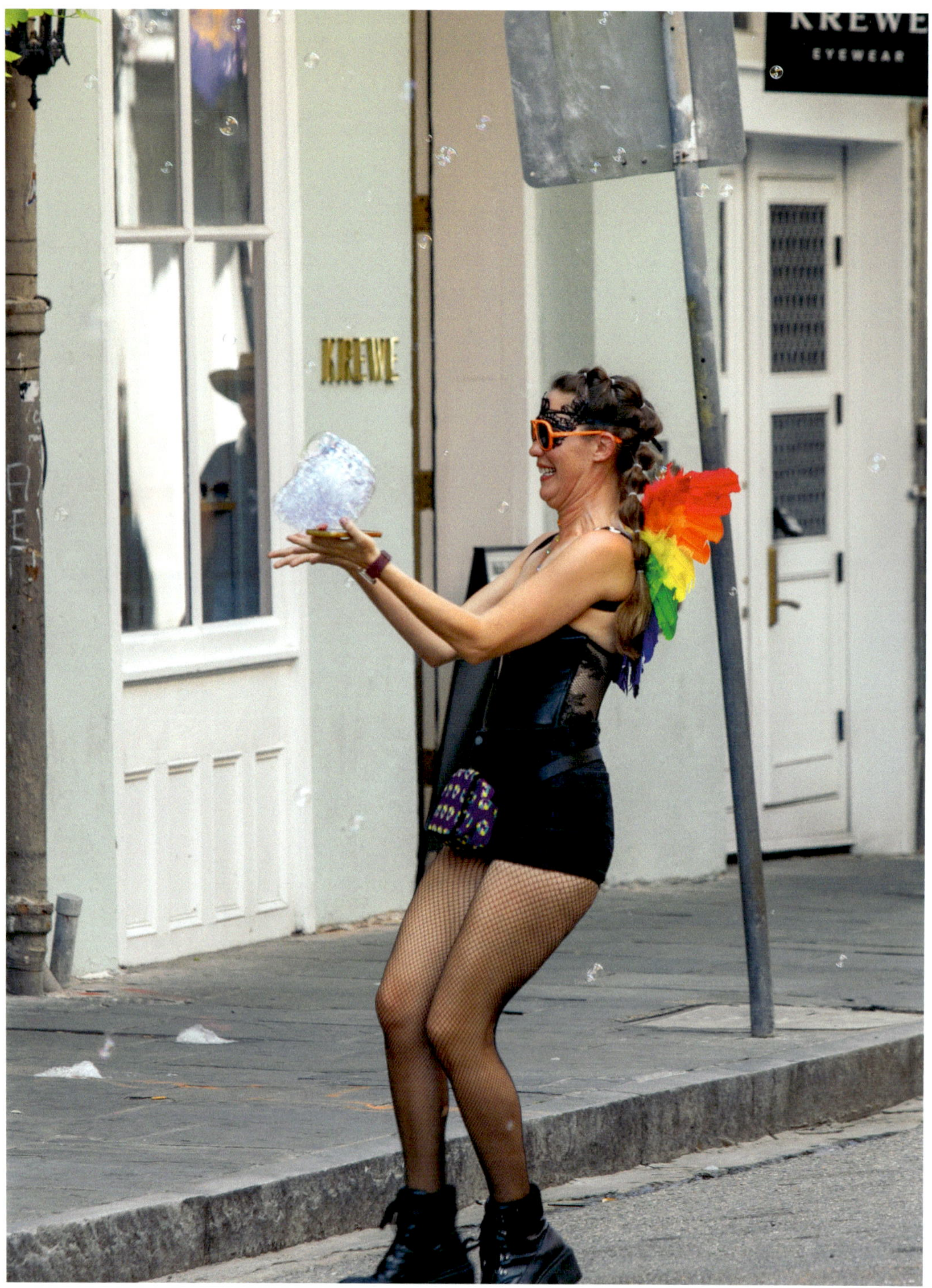

In her little black outfit, adorned with rainbow wings, she captures a giant bubble, a fleeting moment of magic in the French Quarter's enchanting air.

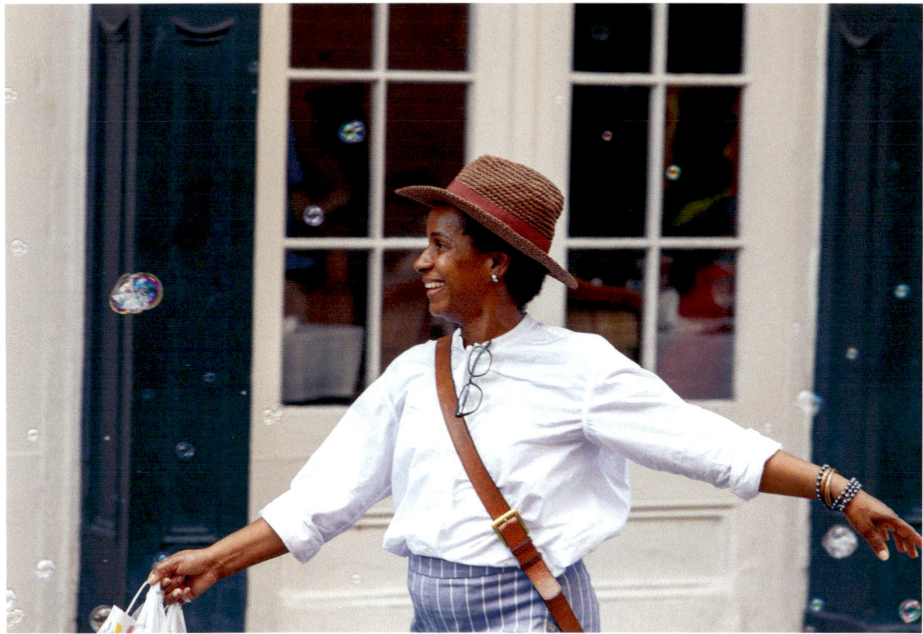

Amid the bubbles floating through the street, she dances, her arms swinging in joyous abandon, turning the French Quarter into her own whimsical ballroom.

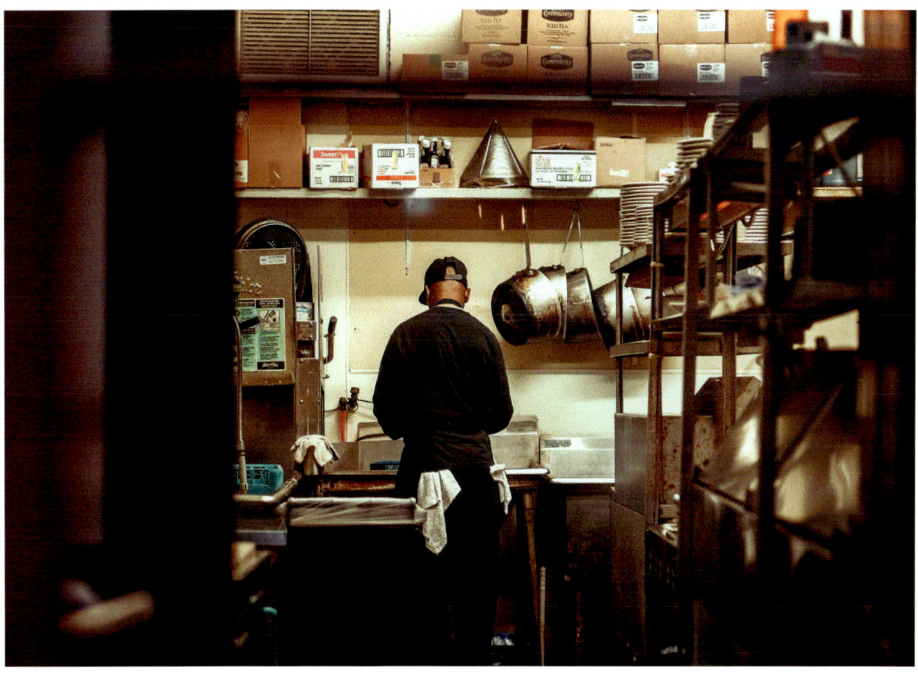

Focused and unyielding, the cook stands with his back to the window, his every move a dance of culinary precision in the heart of the French Quarter.

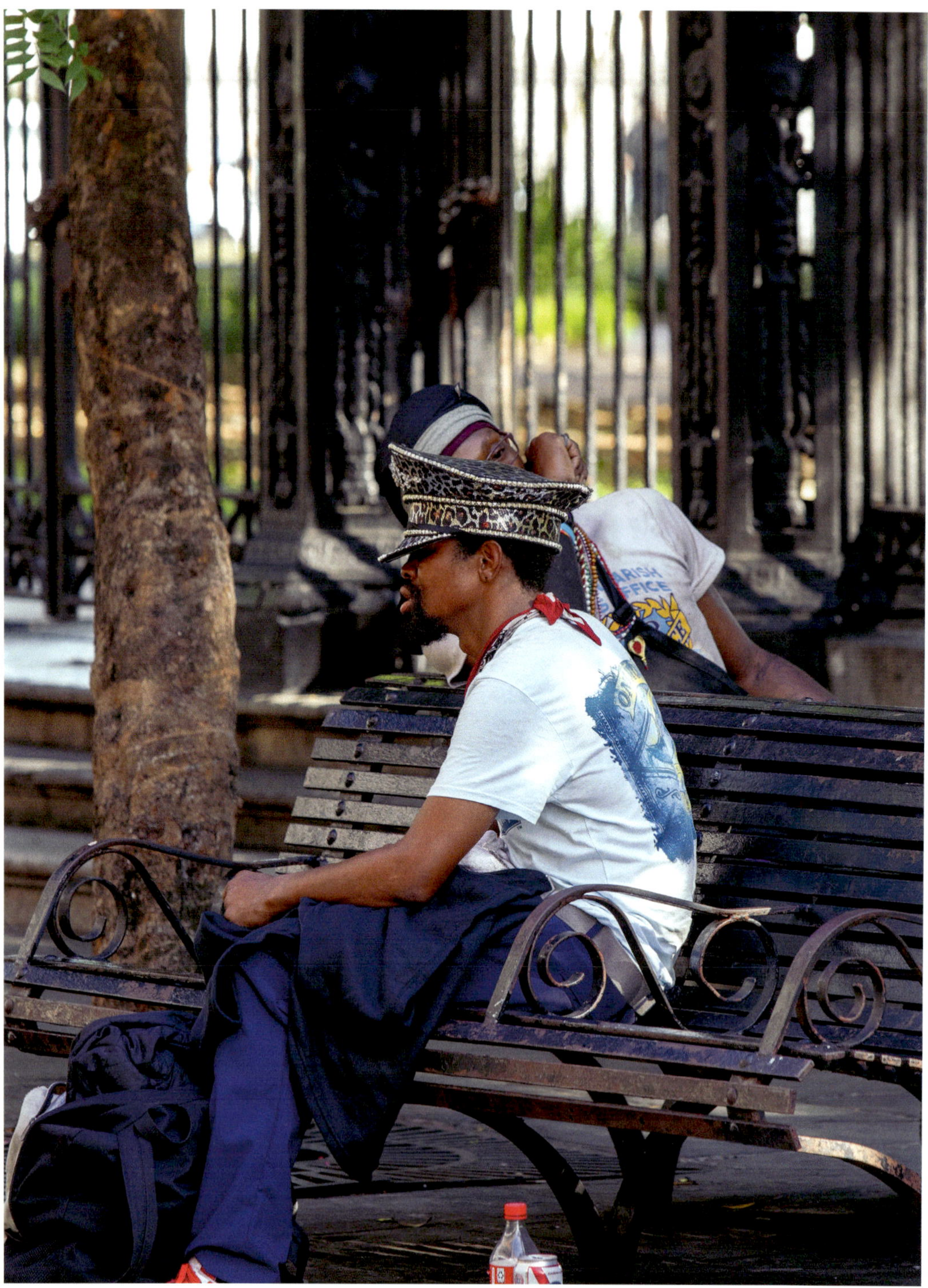

Under the shade of Jackson Square, he takes a break, his leopard captain's hat a bold statement of personality amid the historic serenity.

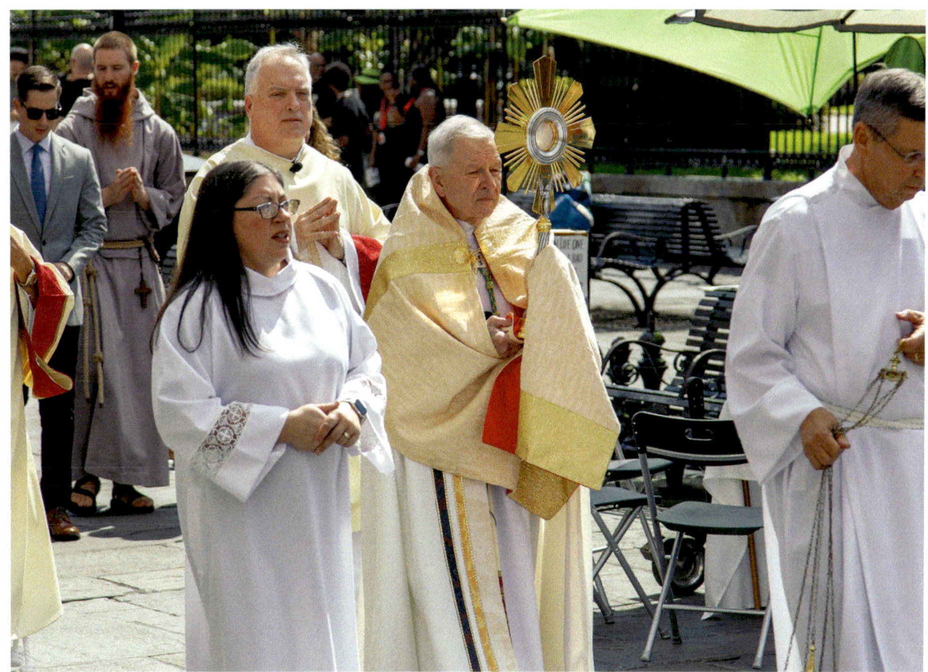

In a solemn march through Jackson Square, the clergy of St. Louis Cathedral lead the faithful, their procession a living tapestry of faith woven into the fabric of New Orleans' spiritual heritage.

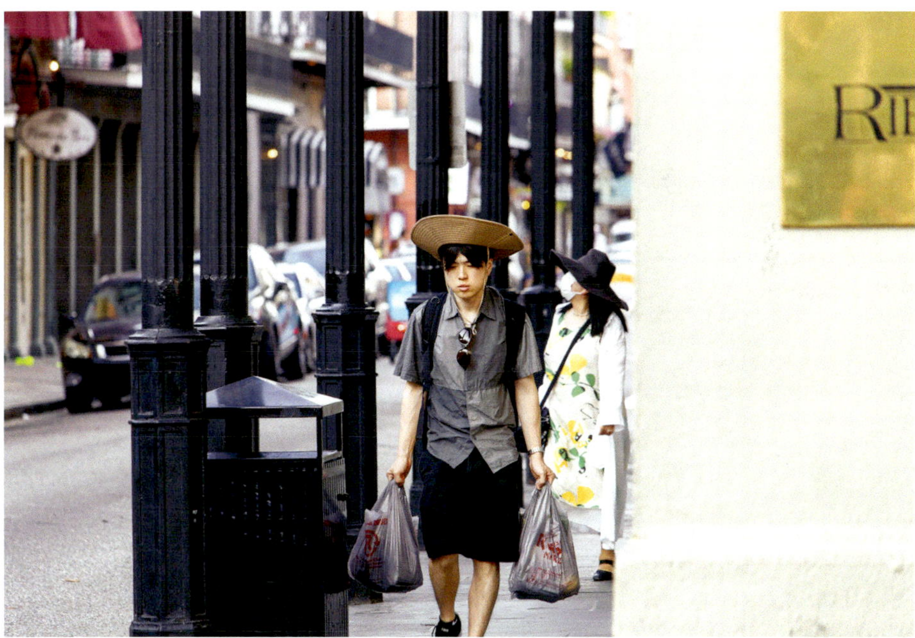

With purpose in his stride, he carries the weight of sustenance, two large sacks of groceries in hand, navigating the French Quarter's charm on his way home.

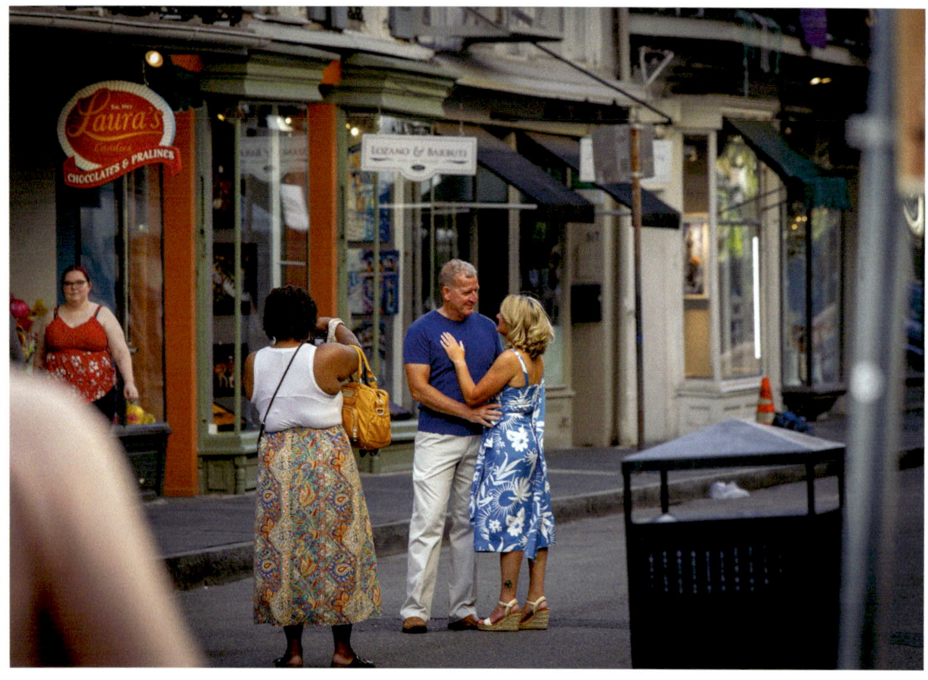

In a moment captured by the lens, they pose, a couple immortalized in the heart of the French Quarter, where every photograph tells a story of love and place.

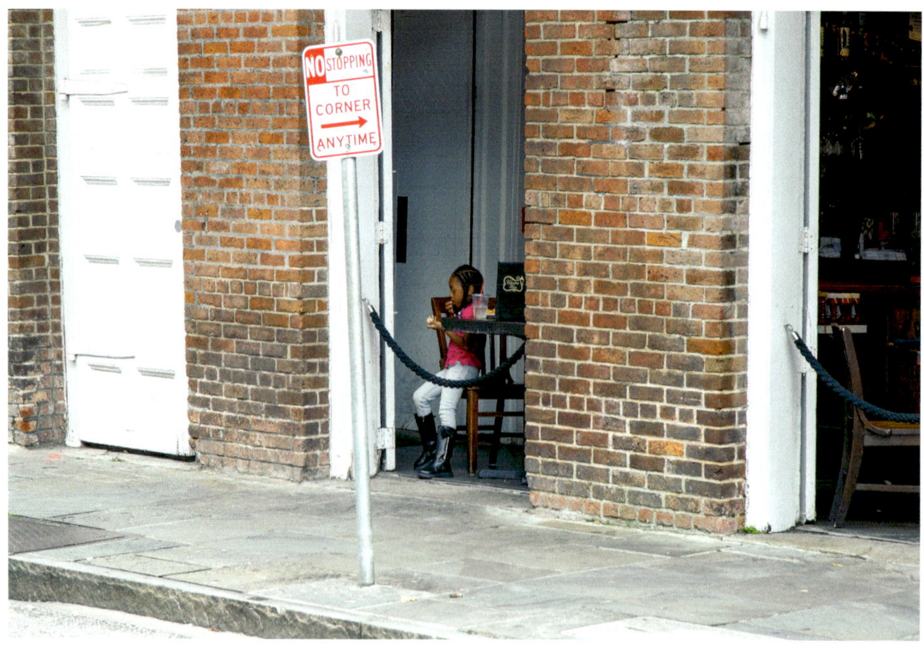

With breakfast in hand, she gazes out, her eyes wide with the wonder of the French Quarter's morning life, a little girl's world unfolding before her.

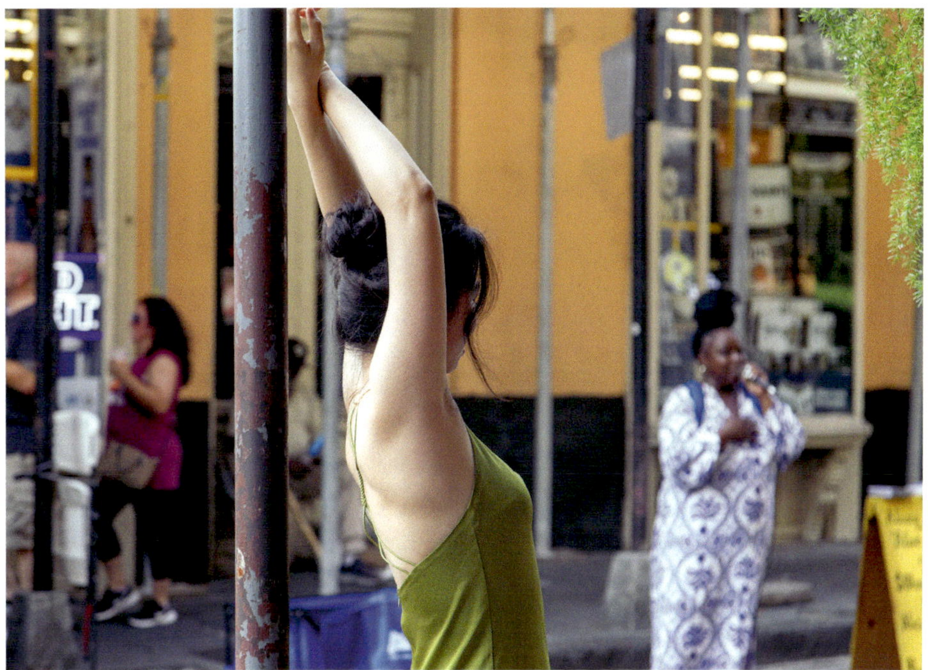

Caught in the rhythm, she dances with the street pole as her partner, the music of the French Quarter weaving through her, an impromptu ballet of urban grace.

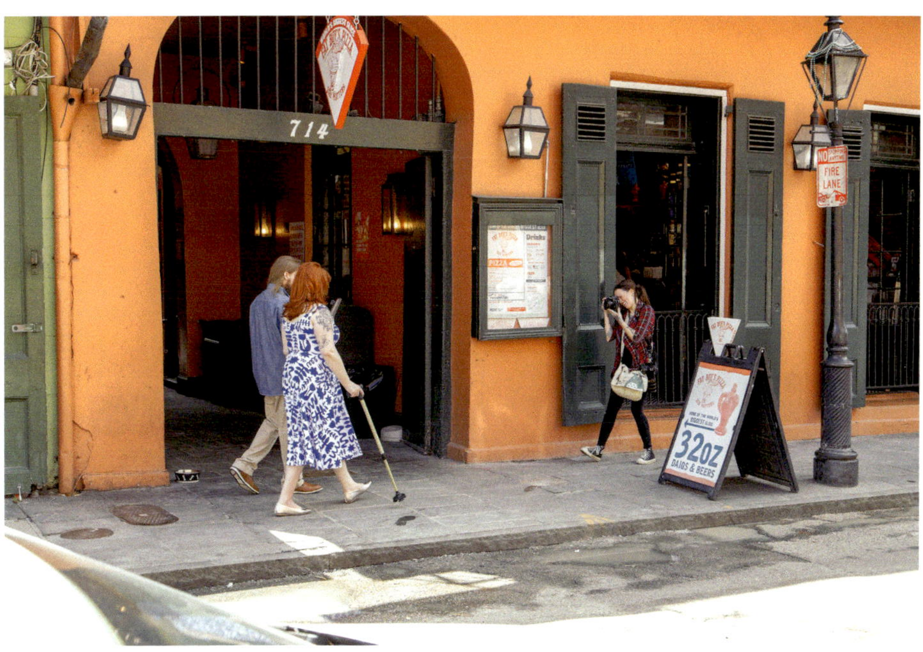

As they stroll, hand in hand, toward the lens, the French Quarter becomes their canvas, each step immortalized, a timeless moment captured in the heart of New Orleans.

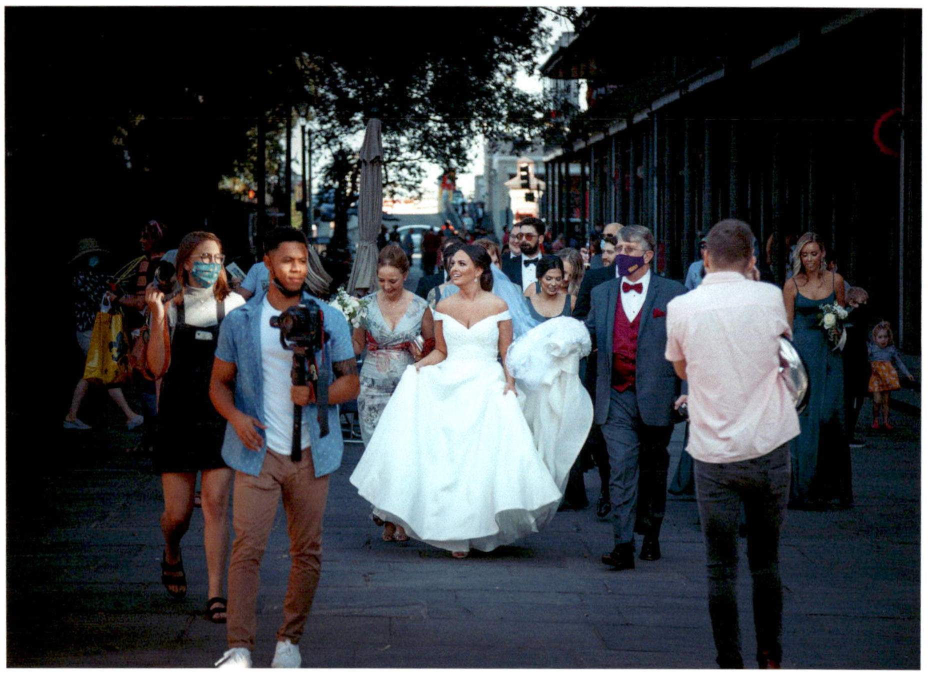

With her entourage in tow, she strides through the French Quarter, a bride announcing her joy to the world, her wedding party a parade of love and celebration.

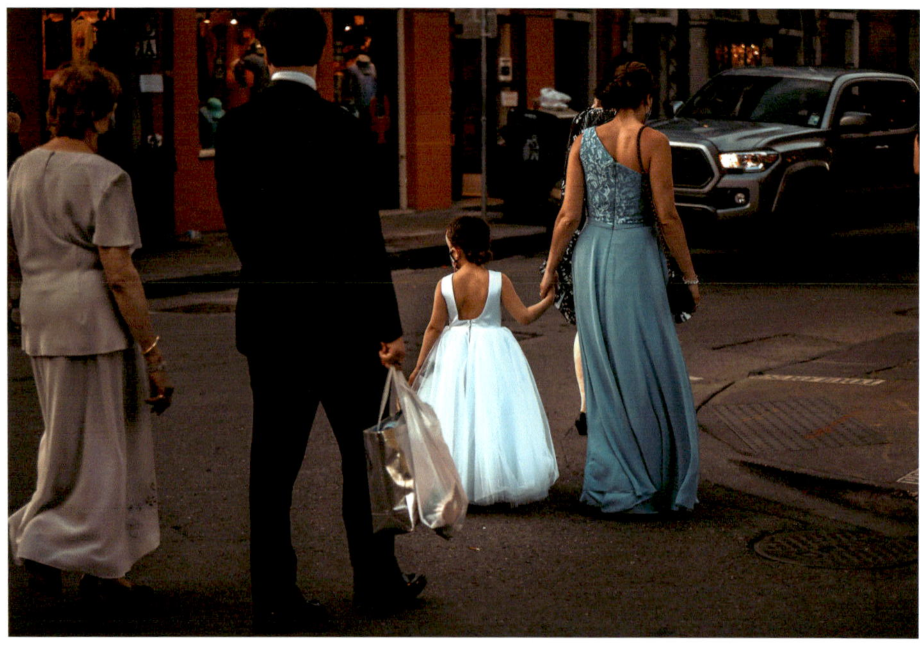

In a tender moment amidst the wedding festivities, the maid of honor holds the flower girl's hand, guiding her through the French Quarter, a symbol of continuity and care in the celebration of love.

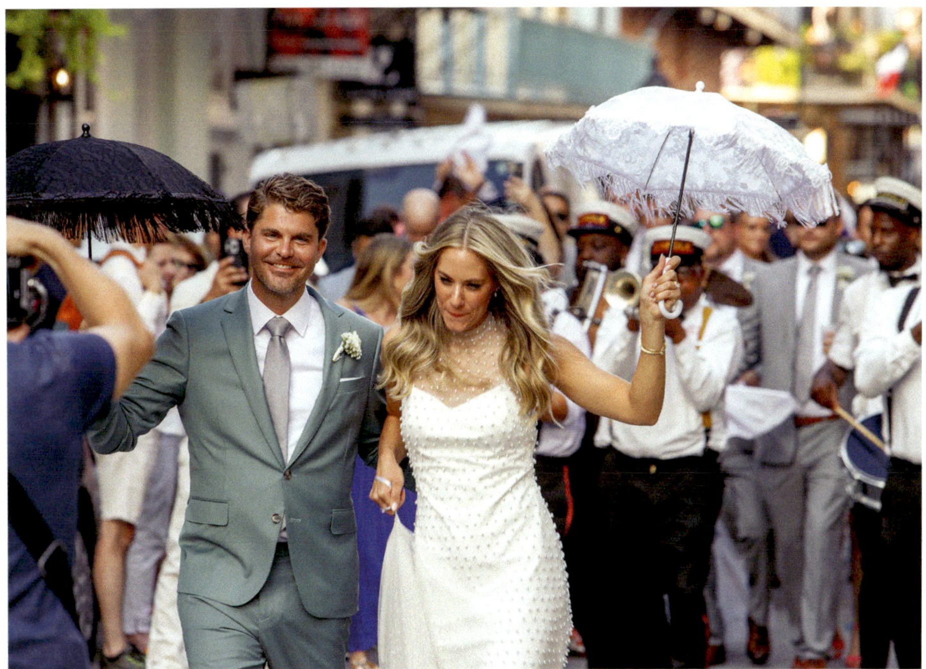

In the heart of the French Quarter, a newly married couple leads a joyous second line, their steps a dance of unity, celebrating love with the rhythm of New Orleans.

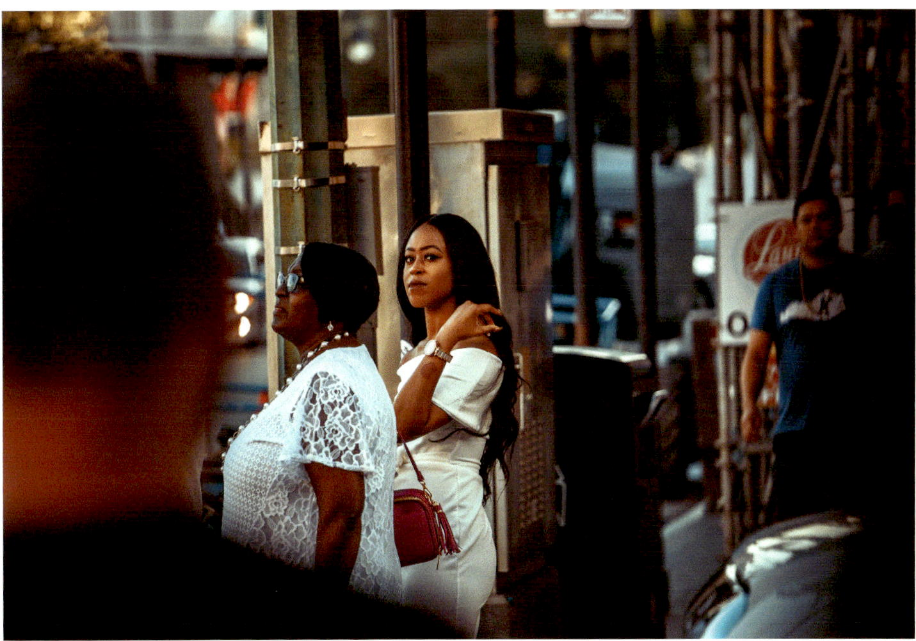

On the way to a rooftop wedding, she flips her hair, catching my lens with a moment of candid beauty, her grace a fleeting glimpse of elegance in the French Quarter's ascent.

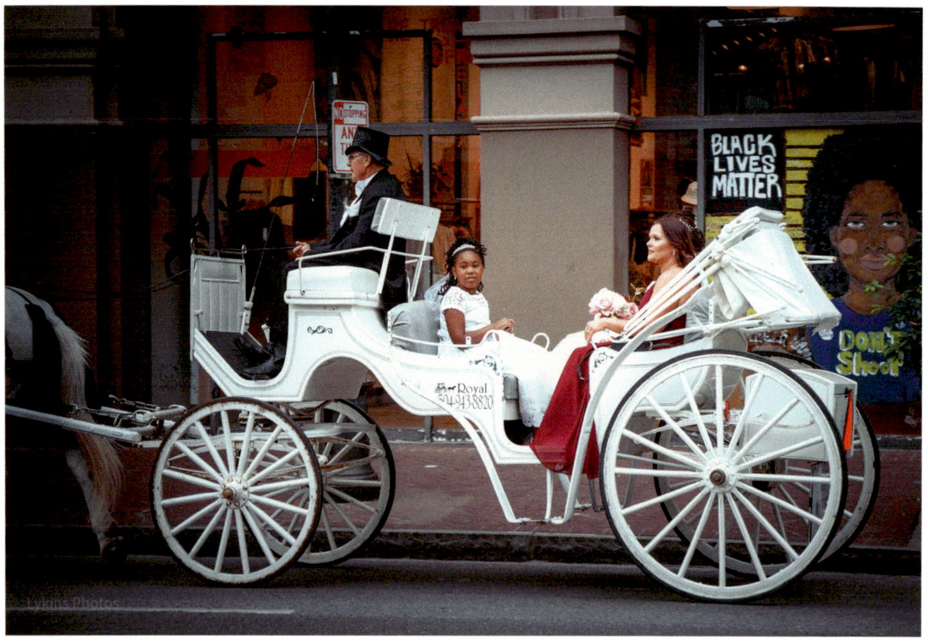

Nestled in an old French Quarter horse-drawn wagon, the flower girl and bridesmaids ride, their journey to the wedding a charming prelude, wrapped in tradition and romance.

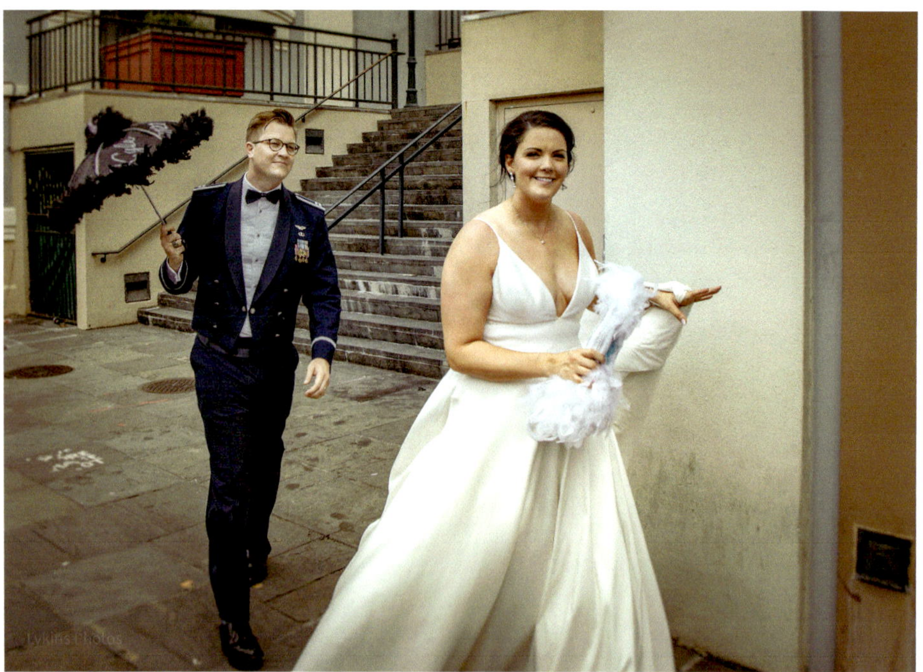

Fresh from the second line, he holds the umbrella aloft, a newly married couple, their joy undimmed, stepping into their new life together under the French Quarter's watchful eyes.

3

The Canines of the Quarter

In the French Quarter, it is not just the humans who revel in the vibrant life; the dogs are equally enchanted by the bustling streets and rich aromas. This chapter is dedicated to these four-legged inhabitants and visitors, whose joy and curiosity add an extra layer of charm to the neighborhood.

Whether they are being walked on a leash, their noses twitching with every new scent, or with their heads joyfully poking out of car windows, the dogs of the Quarter are as much a part of the scene as the people. They trot along, tails wagging, eager to explore every nook and cranny. Their excitement is palpable, a testament to the sensory feast that the Quarter provides.

The smells of Cajun and Creole cuisine wafting from restaurants make their nostrils flare in delight. They sniff at the air, trying to decipher the complex tapestry of spices and flavors. The presence of other dogs, too, adds to the social whirl, with tails wagging in greeting or in the thrill of a new acquaintance.

From tiny teacup breeds nestled in purses to larger breeds proudly strutting beside their owners, each dog brings its own personality to the Quarter. Some are pushed in strollers, their eyes wide with the wonder of it all, while others pull eagerly on their leashes, driven by an insatiable curiosity.

These canine companions are not just pets; they are participants in the daily life of the Quarter. They add a layer of warmth and familiarity, their presence a reminder of the simple joys of life. Through their eyes, we see the Quarter anew, full of adventure and endless discovery.

In this chapter, I have captured moments of these dogs in their element, their expressions as varied as the people around them. Each photograph tells a story of companionship, of shared experiences, and of the unbridled joy of living in, or visiting, one of the most vibrant neighborhoods in the world.

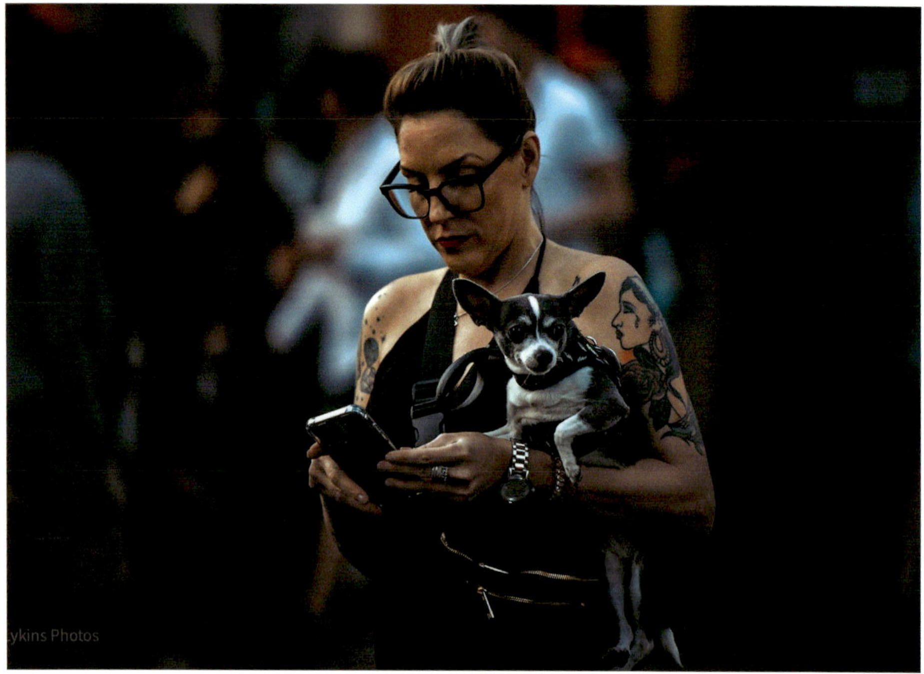

With man's best friend in her arms, she checks her phone, a modern moment in the timeless French Quarter, where even dogs pause for the digital age.

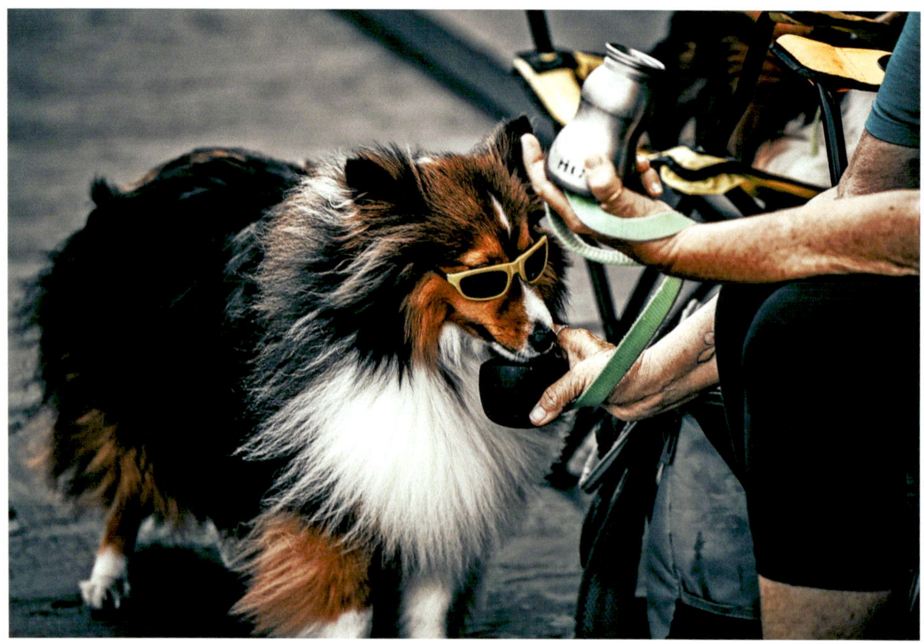

Amid the adventure, a dog takes a well-deserved break, lapping water from a portable bowl, its owner's care a testament to the bond shared in the heart of the French Quarter.

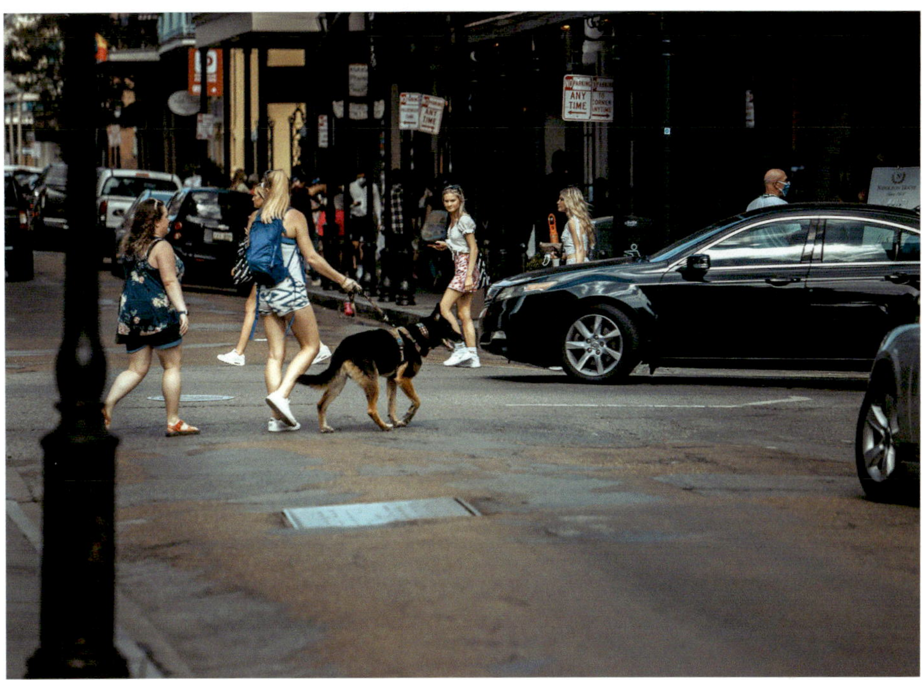

With a confident stride, the German Shepherd leads, navigating the French Quarter's streets with an innate knowledge, its presence a guide through the city's soul.

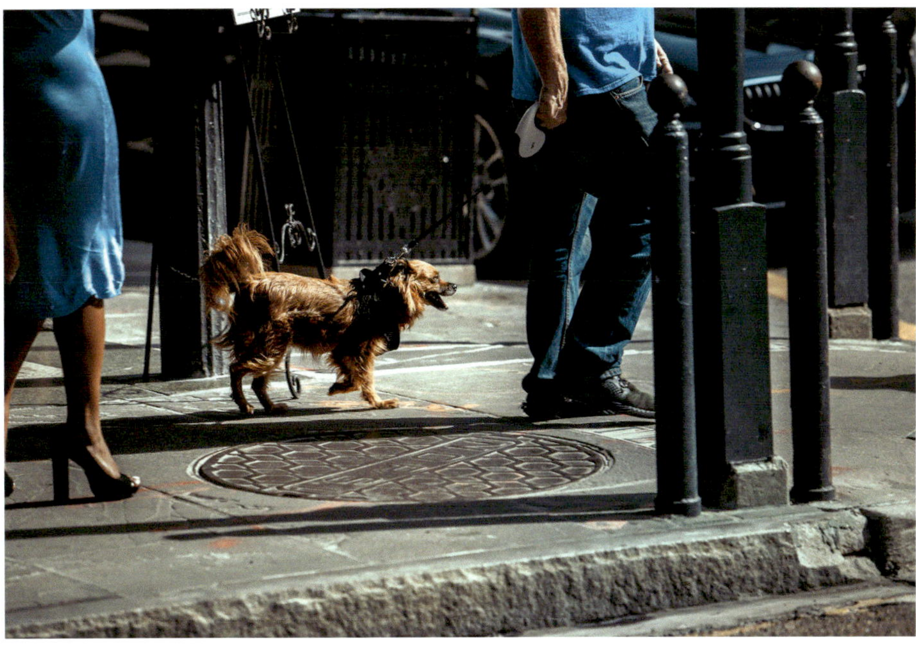

Guided by a gentle leash, the dog trots through the French Quarter, its journey a shared adventure with its owner, exploring the city's vibrant tapestry together.

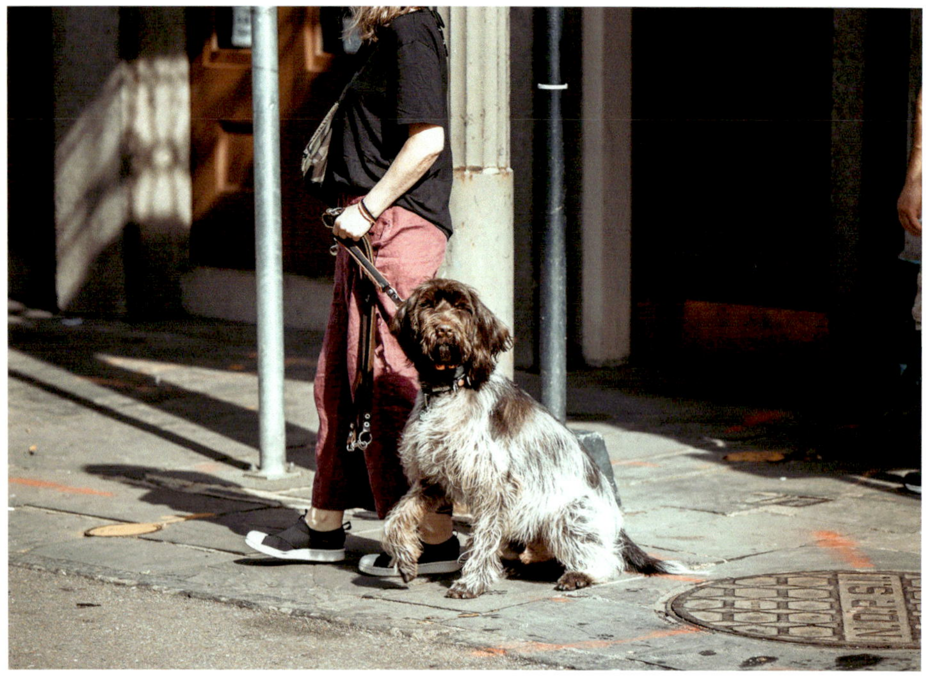

At the crossroad, waiting to venture further, the dog turns, its eyes meeting my lens, capturing a moment of connection in the bustling French Quarter.

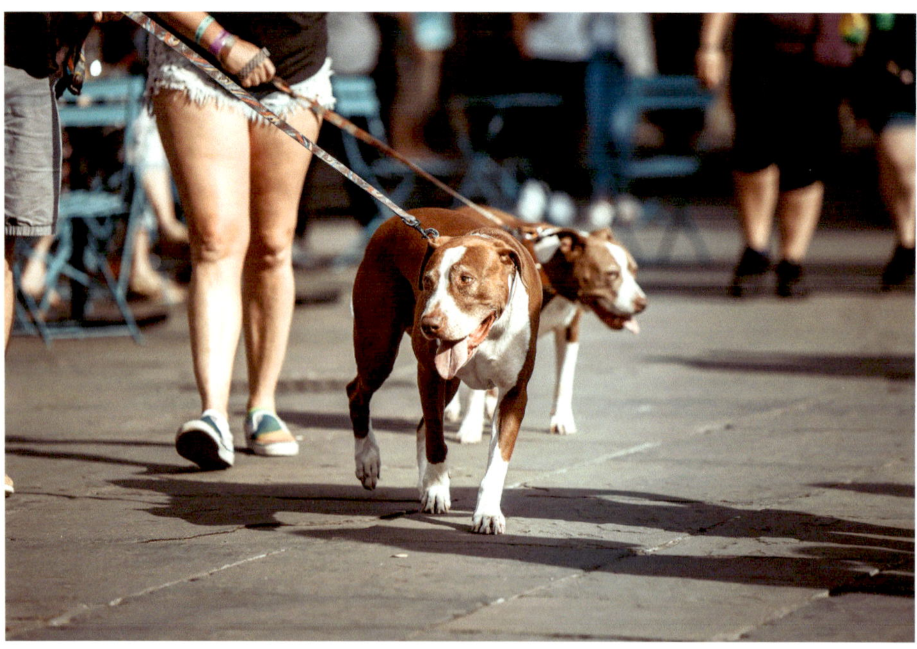

In the morning sun, they walk, a two-headed dog illusion, their synchronized steps with their owner through the French Quarter, a whimsical sight of companionship.

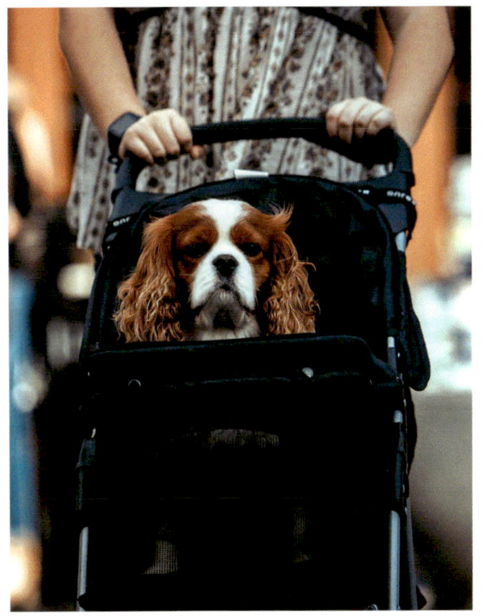

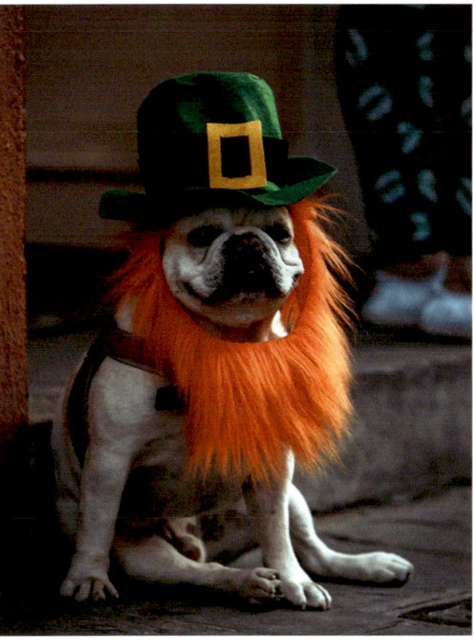

Above left: In the heart of Jackson Square, this pampered pooch rides in style, its stroller a testament to the indulgent love of its owner, navigating the French Quarter's charm with ease.

Above right: Embracing the St. Patrick's Day spirit, this puppy sports a green hat and red beard, a tiny reveler ready to parade through the French Quarter with festive flair.

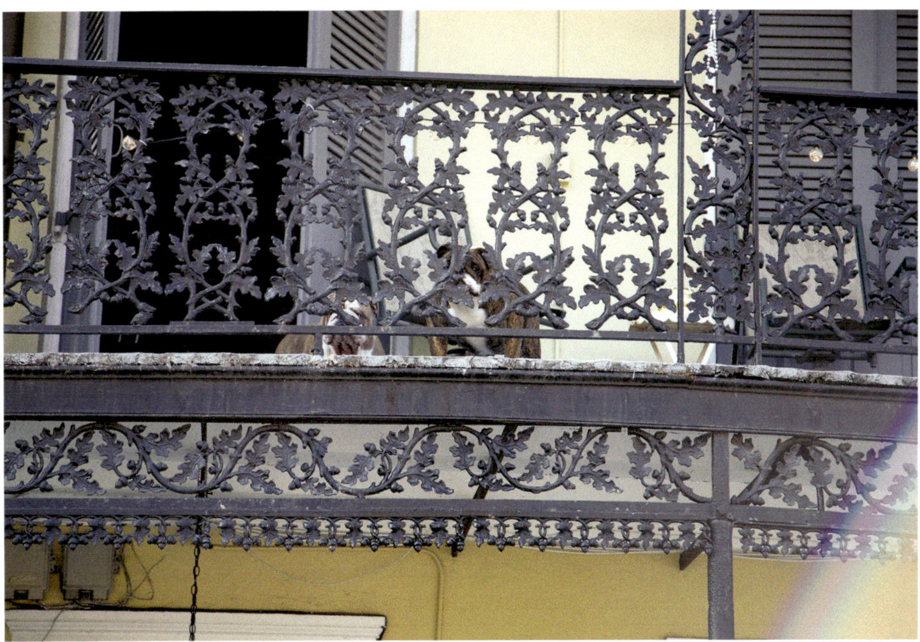

Perched above, two canines survey the scene, their eyes following the passersby, silent observers of the French Quarter's daily drama unfolding below.

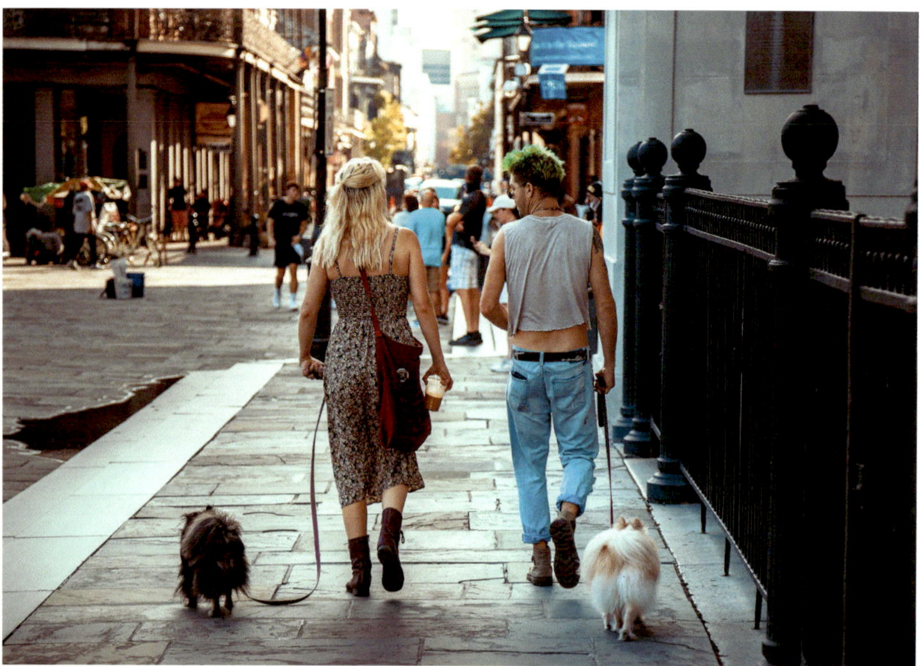

In the waning sun, a couple strolls with their canine companions, their walk through the French Quarter a shared moment of leisure and love, bathed in golden light.

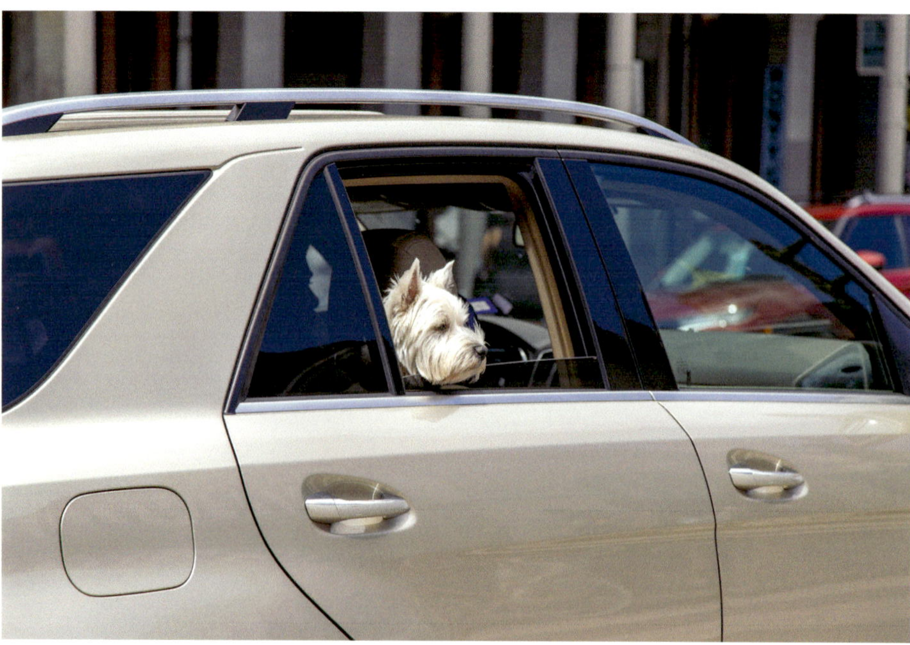

With curiosity in its eyes, the dog peeks from the car's back window, taking in the French Quarter's vibrant streets, a passenger in life's parade.

4

Echoes of the Past

The French Quarter is not just about the people and the pets; it is also about the structures that have stood witness to centuries of life. This chapter delves into the iconic buildings and architecture that define the Quarter, each with its own tale to tell.

Whispers of History: As you wander through the Quarter, the buildings themselves seem to speak. Some whisper gently, their facades weathered by time, telling stories of love, loss, and laughter. Others shout, their vibrant colors and intricate ironwork demanding attention, recounting tales of grandeur, mystery, and sometimes, sorrow.

A Tapestry of Use: These structures serve as homes, restaurants, shops, and even secret hideaways. The balconies, with their iconic wrought-iron railings, are not just architectural features but stages for daily life. Here, people dine, chat, and watch the world go by, their presence adding to the living history of the place.

The Familiar Maze: Every corner turned in the Quarter feels like stepping into a different era, yet there is a comforting familiarity in the shared architectural style. The narrow streets, the courtyards hidden behind gates, the shotgun houses, and the grand hotels—they all contribute to a labyrinth of history where one can easily lose themselves, yet always feel at home.

Stories in Stone: From the grandeur of the St. Louis Cathedral, standing majestically over Jackson Square, to the quaint charm of the old Creole House, each building holds layers of stories. There are tales of hauntings in the LaLaurie Mansion, of rock and roll legends at the Dungeon, and of literary gatherings at places like Lafitte's Blacksmith Shop Bar.

The Living History: These buildings are more than just structures; they are the physical embodiment of the Quarter's soul. They have seen revolutions, celebrations, and quiet moments of reflection. They have housed the rich and the rogue, the famous and the forgotten.

In this chapter, I have captured not just the beauty of these architectural marvels but the essence of their stories. Through these photographs, I invite you to listen to the whispers and shouts of the French Quarter, to feel the weight of history in every brick and beam, and to understand why these buildings are as much characters in the story of New Orleans as the people who inhabit them.

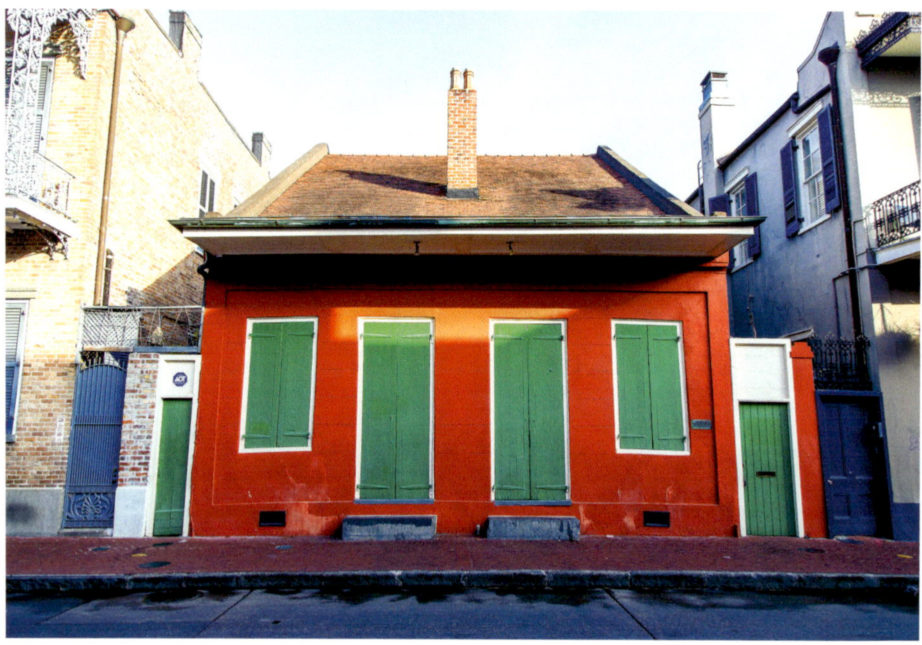

Bathed in the morning sun, the Old Creole House on Bourbon stands, its historic facade a testament to the enduring charm of the French Quarter, where each day begins with a touch of timeless elegance.

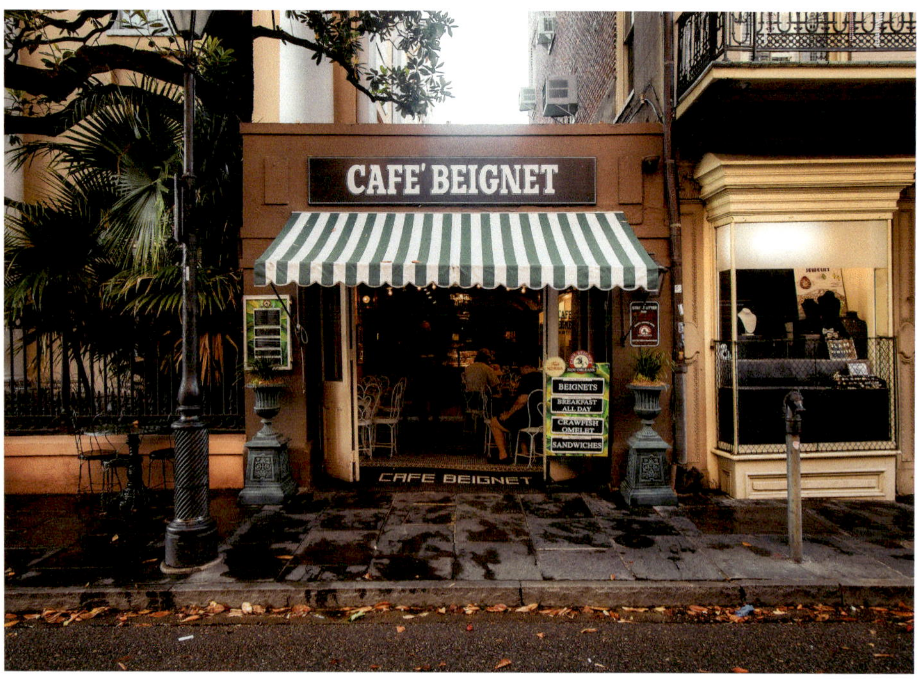

Café Beignet on Royal Street beckons with its welcoming facade, the soft light casting an inviting glow, promising warmth, coffee, and the sweet allure of beignets to all who pass.

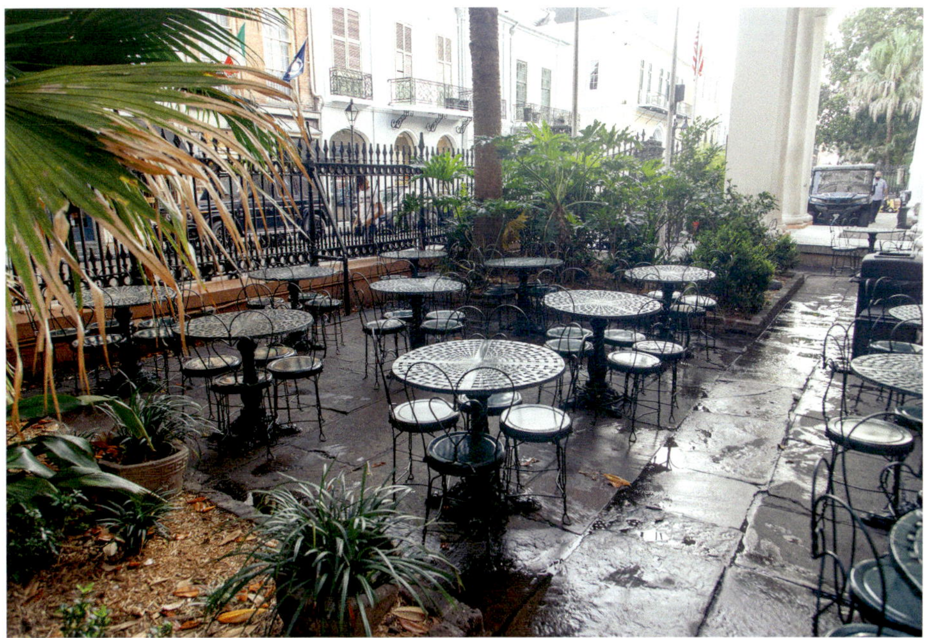

Damp with morning dew, the outdoor seating of Café Beignet waits patiently, each chair and table a silent invitation for patrons to enjoy the day's first moments in the heart of the French Quarter.

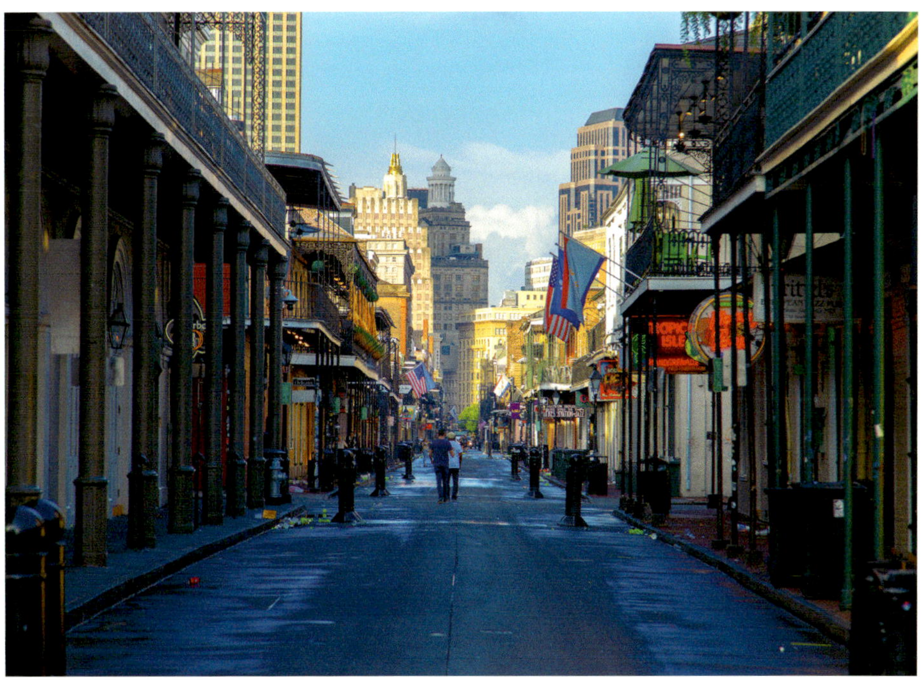

Bathed in the morning sun, Bourbon Street wakes, its pavement wet from the night's wash, the city's heartbeat softly pulsing in the background, ready for a new day's stories.

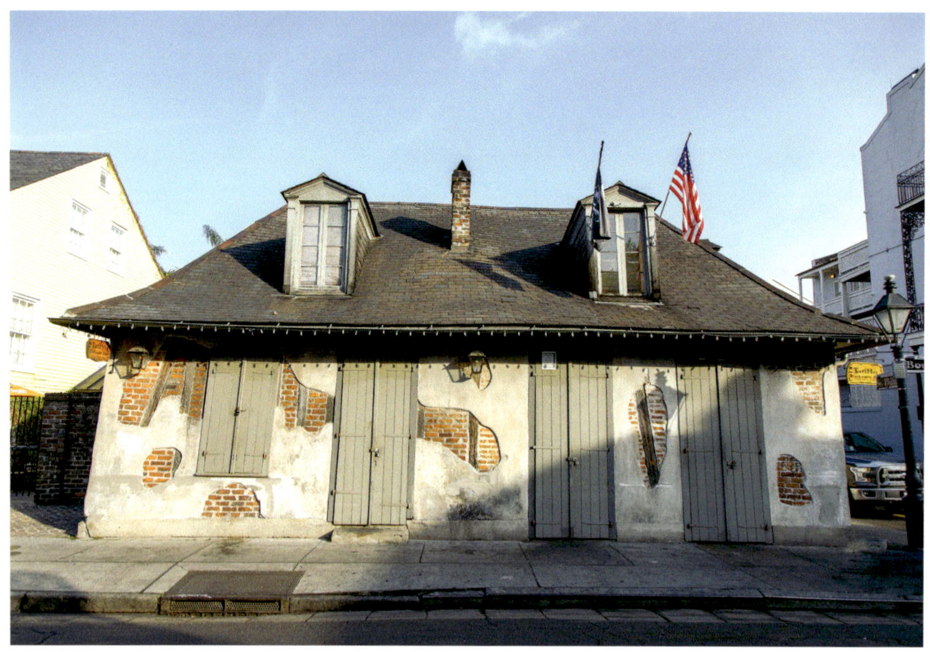

In the early morning light, Lafitte's stands with closed doors, a quiet sentinel of the French Quarter, its history and revelry paused, waiting for the day to unfold.

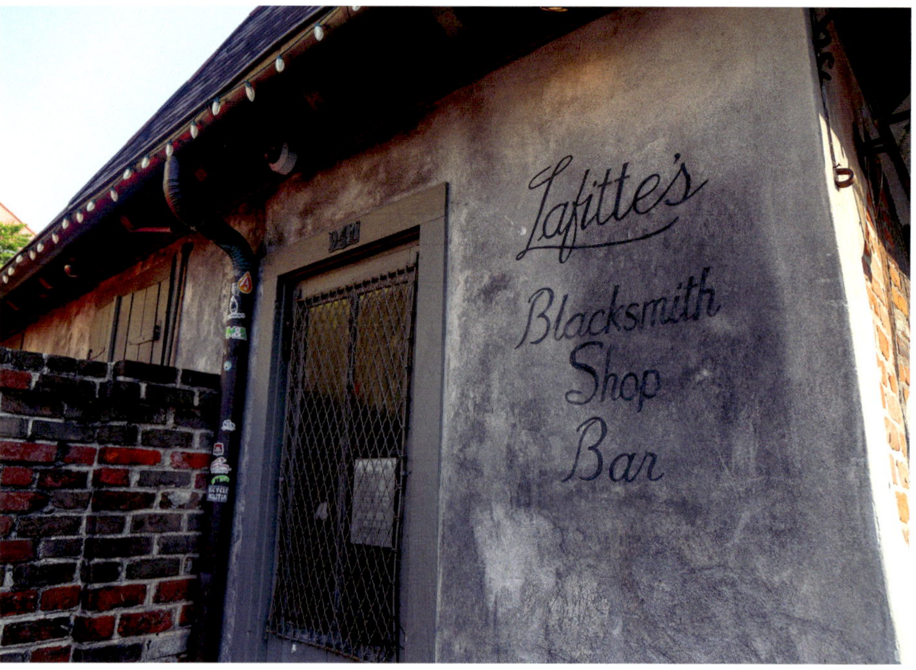

Lafitte's Blacksmith Shop, cloaked in the early morning light, whispers tales of pirates and spirits, its walls holding secrets from New Orleans' past, a living relic of the French Quarter's storied history.

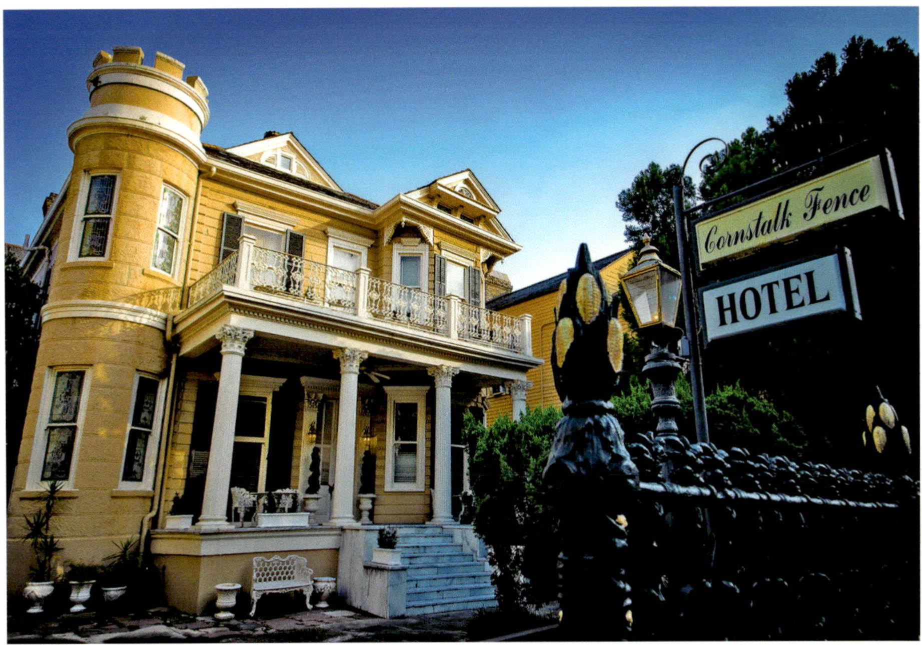

The Corn Stalk Hotel, with its iconic iron fence, stands as a quaint testament to the French Quarter's charm, its history a brief but vivid tale of Victorian elegance and whimsy in New Orleans' heart.

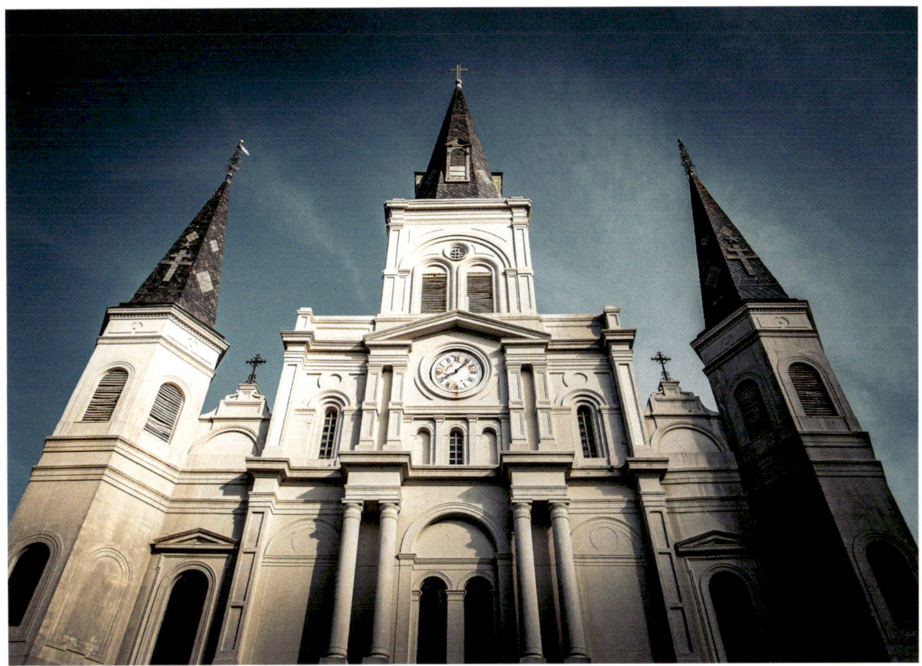

St. Louis Cathedral, with its towering spires and majestic facade, stands as a beacon of faith and history in the French Quarter, its architecture a silent hymn to New Orleans' spiritual and cultural legacy.

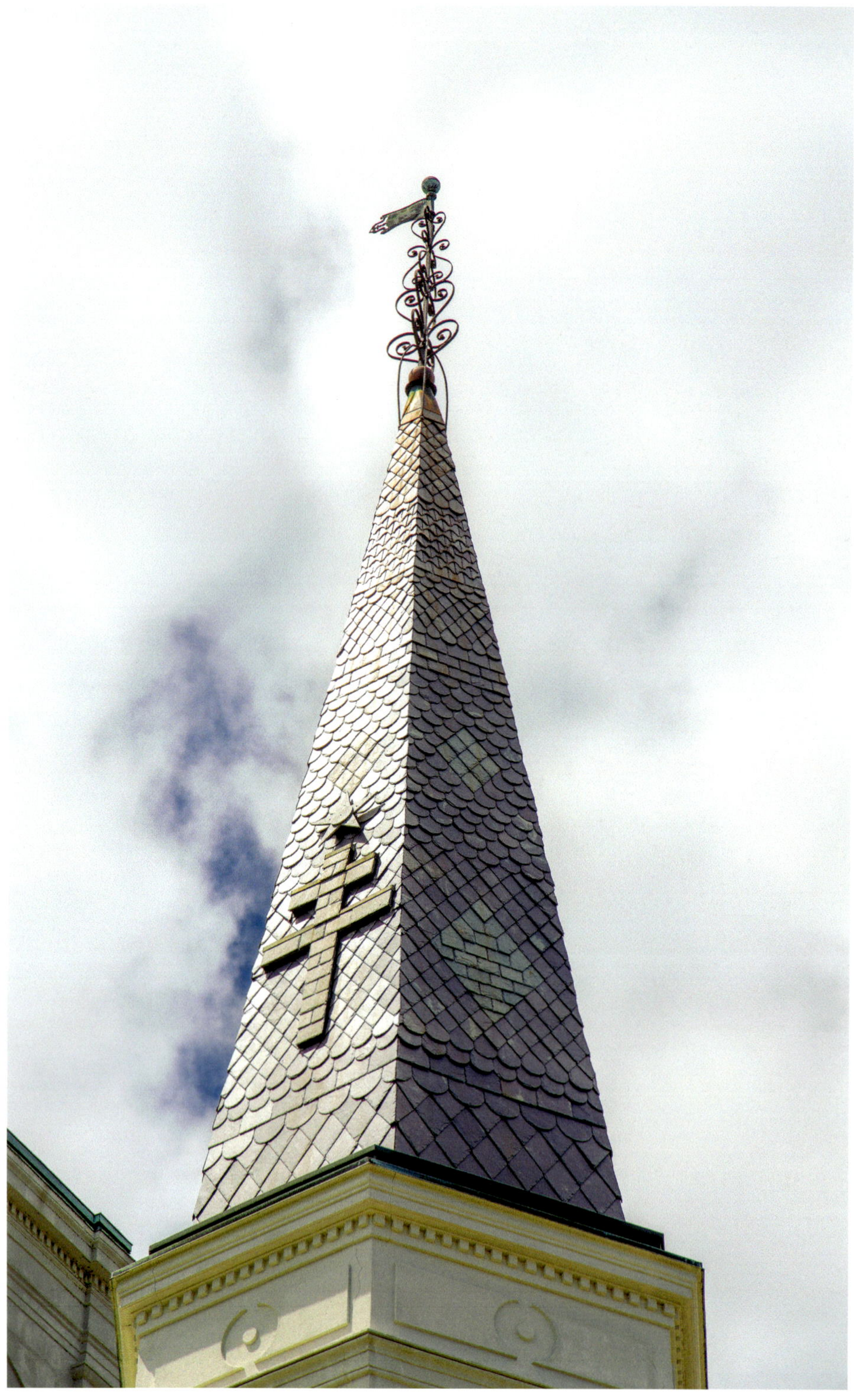

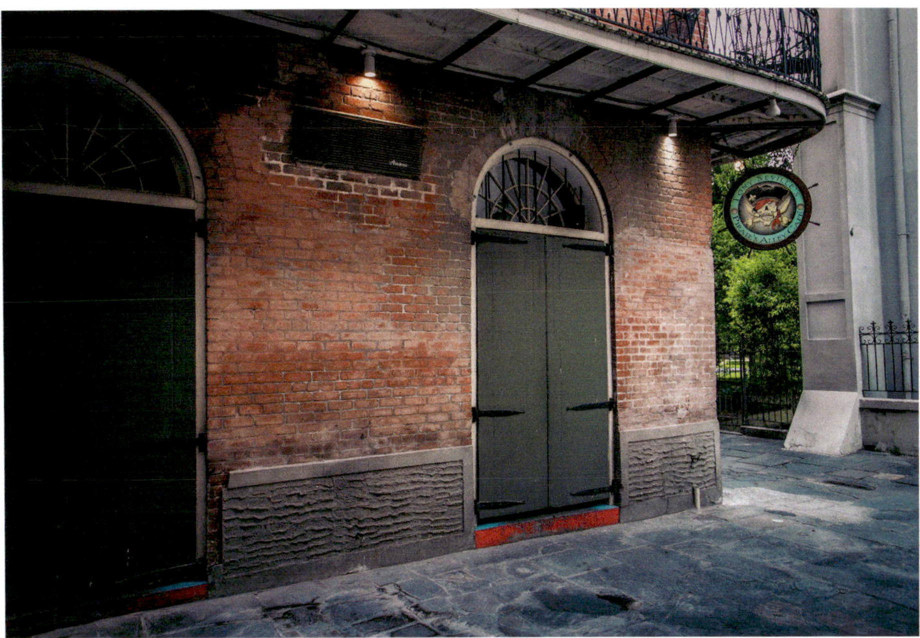

In the hush of early morning, Tony Seville's Pirate Alley Cafe lies closed, its pirate-themed facade a silent promise of adventure and coffee, waiting for the day's tales to begin.

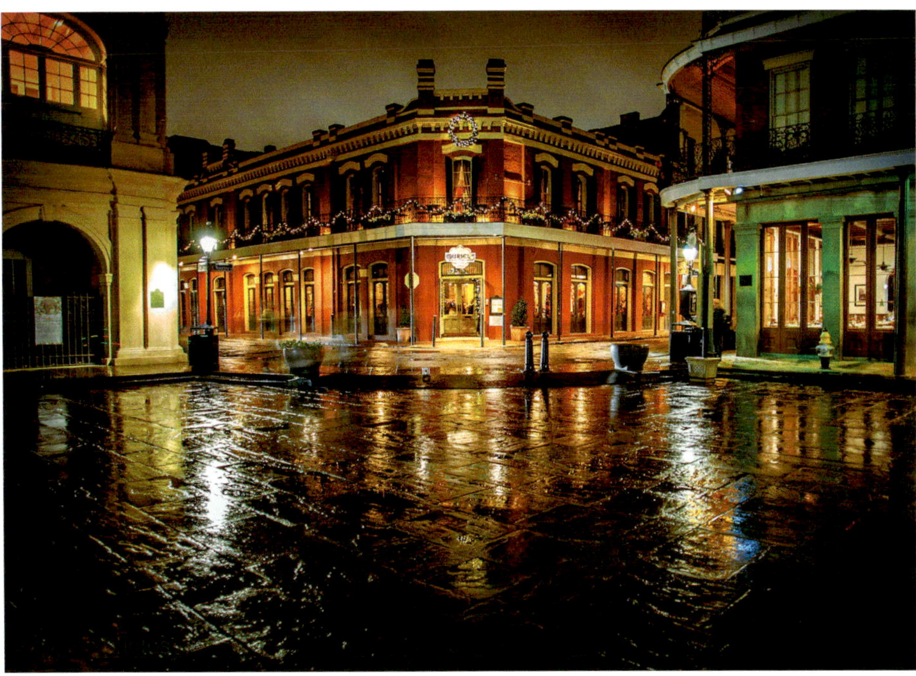

On this rainy night, Muriel's reflection dances in the water, its lights mingling with the cathedral's stone courtyard, creating a shimmering tableau of New Orleans' nocturnal beauty.

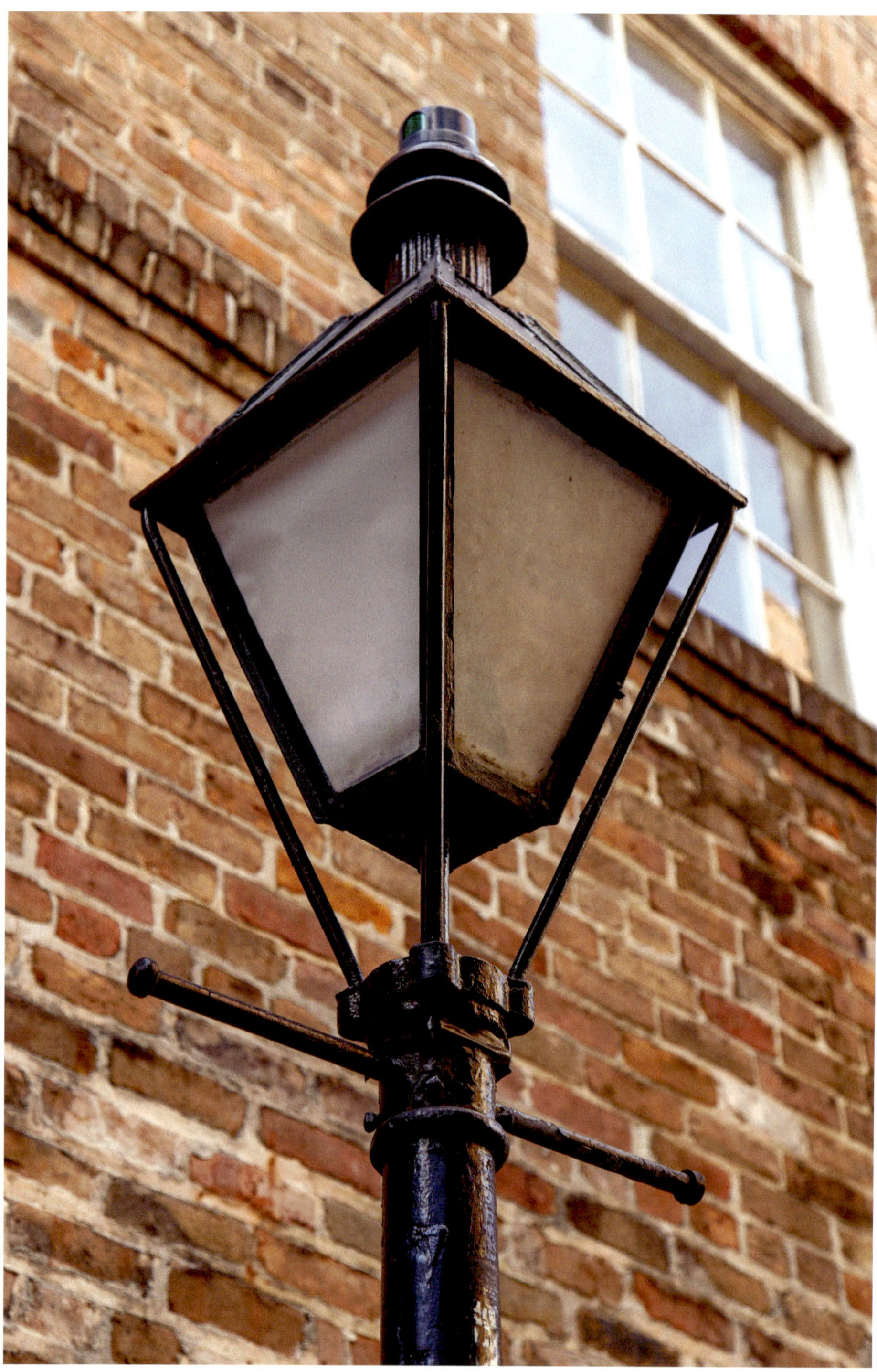

Standing tall yet unlit, an iconic French Quarter streetlight waits for dusk, its form a silent guardian of the historic streets, promising to illuminate the night's mysteries.

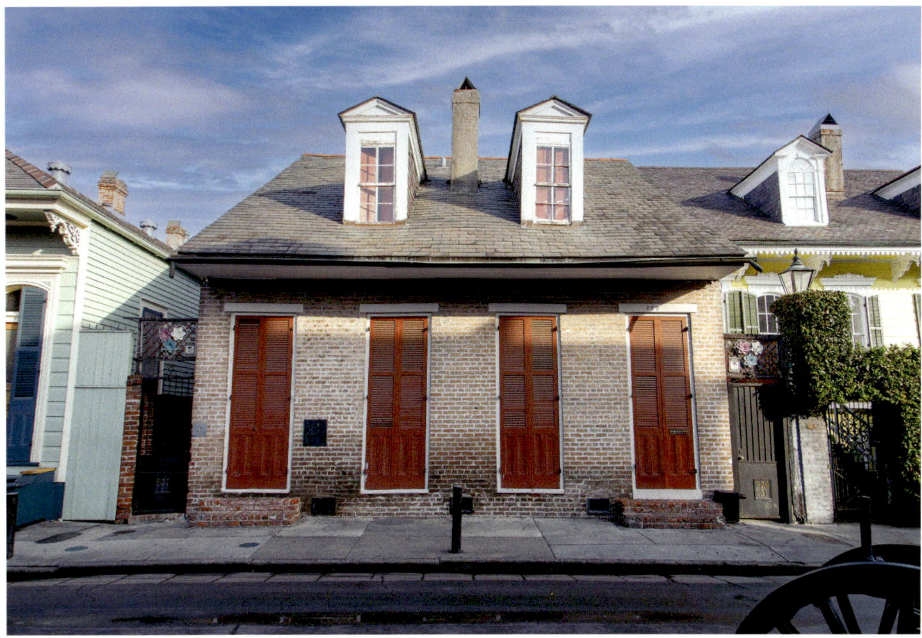

With its brown doors and time-worn facade, this house echoes the Old Creole House, standing as an emblem of the French Quarter's enduring architectural heritage.

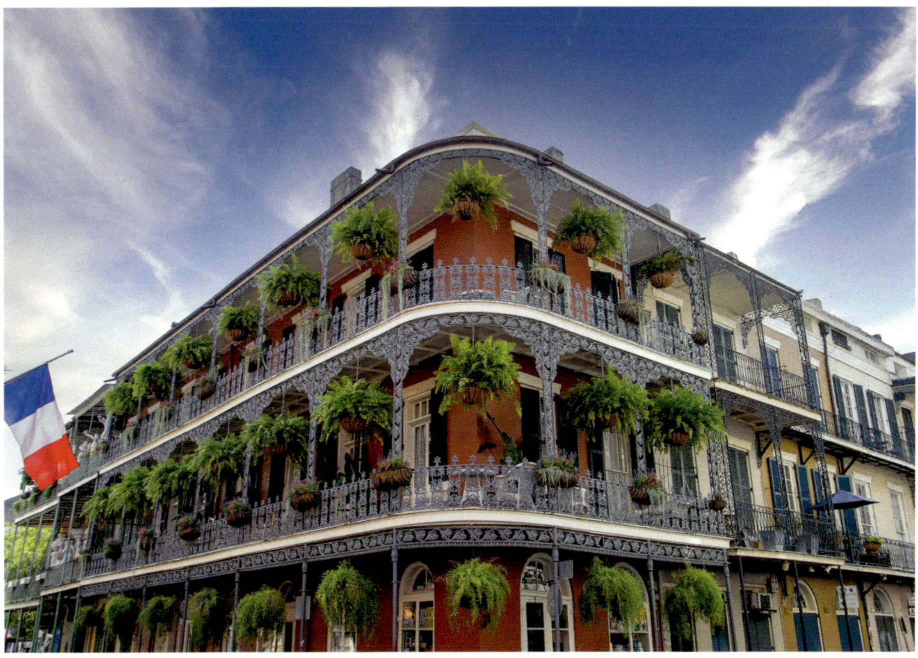

The epitome of French Quarter charm, this house boasts hanging ferns on all three floors, its iron railing a testament to the timeless elegance and lush greenery that define New Orleans' iconic architecture.

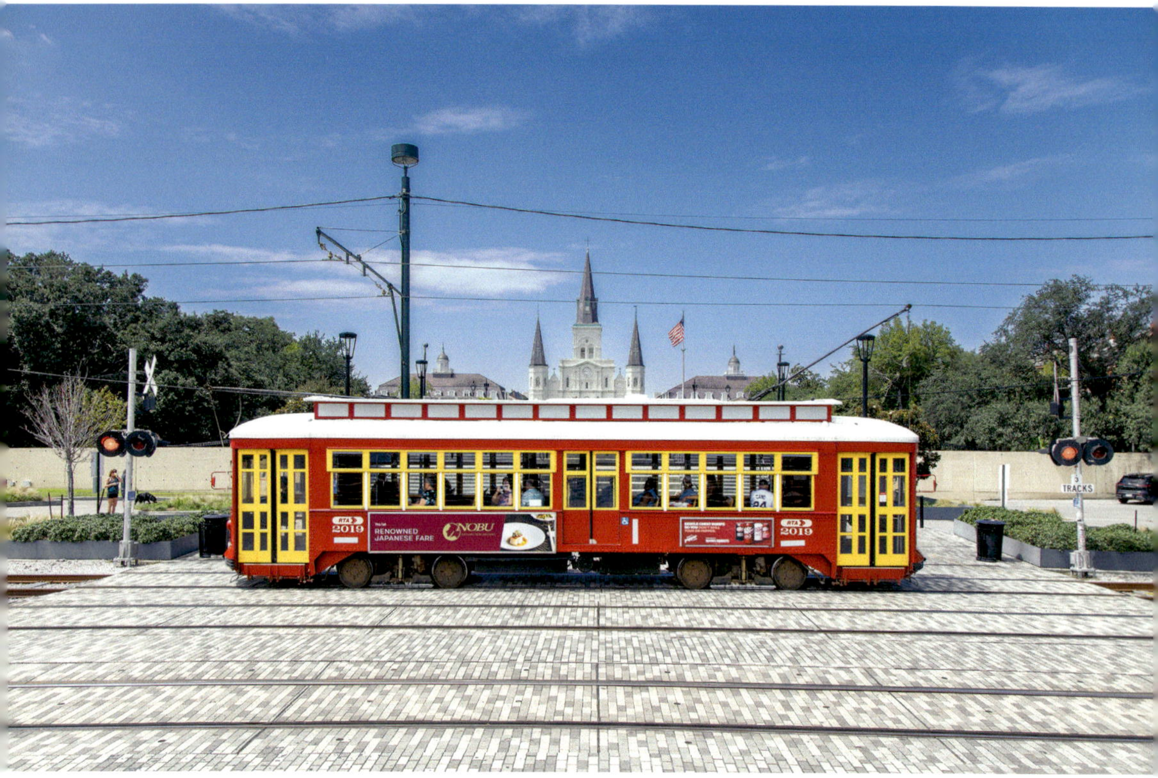

An old trolley glides past the majestic facade of the cathedral, its historic journey along the riverfront a timeless dance of New Orleans' past and present.

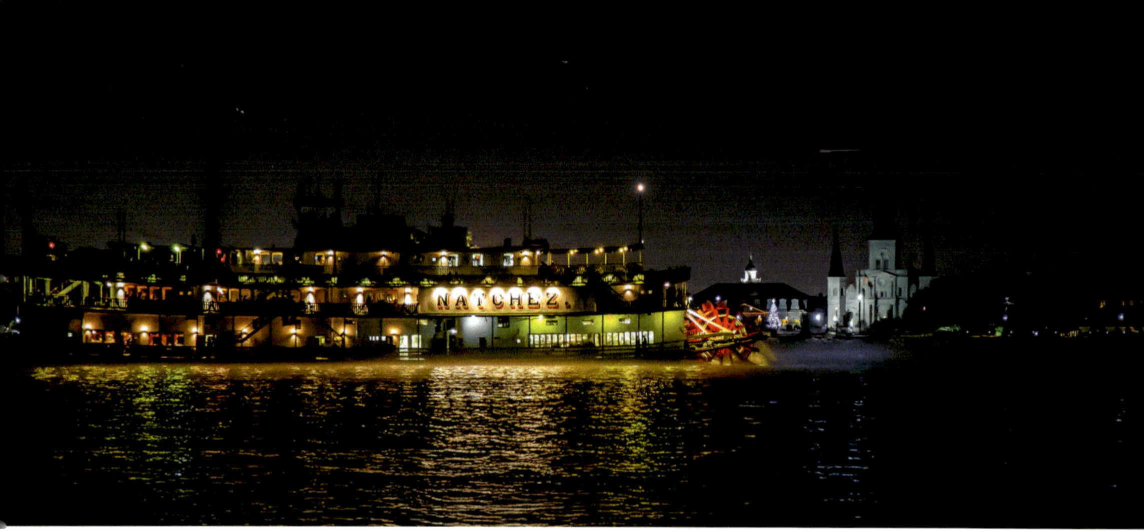

The Natchez Paddle Boat, with its grand wheel churning the waters, passes in front of the cathedral, a floating piece of history against the backdrop of New Orleans' spiritual heart.

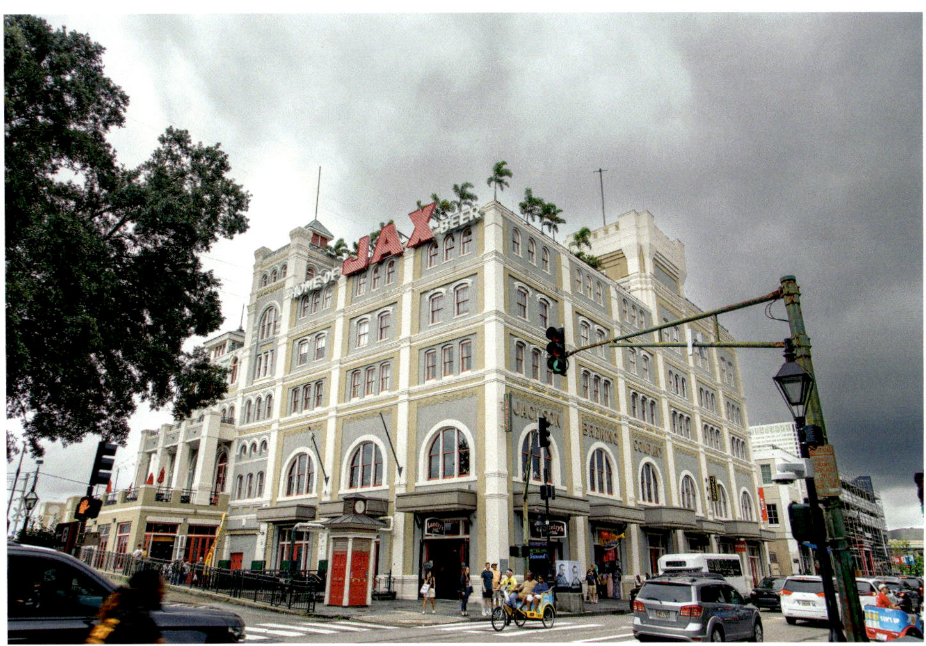

Jax Brewery, once a bustling hub of beer production, now stands as a testament to New Orleans' industrial past, transformed into a vibrant marketplace, its walls echoing with the city's spirit of reinvention.

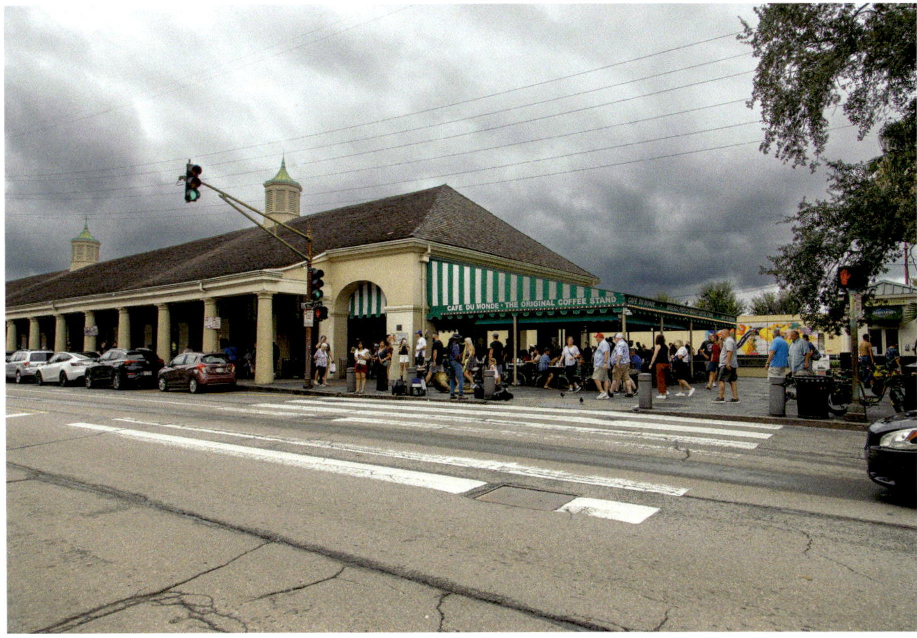

Café du Monde, with its iconic green and white striped awning, is the heartbeat of the French Quarter, where beignets and café au lait have been a tradition since 1862, serving up slices of New Orleans' soul.

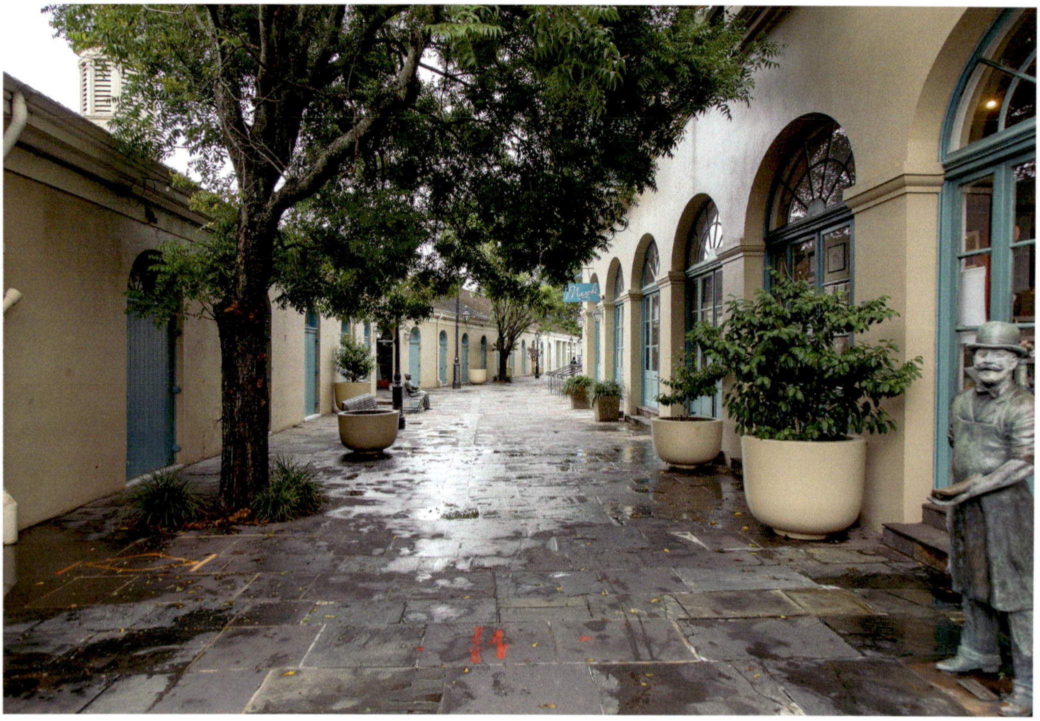

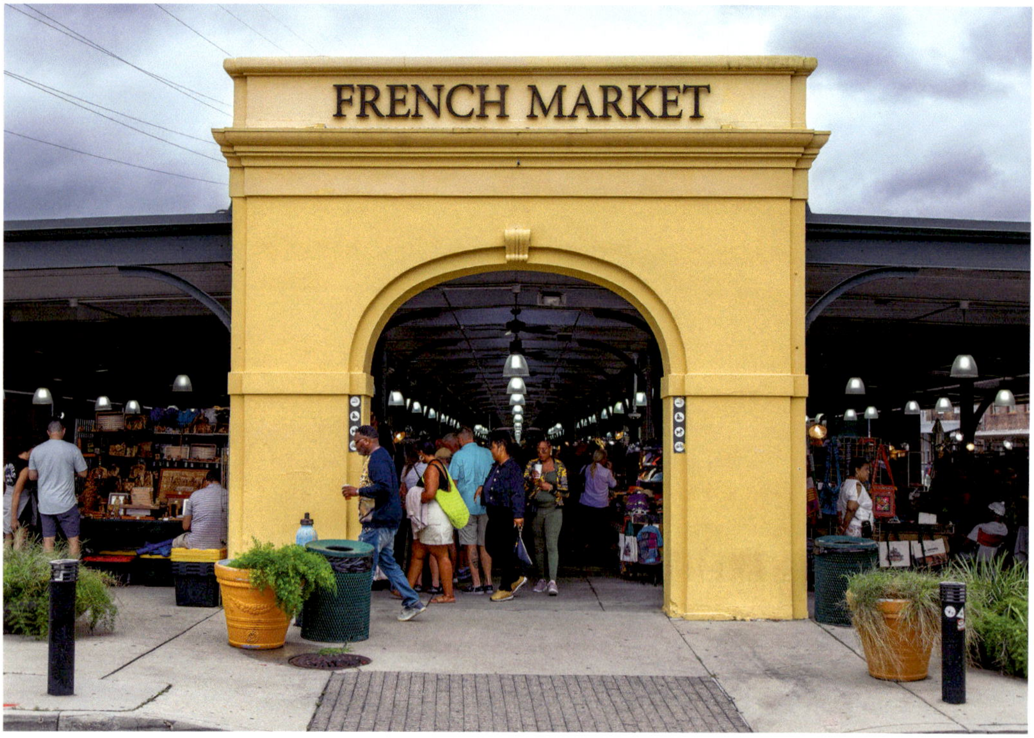

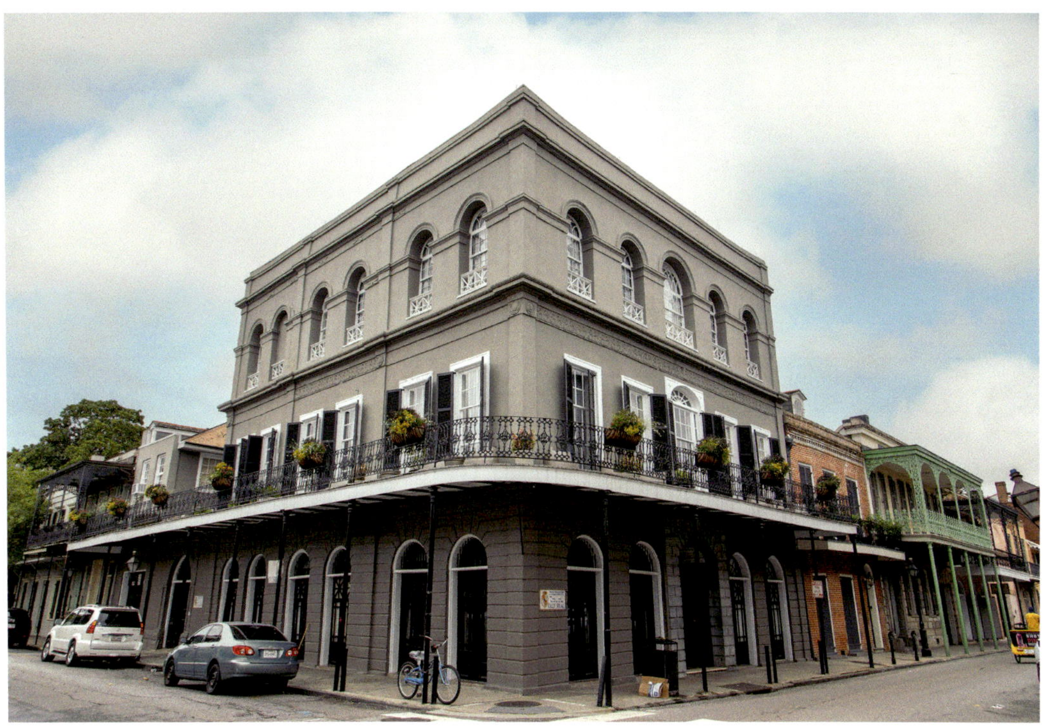

The LaLaurie Mansion, located at 1140 Royal Street in New Orleans' French Quarter, is infamous for its dark history involving Madame Delphine LaLaurie, who was exposed in 1834 for the horrific torture of enslaved individuals after a fire revealed her atrocities. This event led to public outrage, her escape to Paris, and the mansion becoming a symbol of New Orleans' haunted past, often cited in discussions as one of America's most chilling historical sites.

Opposite above: Dutch Alley, a vibrant corridor within New Orleans' French Market, was named in honor of Ernest "Dutch" Morial, the city's first African American mayor, reflecting his legacy and the cultural richness of the area, where art, history, and community converge.

Opposite below: The French Market, a vibrant tapestry of New Orleans' history, began as a Native American trading post, evolving into a bustling hub where cultures blended, from its establishment in 1791 to its enduring role as America's oldest public market, reflecting the city's diverse heritage through centuries of change.

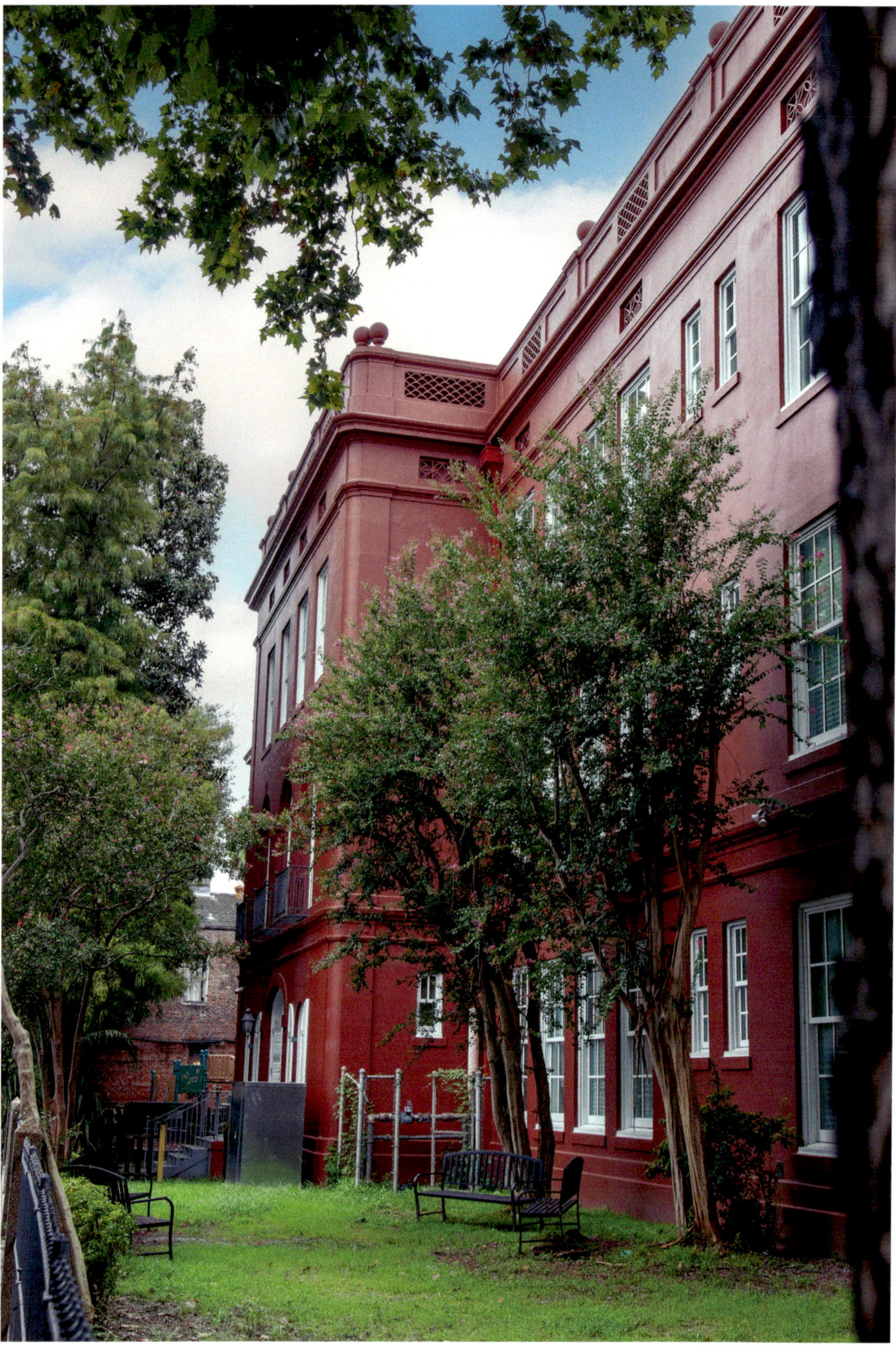

The Homer A. Plessy Community School, nestled at 721 St. Philip Street, stands as the sole testament to education within the French Quarter, a historic beacon where the echoes of learning have resonated since its inception in the nineteenth century, embodying the neighborhood's rich cultural tapestry and enduring community spirit.

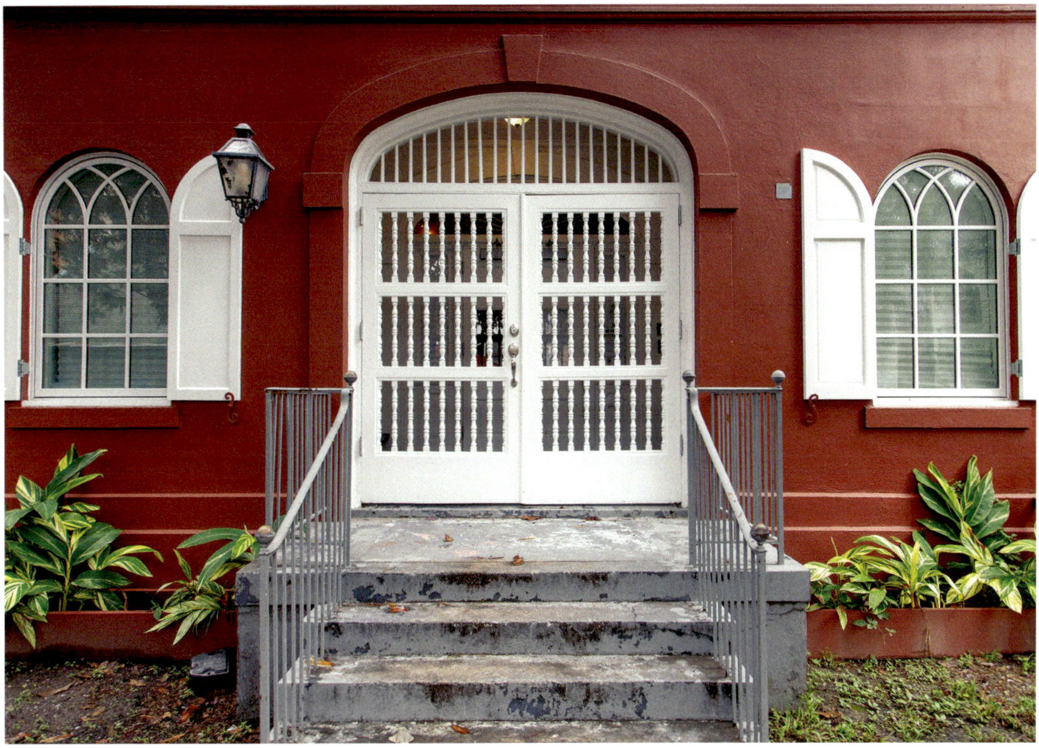

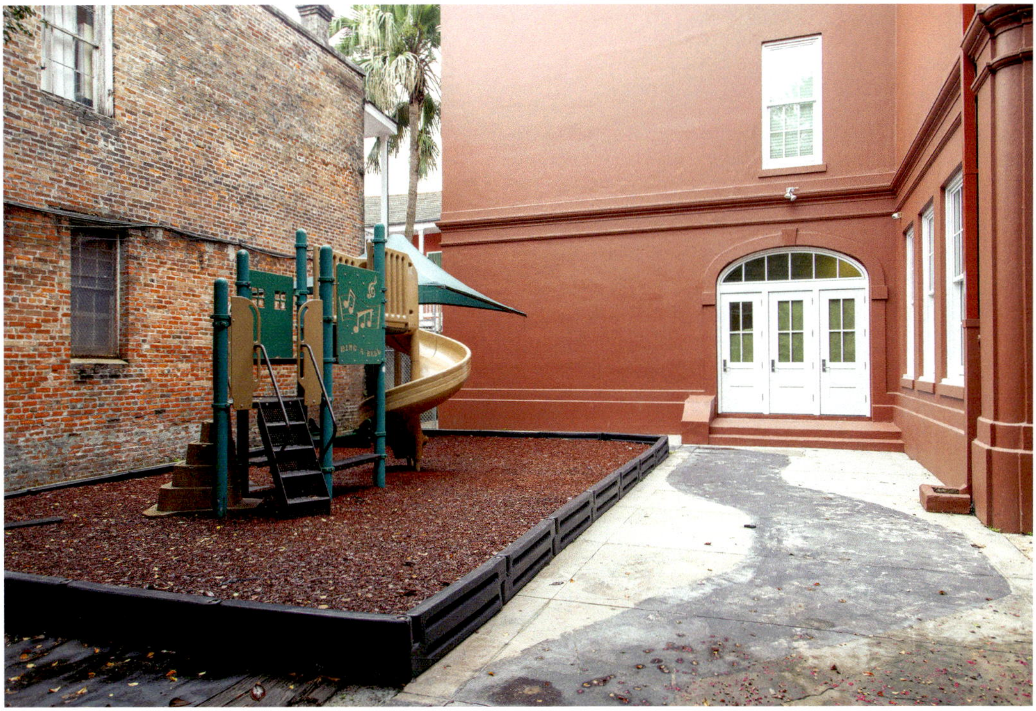

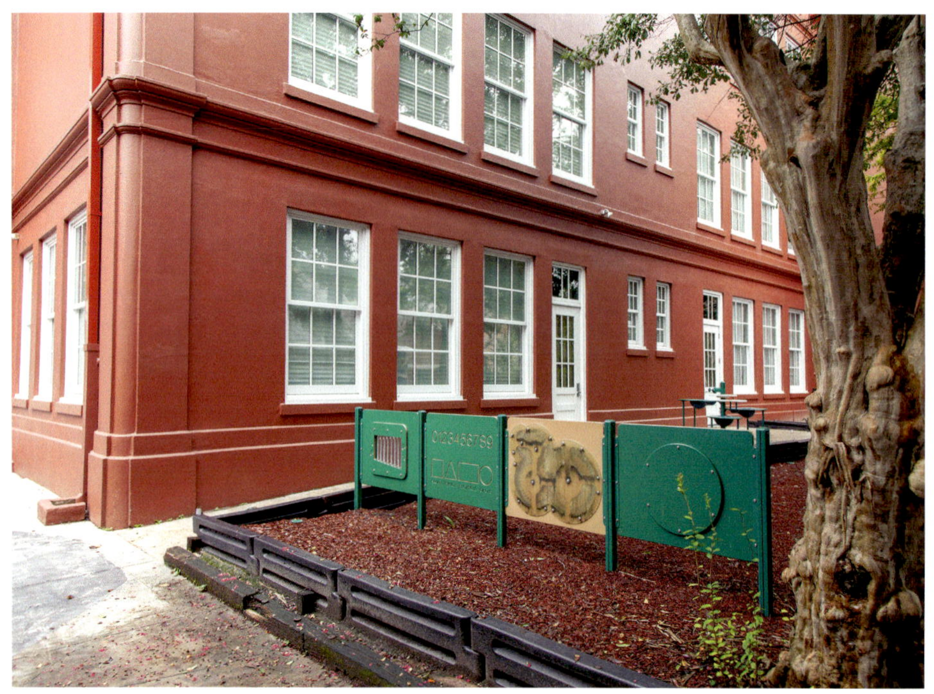

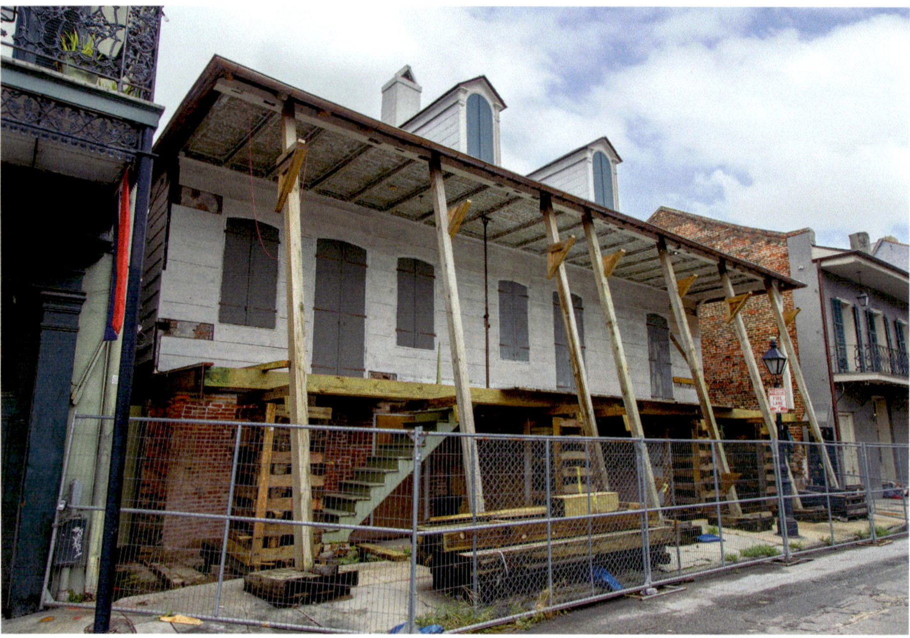

Madame John's Legacy at 632 Dumaine Street, a French Quarter gem, stands as a testament to post-fire resilience, embodying Creole architecture from 1788. This historic house museum, part of the Louisiana State Museum, reflects New Orleans' rich cultural narrative, from its architectural survival to its depiction in literature and film, offering visitors a tangible link to the city's storied past.

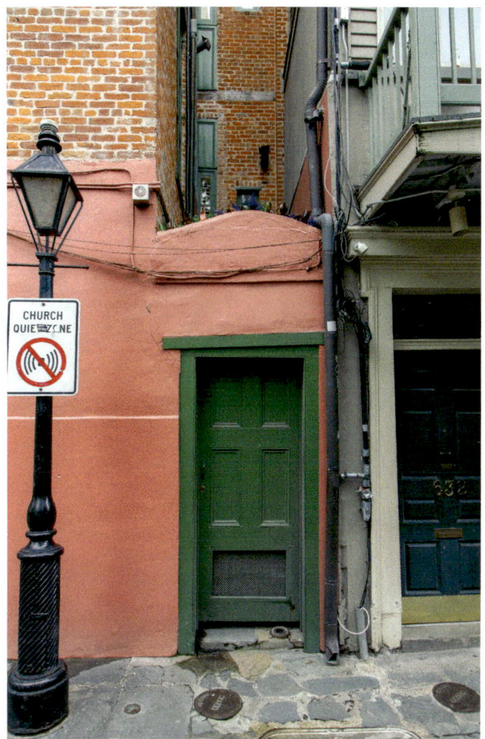

In New Orleans, the tradition of placing broken glass on ledges is not to deter criminals, but rather to keep pigeons from roosting, a quirky yet effective method to maintain the historic facades' pristine condition.

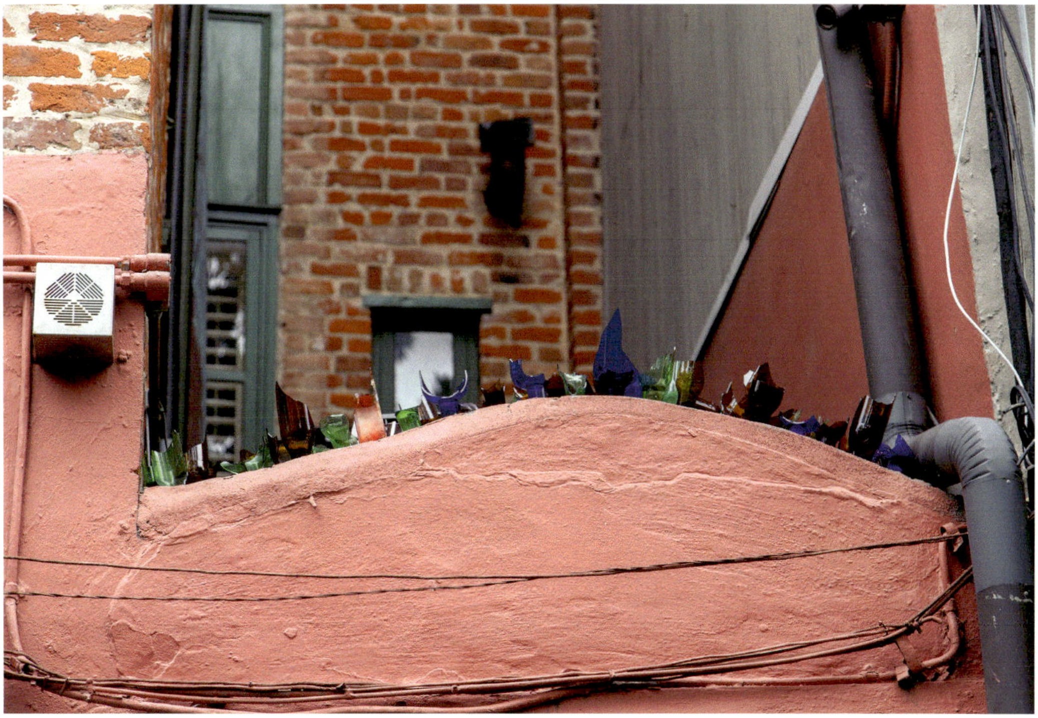

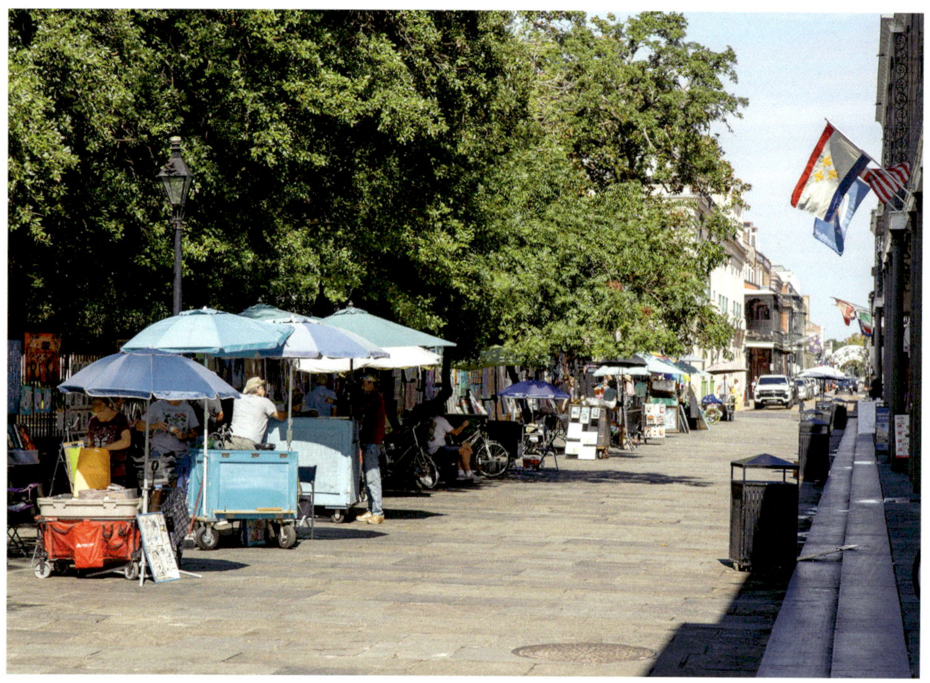

Along Jackson Square, art vendors line up, their colorful displays transforming the sidewalk into an open-air gallery, where the spirit of New Orleans' creativity meets the cobblestones.

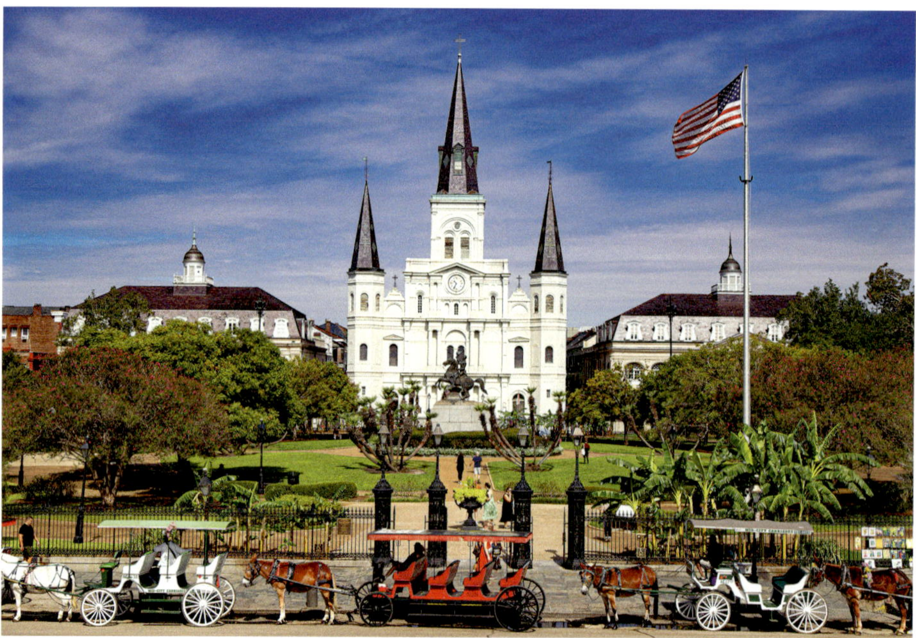

In front of Jackson Square, a picturesque lineup of horses and buggies awaits, their reins held patiently, offering a nostalgic journey through the French Quarter's historic streets.

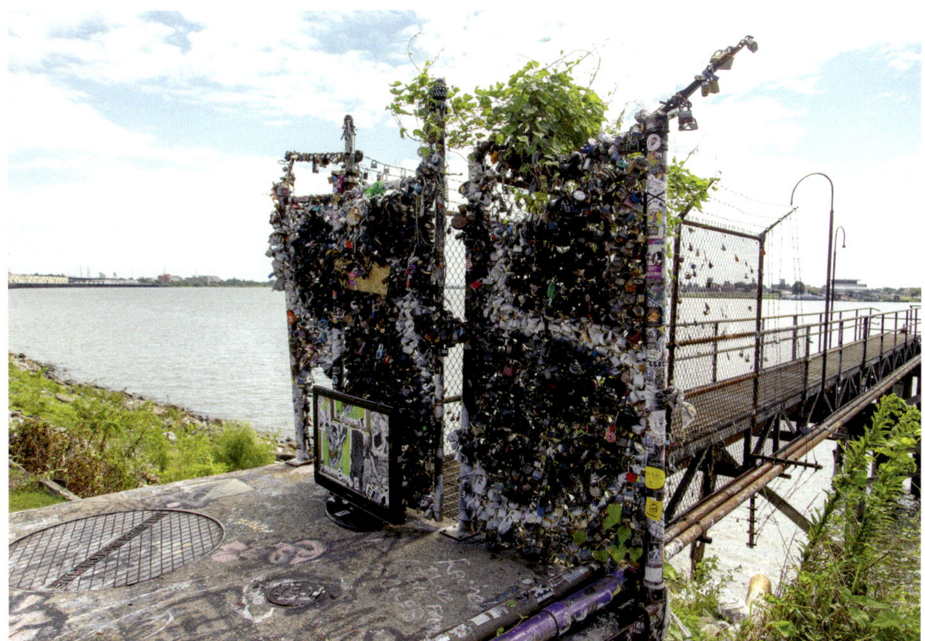

From the heart of Paris to the banks of the Mississippi, love locks symbolize eternal affection, where couples seal their commitment with a click, leaving behind a testament to love that's meant to last, even if the structures they adorn sometimes cannot.

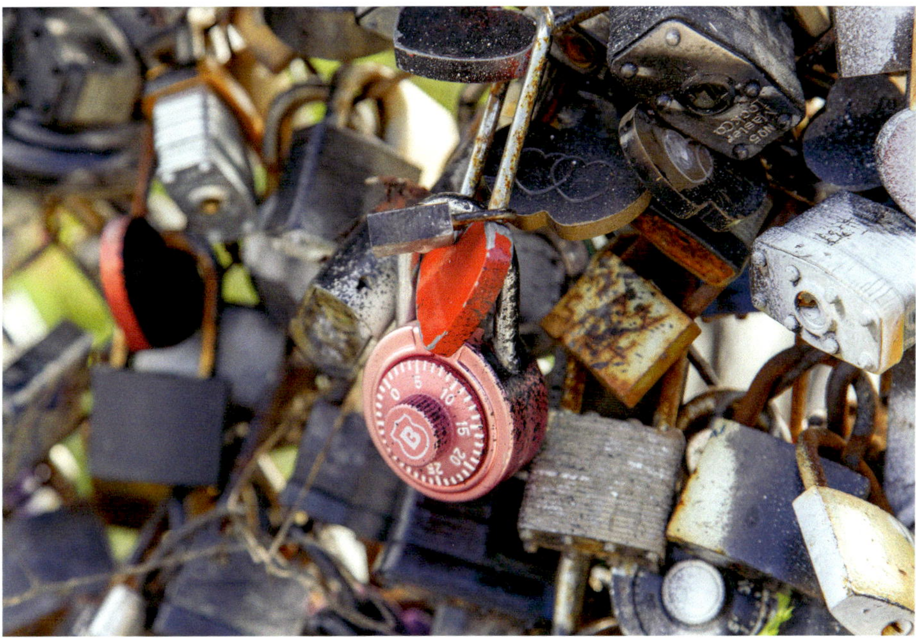

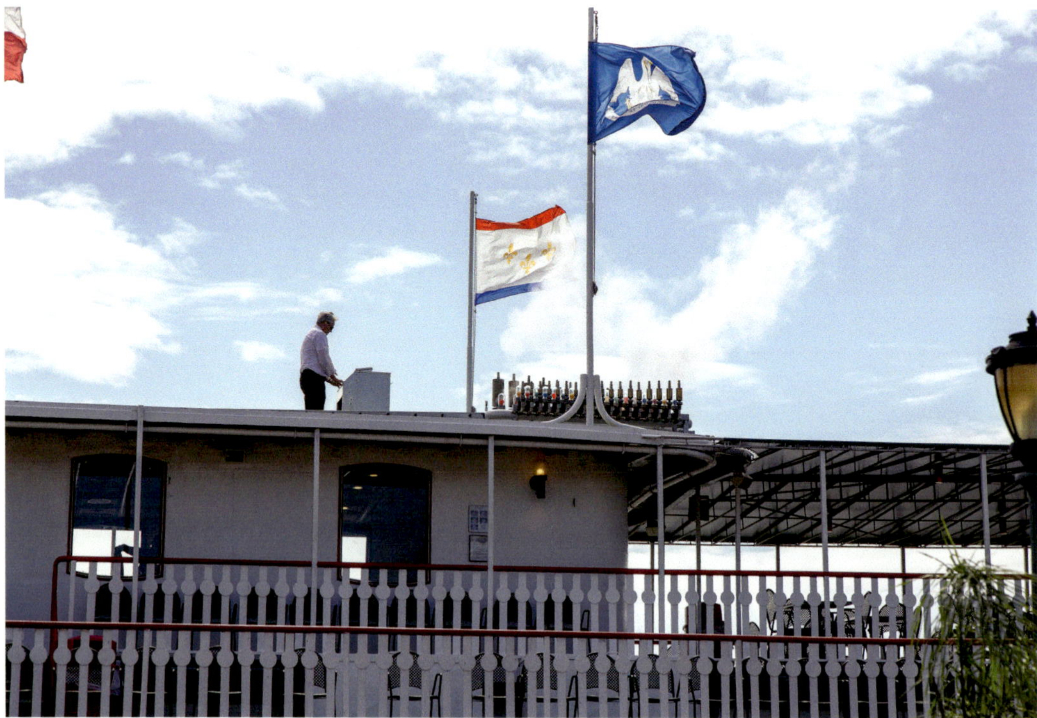

Harnessing the steam from The Natchez Paddle Boat, the organ player fills Sunday morning with music, each note a puff of history, enchanting the gathering crowd with a melody that dances on the river's breeze.

Opposite page: The Andrew Jackson Hotel, a historic boutique in New Orleans' French Quarter, blends eighteenth-century charm with modern comfort. Once a courthouse where Andrew Jackson was fined, it now offers twenty-one rooms steeped in history. Its location near Bourbon Street provides vibrant access, yet it maintains a serene, haunted ambiance, offering guests a dive into the city's past with Southern hospitality.

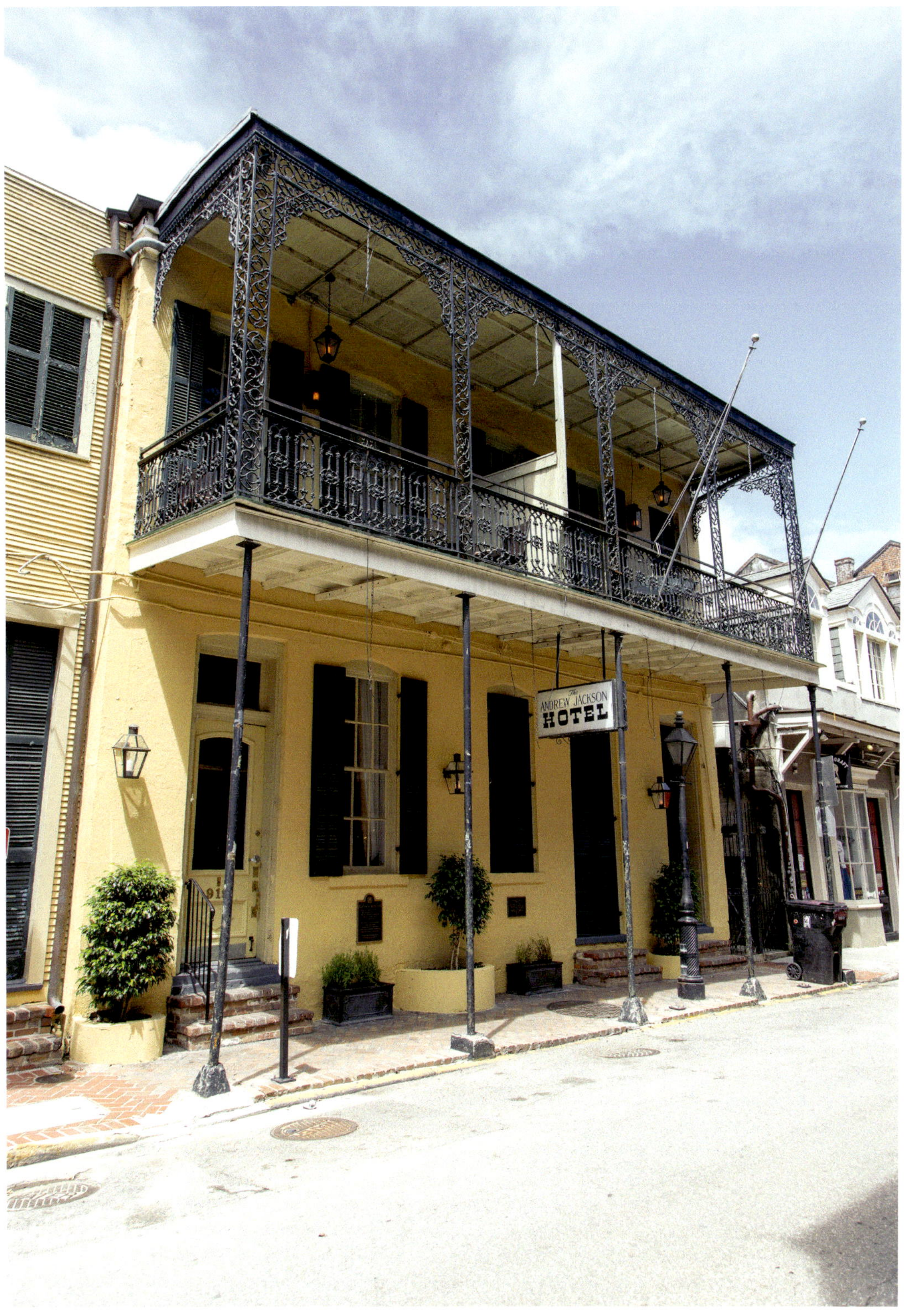
The
ANDREW JACKSON
HOTEL

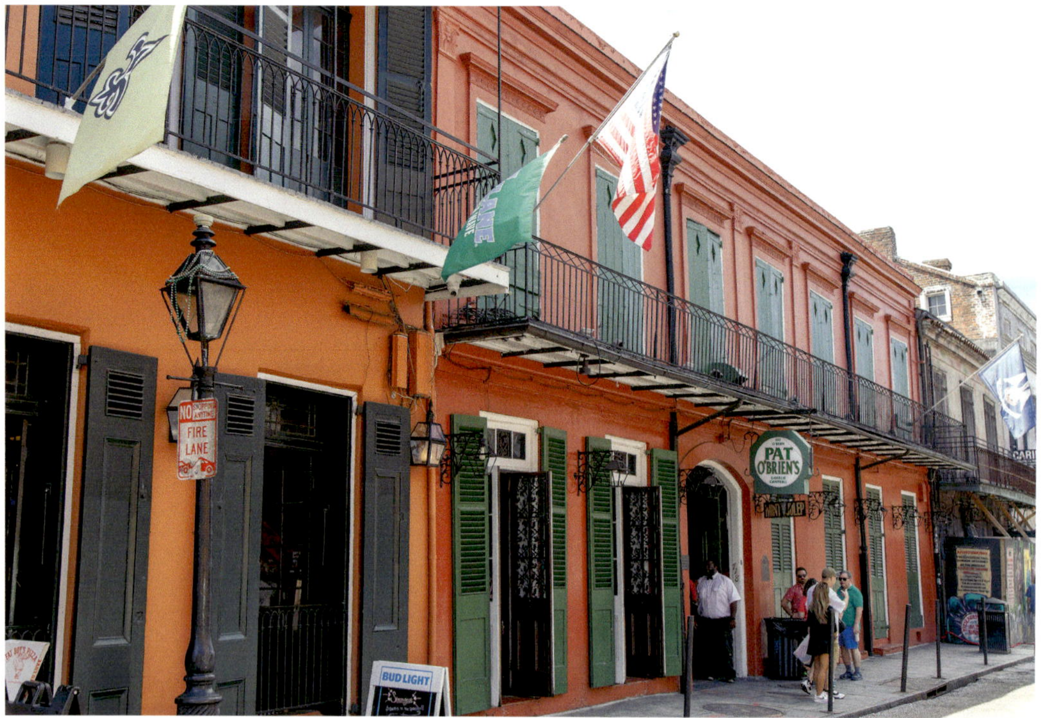

Pat O'Brien's, affectionately known as Pat O's, is an iconic New Orleans bar located in the French Quarter. Famous for its Hurricane cocktail, served in a signature glass, Pat O's has been a staple since 1933. Its lush, tropical courtyard, complete with a flaming fountain, provides a vibrant atmosphere where jazz music fills the air. Beyond its drinks, Pat O's is celebrated for its piano bar, where patrons can sing along to classic tunes. This historic bar not only embodies the spirit of New Orleans' nightlife but also its resilience, having survived Prohibition by selling legal wine and spirits as a "soft drink stand." Today, it is a must-visit destination for locals and tourists alike, offering a slice of the city's soul in every sip.

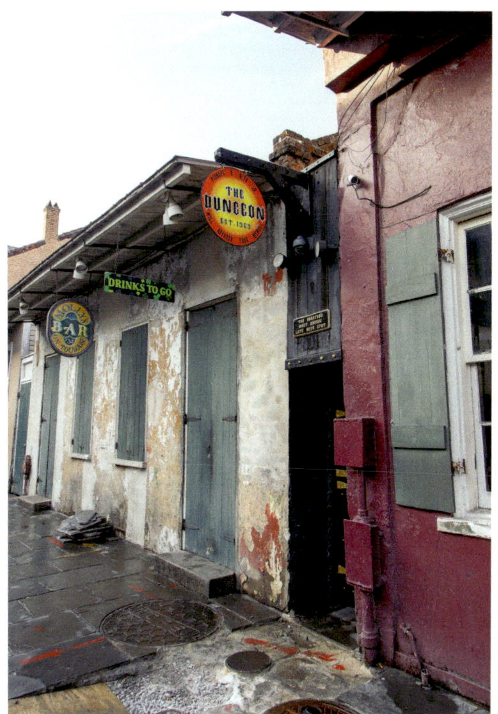

The Dungeon in the Quarter, a late-night haunt in New Orleans' French Quarter, is where gothic ambiance meets rock 'n' roll, offering a subterranean escape with its dark decor, heavy metal tunes, and a reputation for being an underground legend among locals and tourists alike.

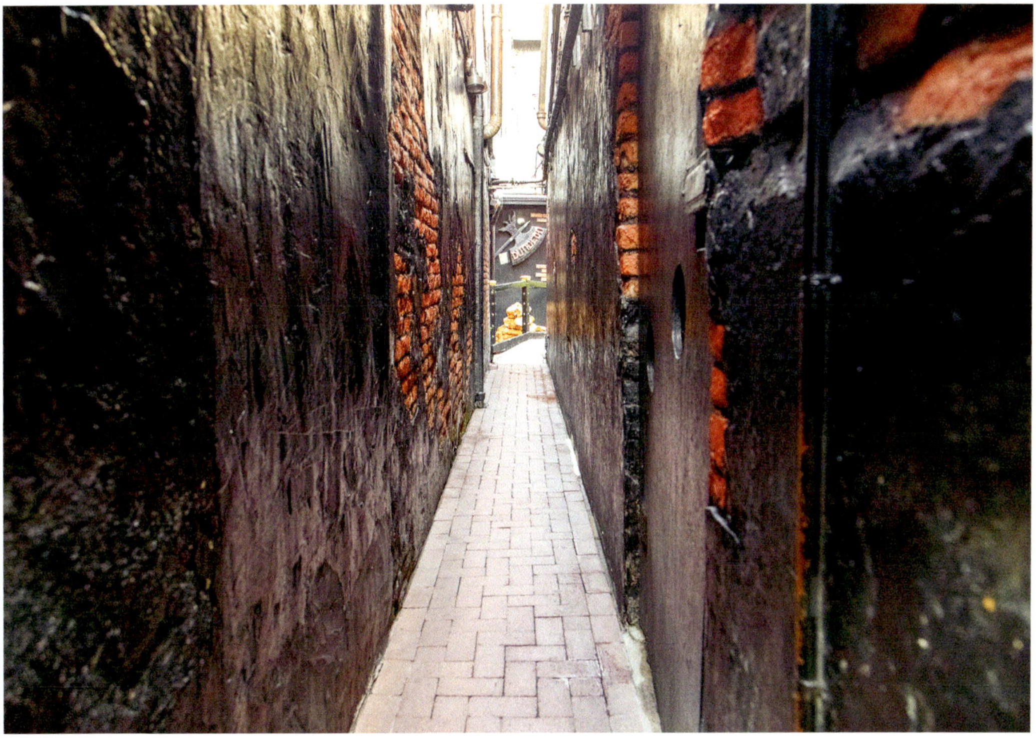

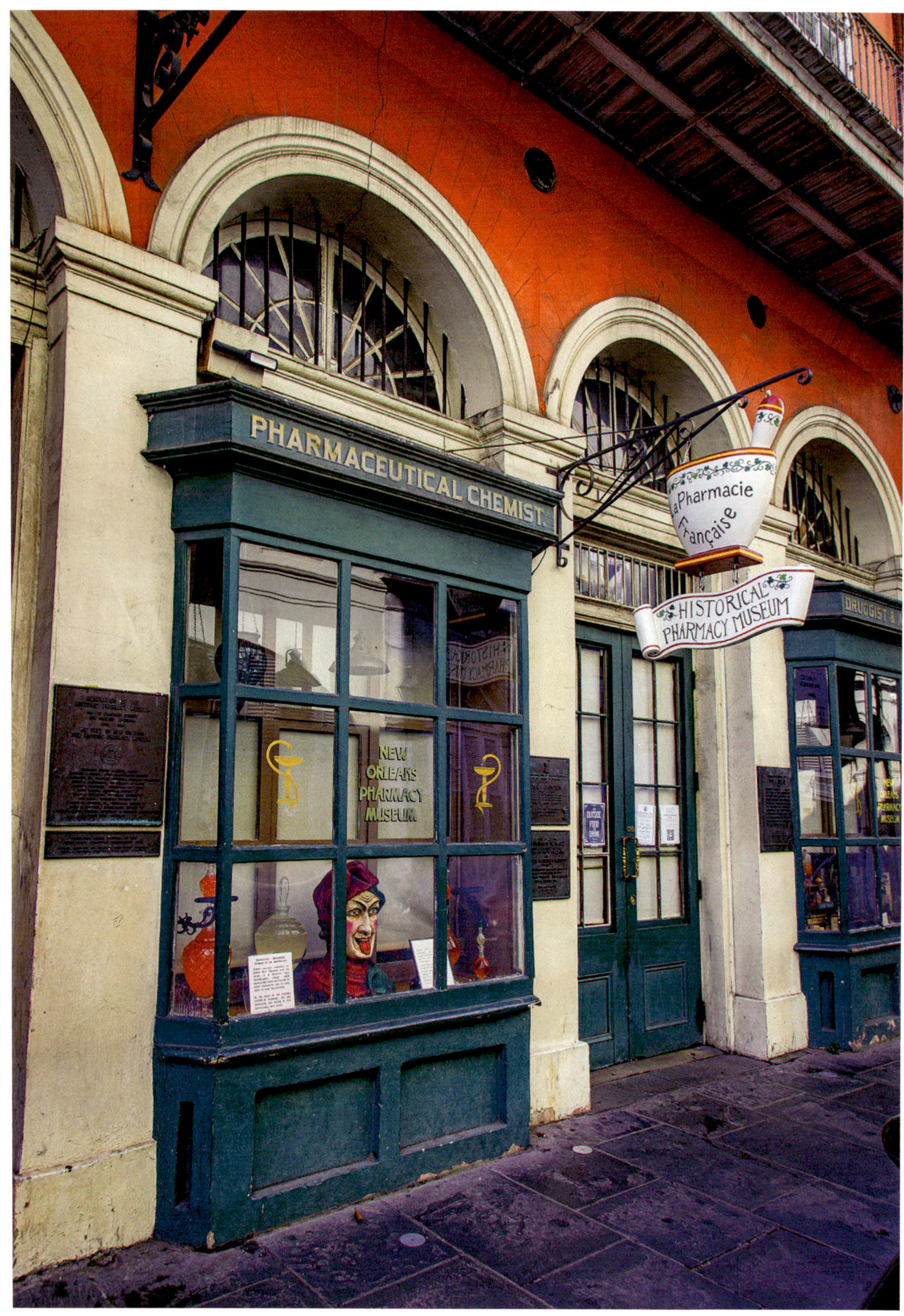
PHARMACEUTICAL CHEMIST.
La Pharmacie Française
HISTORICAL PHARMACY MUSEUM
NEW ORLEANS PHARMACY MUSEUM

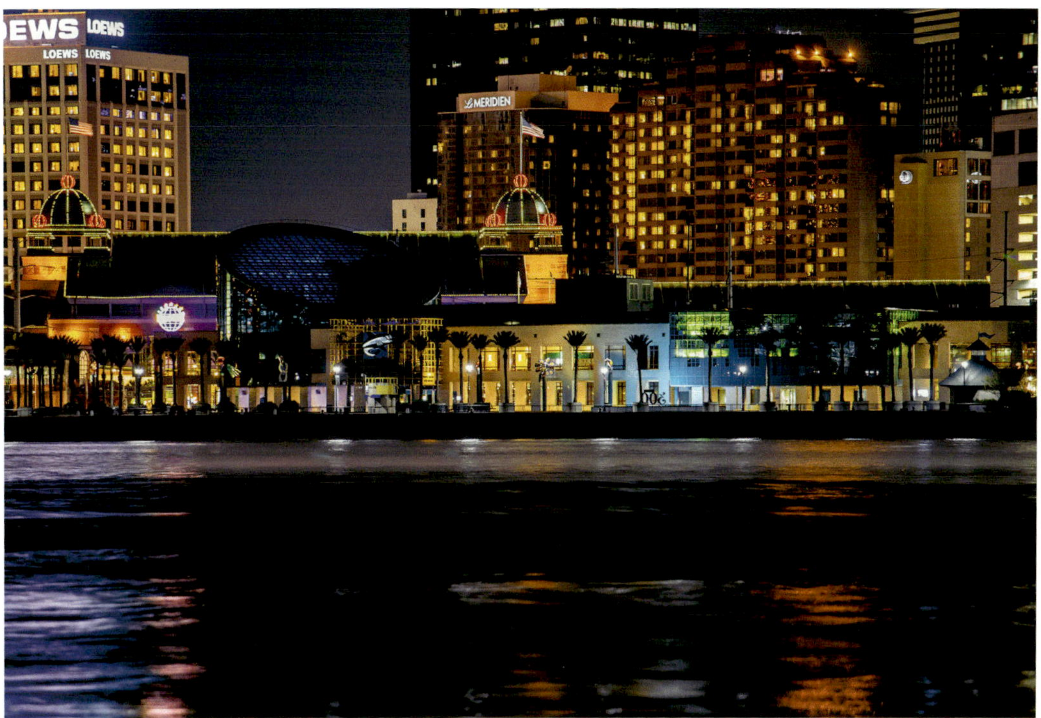

From Algiers Point, the Audubon Aquarium at night transforms into a beacon of urban beauty, its lights reflecting off the Mississippi, offering a serene contrast to the bustling city life across the river.

Opposite page: The New Orleans Pharmacy Museum, housed in an 1823 French Quarter building, was once Louis J. Dufilho Jr.'s apothecary, America's first licensed pharmacist. It showcases nineteenth-century pharmaceutical history with an extensive collection of medical antiques, including apothecary jars, surgical tools, and voodoo artifacts, reflecting New Orleans' medical and cultural heritage. This museum, on the National Register of Historic Places, offers a glimpse into early pharmacy practices, blending history with the mystique of the French Quarter.

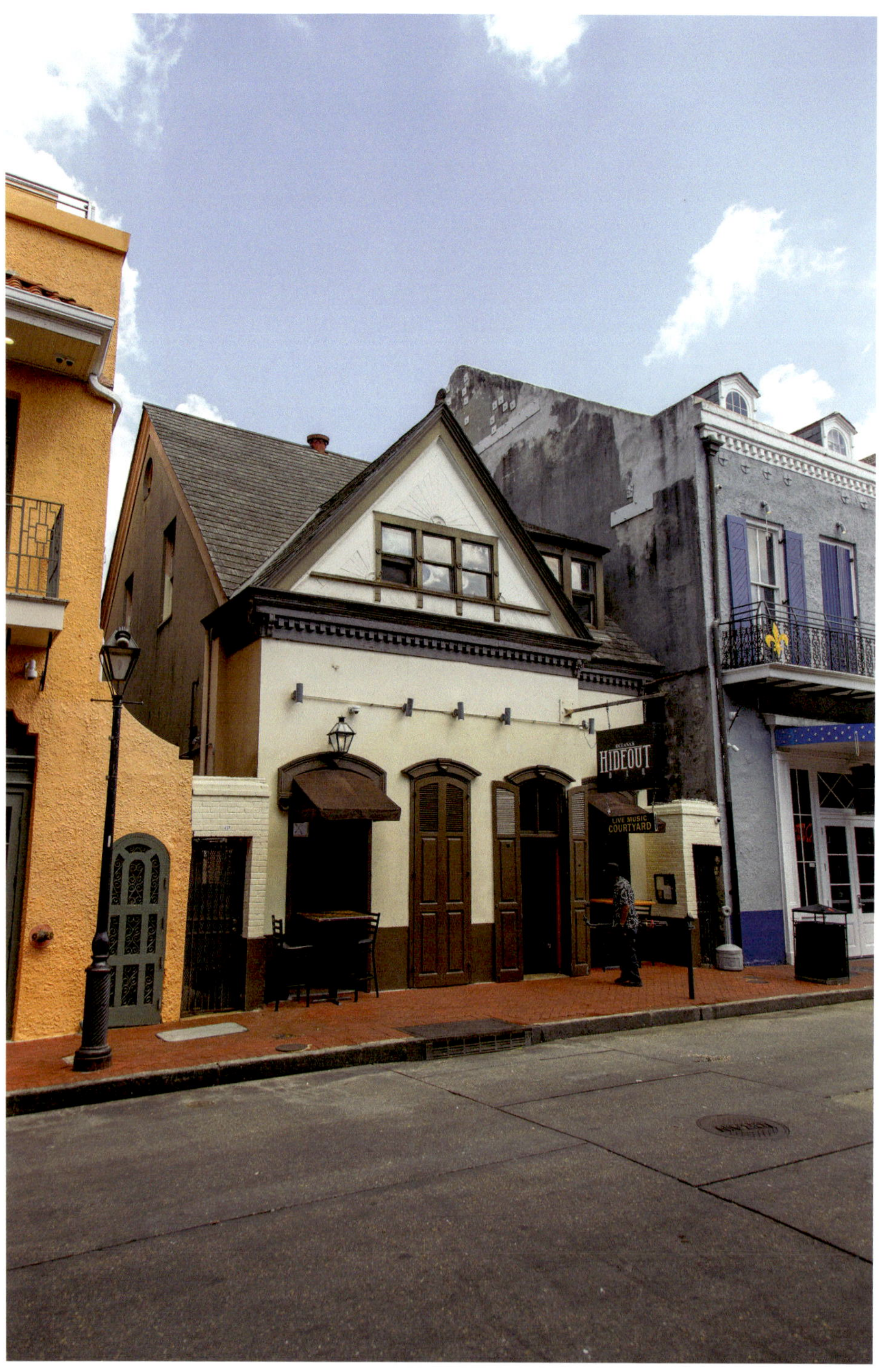

Tucked away in the French Quarter, The Hideout offers a speakeasy retreat with Southern bites, live tunes, and a courtyard escape, where New Orleans' charm whispers rather than shouts.

5

The Symphony of the Streets

In the French Quarter, the streets themselves are stages where talent and passion come alive. This chapter celebrates the entertainers who fill the air with music, stories, and spectacle, making every corner a potential theater.

A Cornucopia of Talent: From the moment you step into the Quarter, you are greeted by a symphony of sounds and sights. Tanya Huang's violin might serenade you with classical melodies, her bow dancing across the strings with a precision that transports you to concert halls. On another corner, Terry from Haunted History might pull you into a circle, his voice weaving tales of ghosts and legends that chill the spine.

The Jazz Ambassadors: Then there is Effrim Towns, whose trumpet with The Dirty Dozen Brass Band fills the air with the soul of New Orleans. Jazz, the heartbeat of the city, is not just heard but felt, vibrating through the cobblestones and into your very being. These musicians, with their horns and drums, are the modern-day minstrels, carrying forward the legacy of jazz.

Living Statues and Street Performers: Beyond the musicians, the Quarter hosts an array of performers. Living statues stand in silent defiance of time, their stillness a stark contrast to the bustling life around them. Magicians, dancers, and acrobats perform feats that defy logic, drawing gasps and applause from passersby.

The Essence of the Quarter: These entertainers are not mere performers; they are the spirit of the French Quarter. They embody its creativity, its resilience, and its joy. Each act, whether a solo violinist or a full brass band, contributes to the rich cultural tapestry that makes the Quarter unique.

A Living Legacy: Through their performances, these artists keep the traditions of New Orleans alive, blending the old with the new. They are as integral to the Quarter's identity as its historic buildings, their talents echoing through the streets, ensuring that the music, stories, and magic never fade.

In this chapter, I have captured moments of these entertainers in action, their passion and skill evident in every frame. Through these photographs, I invite you to experience the spontaneous concerts, the impromptu storytelling sessions, and the unexpected performances that make the French Quarter not just a place, but a living, breathing celebration of art and life.

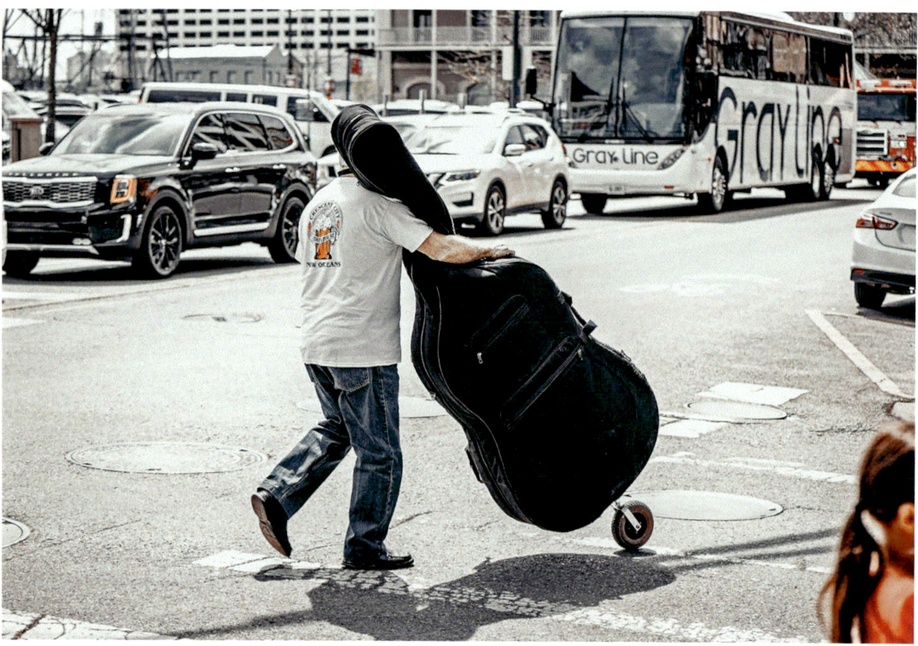

With his bass in tow, or push, he rolls through the streets, a musician on a mission, the heartbeat of New Orleans' rhythm echoing with each turn of the wheel.

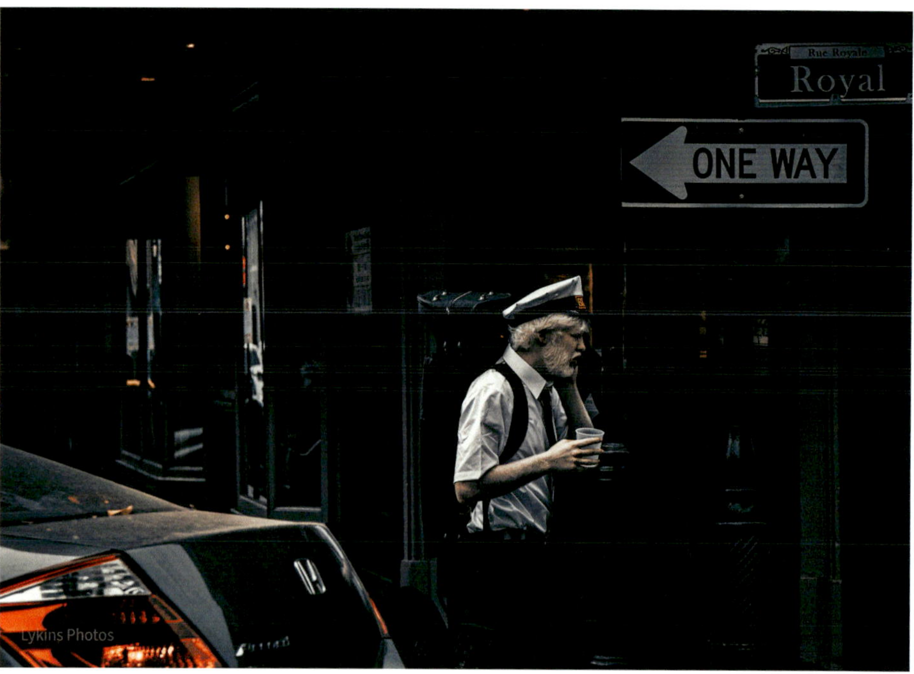

Taking a moment's rest, a member of the Big Fun Brass Band pauses, their instrument at their side, the vibrant energy of New Orleans' music scene still pulsing through their veins.

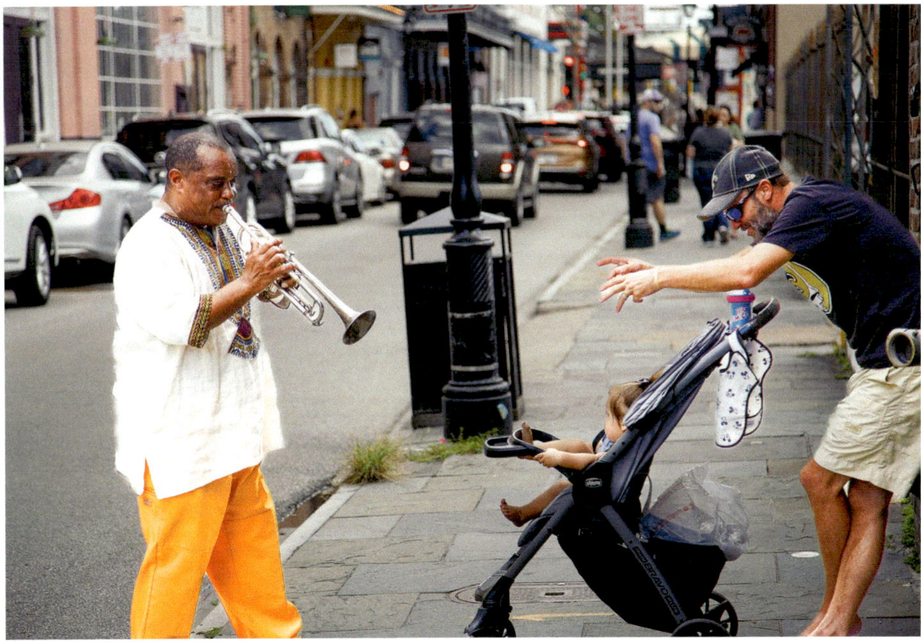

Efrem Towns, trumpet in hand, serenades a captivated baby and her father on the streets of the Quarter, where every note is a gift, weaving the magic of New Orleans' soul.

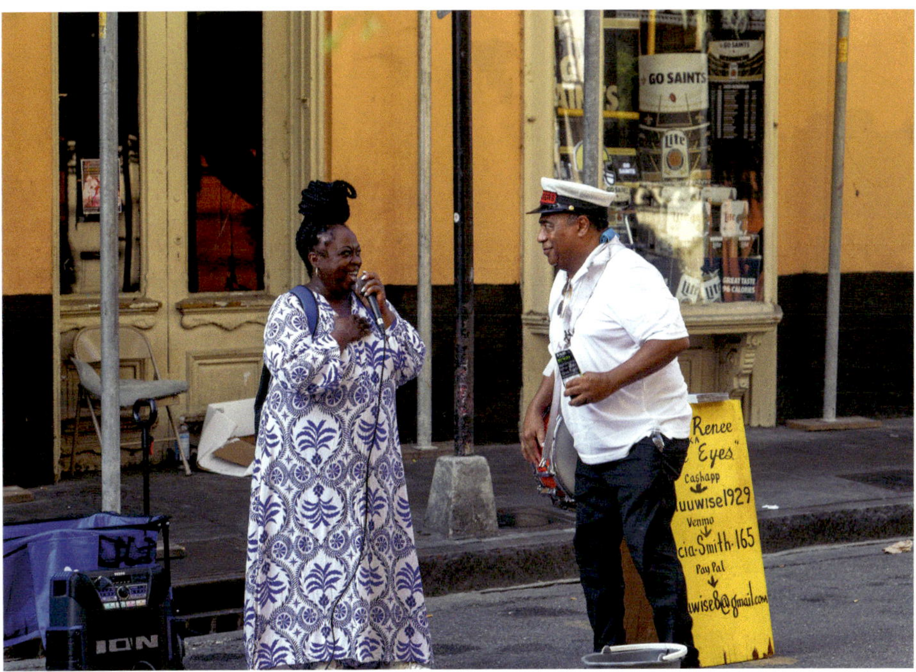

In the heart of the Quarter, Alicia Renee, known as Blue Eyes, shares a soulful moment with another performer, their music blending into a spontaneous street symphony.

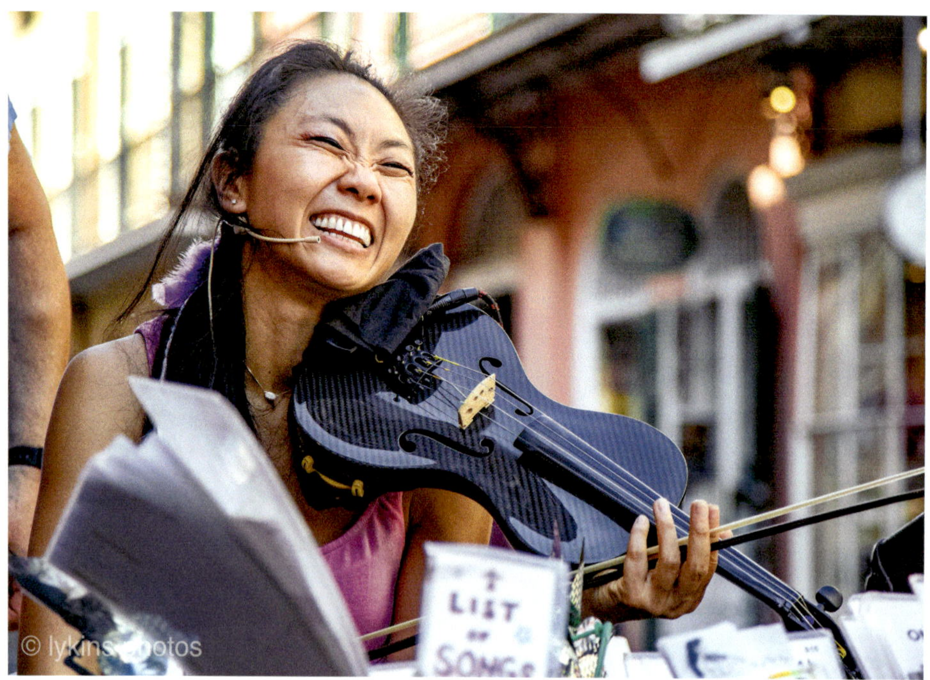

Between melodies, Tanya Huang's laughter rings out, a joyful interlude in her street performance, capturing the spirit of New Orleans' vibrant street culture.

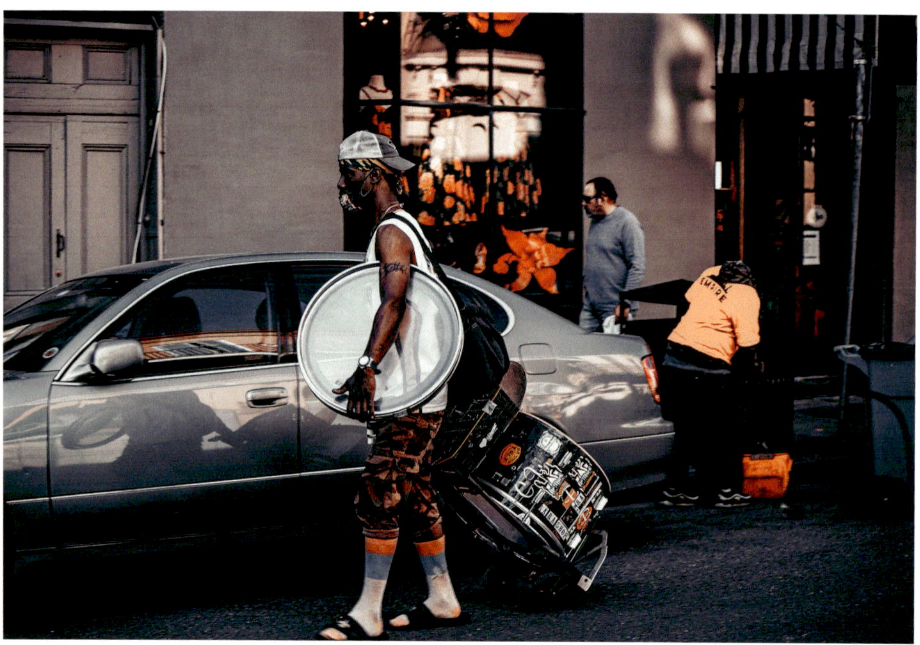

Three years ago, in the vibrant stretch of the French Quarter, I captured a drummer, his rhythm echoing off the historic buildings, a living testament to New Orleans' pulsating heart.

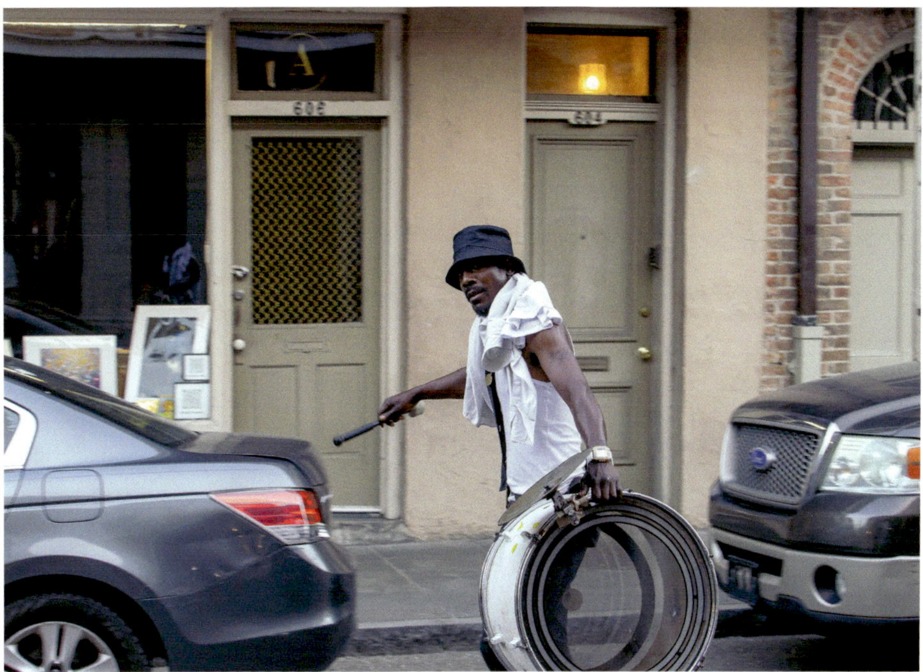

This day, I found him again, nearly in the same spot, the same passionate drummer, his beats as timeless as the city's spirit, proving some things in New Orleans never change.

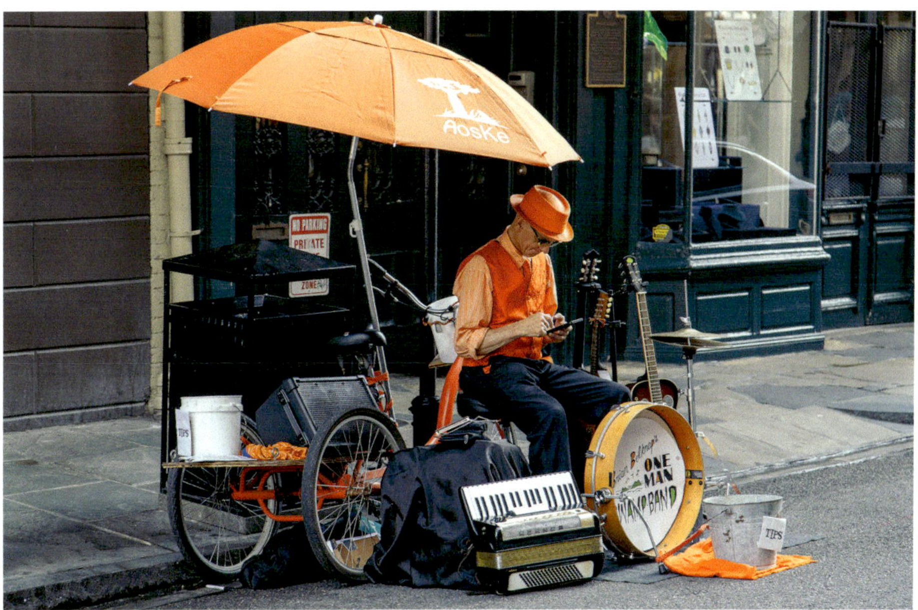

Caught in a rare moment of stillness, Brian Belknap, the dynamo behind the One Man Swamp Band, checks his phone during a break, his instruments resting around him, a brief pause in the symphony of his life on the streets.

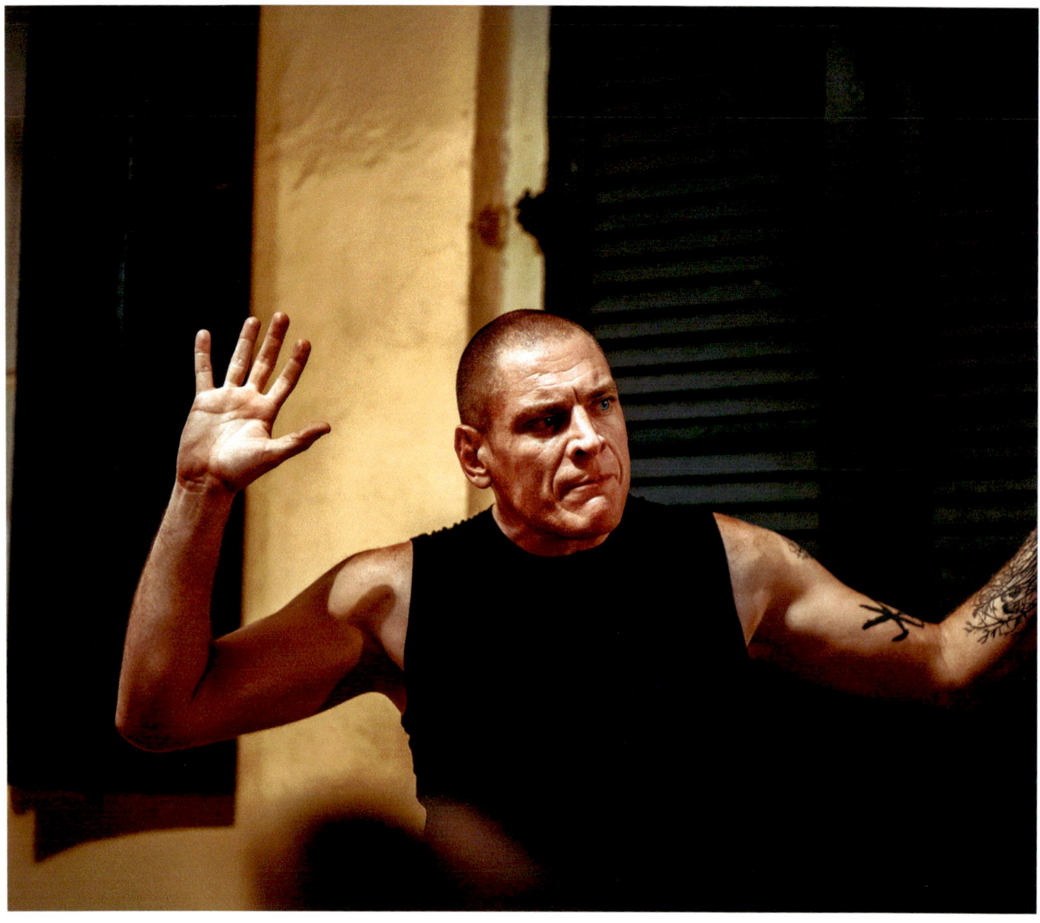

Meet Terry, the French Quarter's living legend. With a passion for the past and an encyclopedic knowledge of New Orleans' spectral tales, Terry does not just guide you; he resurrects history. His tours are not just walks through the Quarter—they are journeys through time, where every shadow whispers secrets. Terry is not just a guide; he is the keeper of New Orleans' haunted legacy.

6

The Signs of Life

In the French Quarter, even the street signs and business fronts tell stories. This chapter explores the unique signage and the vibrant commercial life that defines this historic neighborhood.

The Street Signs: The street signs of the French Quarter are more than just directional aids; they are pieces of art and history. While you might expect traditional signs mounted on poles, the Quarter has its own charm with names often embedded in the sidewalk. These signs, with their distinctive blue and white tiles, are a nod to the past, a time when horse-drawn carriages made these low-lying markers practical for drivers to read. The names themselves? A blend of French and Spanish influences. Streets like Bourbon, Royal, and Chartres echo the French heritage, named after nobility or saints. Yet, the Spanish era left its mark too, with streets like Decatur, named after a U.S. naval hero, reflecting the broader historical influences post-Spanish rule. This mix of names tells a story of colonial exchange, where French and Spanish cultures melded, creating the unique Creole identity of New Orleans.

Businesses: The Heart of the Quarter: From the iconic signs of Pat O'Brien's to the neon lights of Bourbon Street's bars, the business signs are as much a part of the Quarter's identity as its architecture. Each sign, whether for a restaurant, hotel, or bar, represents not just a business but a piece of the city's soul.

Restaurants: From the Creole dishes at places like Cafe Maspero, with its historic sign, to the modern eateries, these establishments are where culinary traditions thrive. The signs often reflect the age and reputation of the eatery, some becoming landmarks themselves.

Hotels: The signs of hotels like the Andrew Jackson or the Le Richelieu not only guide guests but also promise a taste of New Orleans' hospitality, their designs often echoing the architectural style of the buildings.

Bars: The neon lights of bars like Lafitte's Blacksmith Shop or the vibrant facade of the Tony Seville's Pirate Alley Café are more than just invitations for a drink; they are beacons of the Quarter's nightlife, each with its own history and character.

The Cultural Tapestry: These signs and businesses are more than just markers or commercial entities; they're threads in the rich tapestry of the French Quarter. They reflect its history, its resilience, and its continuous evolution. From the oldest establishments that have seen centuries pass to the new ventures that keep the Quarter vibrant, each sign tells a story of survival, celebration, and the ever-present spirit of New Orleans.

In this chapter, through photographs, I have captured these signs not just as they are but as symbols of the lifeblood of the Quarter. They guide us, entertain us, and remind us of why this place, with its blend of French and Spanish heritage, remains a unique corner of America, where every corner turned is a page from a living history book.

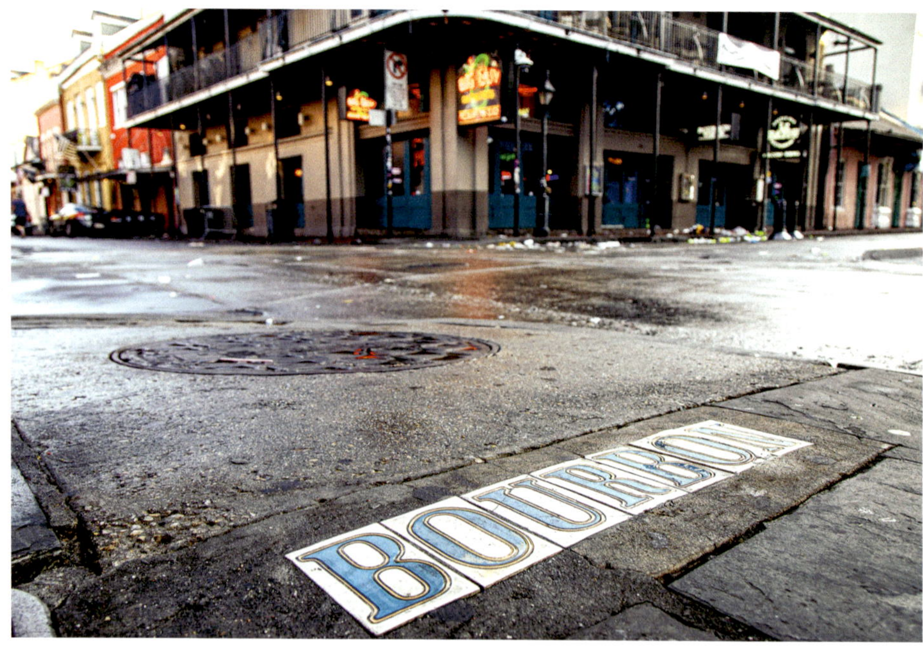

The charming street name tiles in the French Quarter are a pedestrian's delight for navigation, but a driver's challenge, often leading to a slow, careful dance through history.

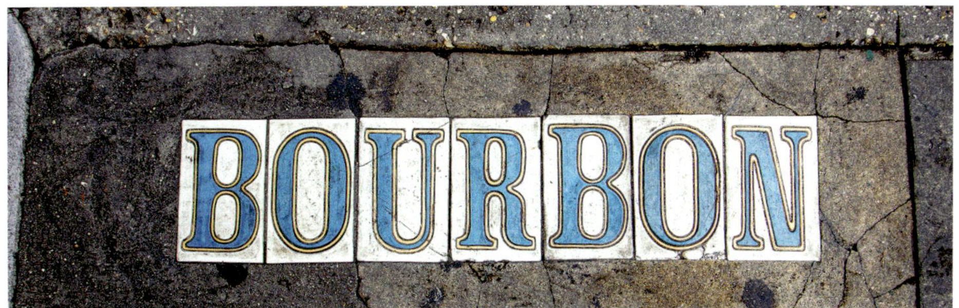

Bourbon Street, heart of New Orleans' French Quarter, evolved from a residential area to a global nightlife icon since 1721. Named for France's House of Bourbon, it reflects the city's cultural blend, shaped by fires, Spanish rule, and American influence. Known for jazz, cocktails, and twenty-four-hour revelry, it is where history meets hedonism, embodying New Orleans' spirit of celebration, resilience, and musical heritage, making it a must-visit for its unique ambiance.

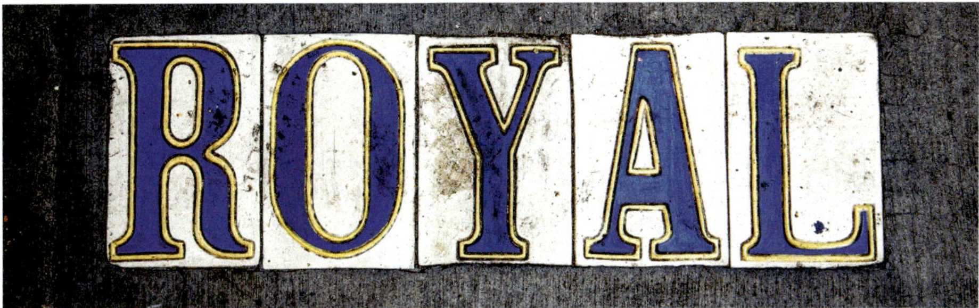

Royal Street, a historic artery of New Orleans, contrasts Bourbon's revelry with elegance. Lined with antique shops, galleries, and landmarks like Hotel Monteleone, it is a pedestrian-friendly corridor showcasing the city's architectural heritage. While it hosts cultural events and daily music, Royal Street also navigates gentrification, balancing preservation with modern challenges, embodying New Orleans' complex soul where history, culture, and contemporary life intertwine.

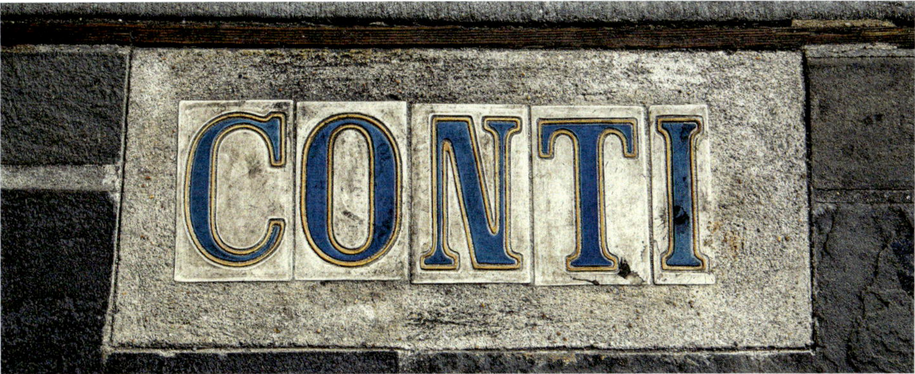

Conti Street in New Orleans' French Quarter, a historic corridor, blends old-world charm with vibrant culture. Home to landmarks like the Prince Conti Hotel, it is where history meets modern allure, offering a glimpse into the city's soul through its architecture, bars, and cultural museums.

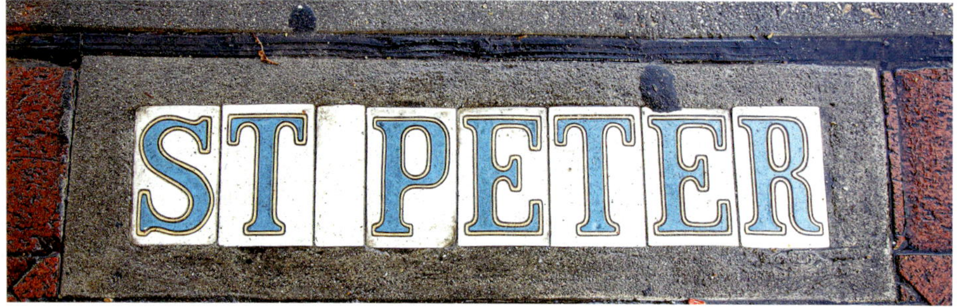

St. Peter Street in New Orleans' French Quarter, dating back to the city's founding in 1718, reflects the area's French and Spanish heritage. Named after St. Peter, it is known for historic architecture, including the site of the original St. Louis Cathedral. The street has witnessed significant events like the Great New Orleans Fires, leading to its predominantly Spanish architectural style. Today, it is a blend of residential charm and cultural landmarks, embodying the Quarter's rich history.

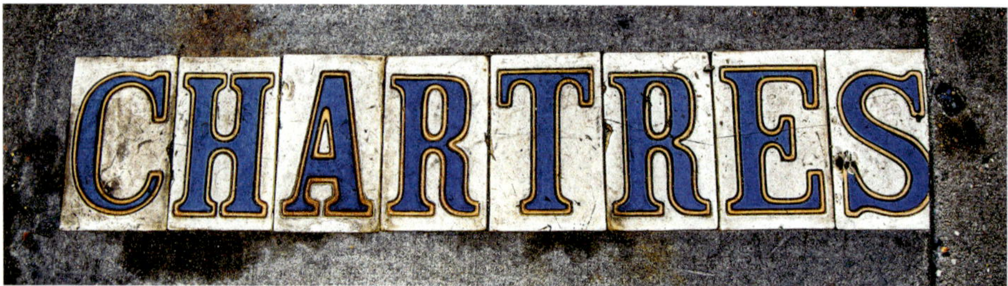

Chartres Street in New Orleans, named after the French city of Chartres, is a historic artery of the French Quarter, dating back to the city's founding in 1718. It is renowned for its architectural heritage, housing landmarks like the St. Louis Cathedral and the Beauregard-Keyes House. Over centuries, it evolved from residential to commercial, reflecting New Orleans' cultural blend, with significant historical events like the Louisiana Purchase influencing its development. Today, it is a blend of history, culture, and commerce, epitomizing the city's charm.

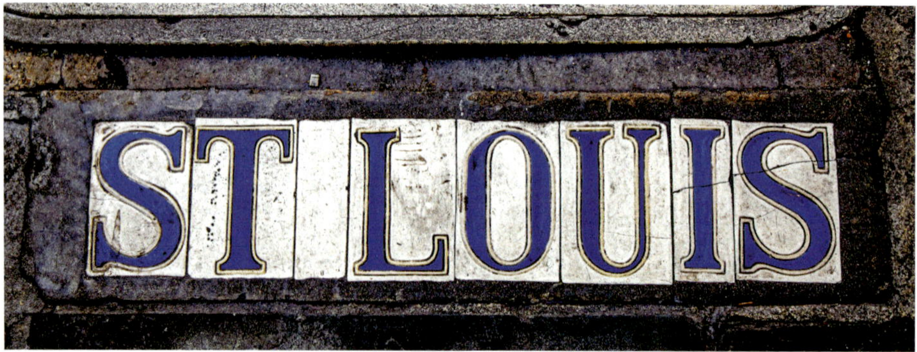

St. Louis Street in New Orleans, named after King Louis IX of France, runs through the heart of the French Quarter. Its history intertwines with that of the St. Louis Cathedral. Established in the early eighteenth century, the street has witnessed the city's evolution, from French and Spanish colonial periods to modern times, reflecting New Orleans' rich cultural tapestry with its architecture and proximity to historic landmarks.

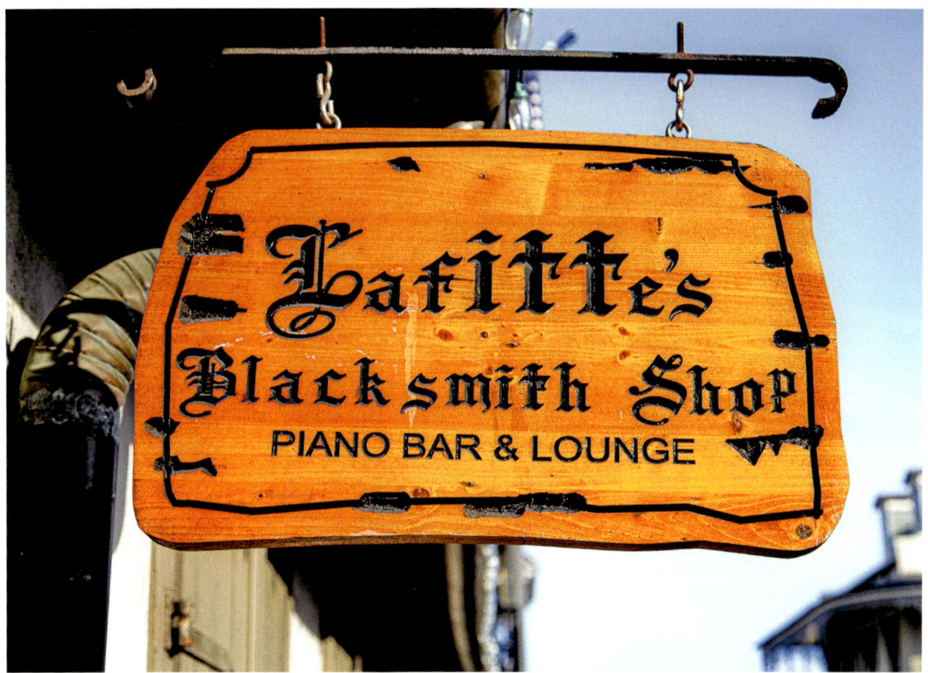

Lafitte's newer wooden sign, crafted to echo the eighteenth century, beckons visitors into one of New Orleans' most historic bars, blending modern craftsmanship with the lore of Jean Lafitte.

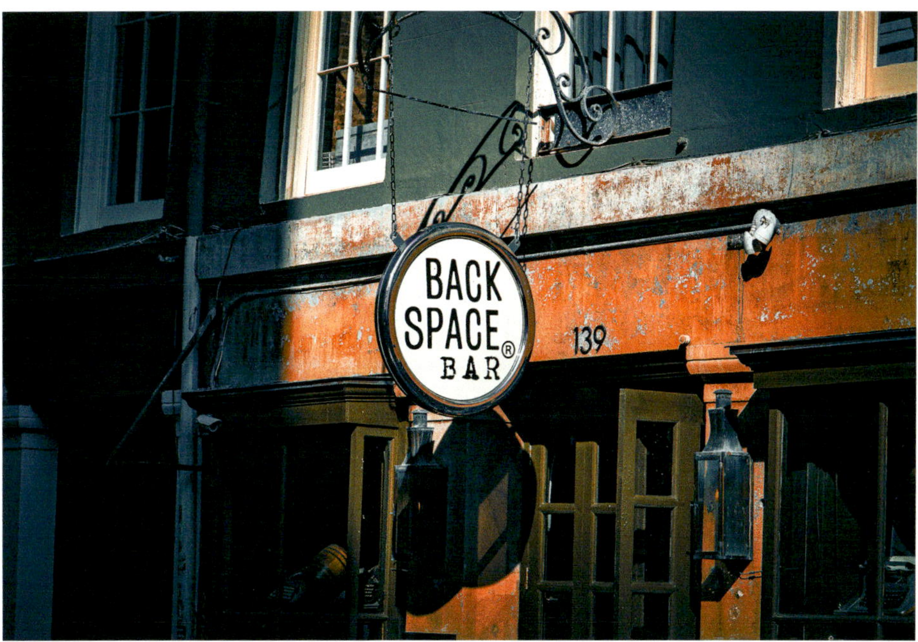

The sign at Backspace Bar in New Orleans' French Quarter is a clever play on words, visually representing the concept of "backspace" through its design.

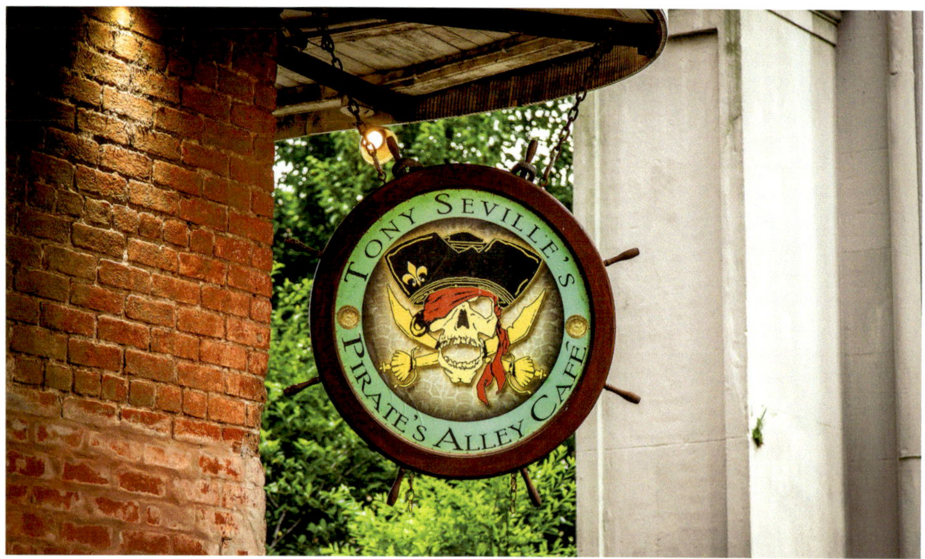

Tony Seville's Pirate Alley Cafe in New Orleans features a sign that cleverly incorporates the theme of piracy into its design. The sign, resembling a pirate ship's steering wheel, not only serves as a beacon for visitors but also encapsulates the cafe's nautical and pirate motif. This unique sign, with its spokes and central hub, evokes the imagery of steering through the historic and somewhat mystical Pirate's Alley, inviting patrons into an establishment where every detail, from decor to ambiance, celebrates the city's rich pirate lore and maritime history.

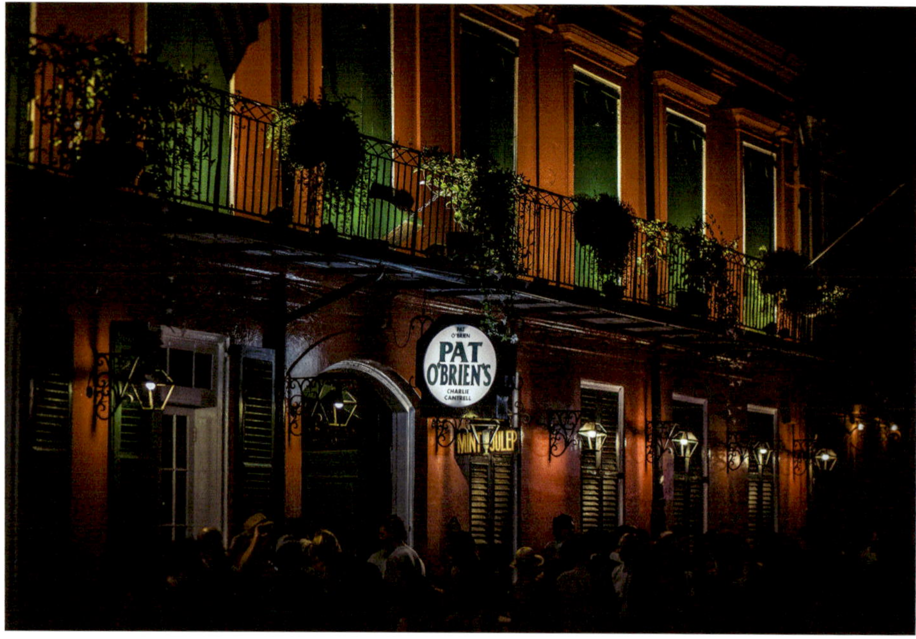

Pat O'Brien's sign at night, a glowing beacon in the French Quarter, guides the lost and weary to its doors, promising warmth, music, and the iconic Hurricane cocktail.

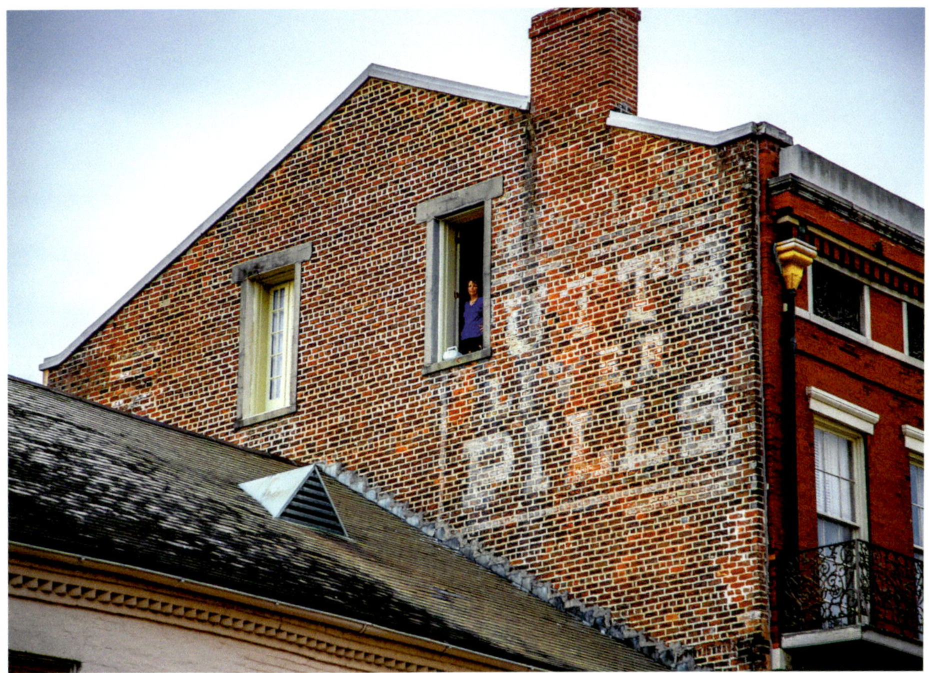

On a weathered brick wall, the faint echo of "Butt's Liver Pills" reminds us that even in New Orleans, where time dances differently, some signs of the past refuse to fade away.

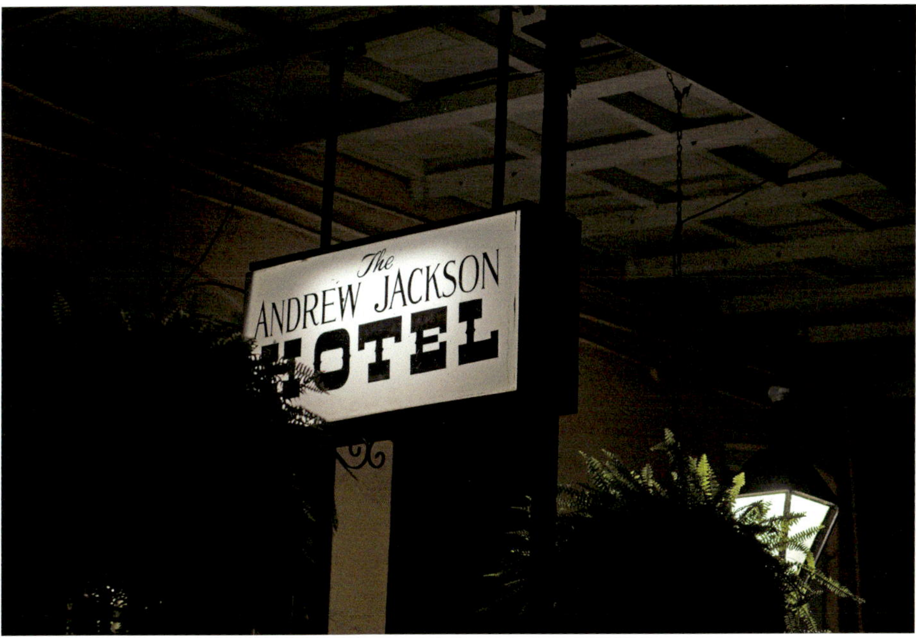

Under the cloak of night, the Andrew Jackson Hotel's sign glows, beckoning like a spectral guide for those wandering the haunted streets of the French Quarter.

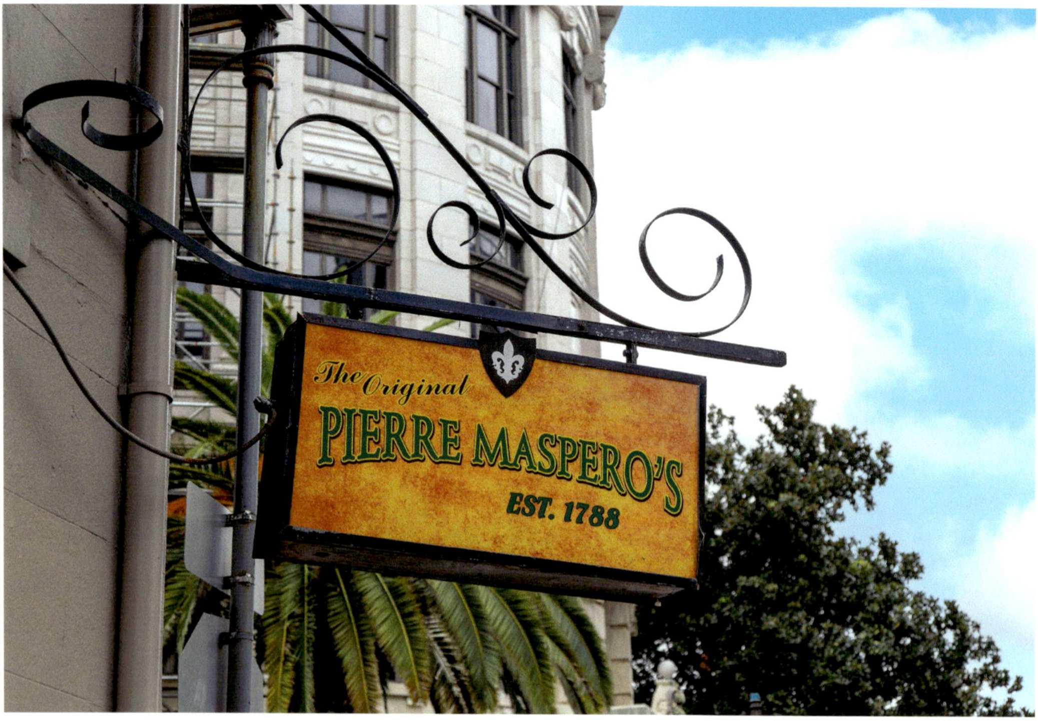

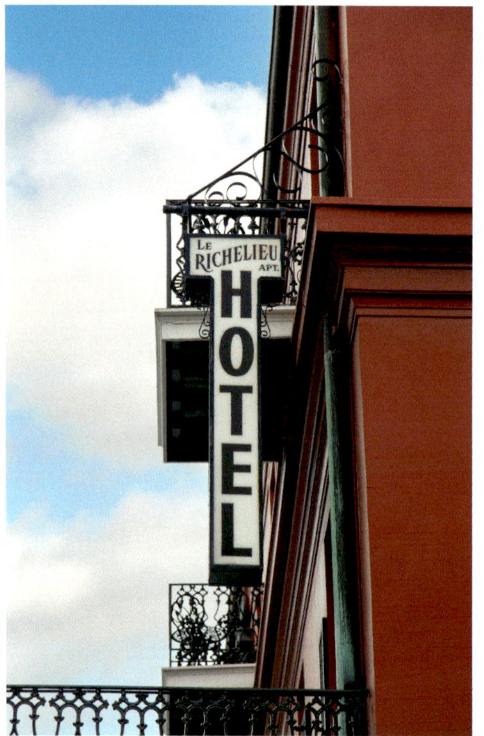

Above: Pierre Maspero's sign stands as a testament to time, inviting diners into a piece of New Orleans history, since 1788, where every meal is steeped in tradition.

Left: The Le Richelieu Hotel sign, a beacon of elegance, promises a stay wrapped in the luxurious history and charm of New Orleans' French Quarter.

7

Wheels of the Quarter

In the French Quarter, wheels are not just for transportation; they are a way of life, a spectacle, and a symbol of freedom. This chapter celebrates the bicycles and motorbikes that weave through the streets, adding to the dynamic rhythm of the neighborhood.

THE PEDAL PUSHERS: Bicycles are as common in the Quarter as the cobblestones they roll over. From the early morning commute of locals heading to work, their bikes laden with bags, to the late-night rides of those returning from a long shift, bicycles are a practical choice in this pedestrian-heavy area.

Leisurely Rides: Some pedal at a leisurely pace, enjoying the sights, sounds, and smells of the Quarter. These riders often stop to take photos, chat with locals, or simply soak in the atmosphere.

The Showmen: Then there are those who turn their ride into an art form. Popping wheelies, balancing on one wheel, or performing tricks, these cyclists turn the streets into their personal stage, drawing cheers and applause.

THE MOTORCYCLE MAVERICKS: Motorbikes, with their roar and gleam, add a different kind of energy to the Quarter. Often seen as symbols of freedom and rebellion, these riders are part of the Quarter's eclectic mix.

The Ghost Riders: Despite their rough and tumble appearance, these bikers are often friendly locals or enthusiasts who love the Quarter's vibe. They cruise through, their bikes gleaming under the streetlights.

Community and Culture: Motorcycle culture in the Quarter is not just about the ride; it is about community. Gatherings, rides, and events centered around bikes are common, showcasing a love for these machines and the freedom they represent.

A SYMBOL OF FREEDOM: Both bicycles and motorbikes in the French Quarter represent more than just modes of transport. They symbolize the freedom of movement, the joy of being part of this vibrant community, and the spirit of adventure. Whether it is the daily commute, a leisurely exploration, or a display of skill, these wheels contribute to the lively, ever-moving pulse of the Quarter.

CAPTURING THE MOTION: In this chapter, I have captured the dynamic energy of these riders. From the focused faces of cyclists navigating the crowded streets to the proud stance of bikers beside their gleaming machines, each photograph tells a story of movement, freedom, and the unique lifestyle of the French Quarter.

Through these images, I invite you to feel the wind in your hair, hear the hum of wheels on pavement, and experience the camaraderie and joy that these riders bring to the streets of New Orleans' oldest neighborhood.

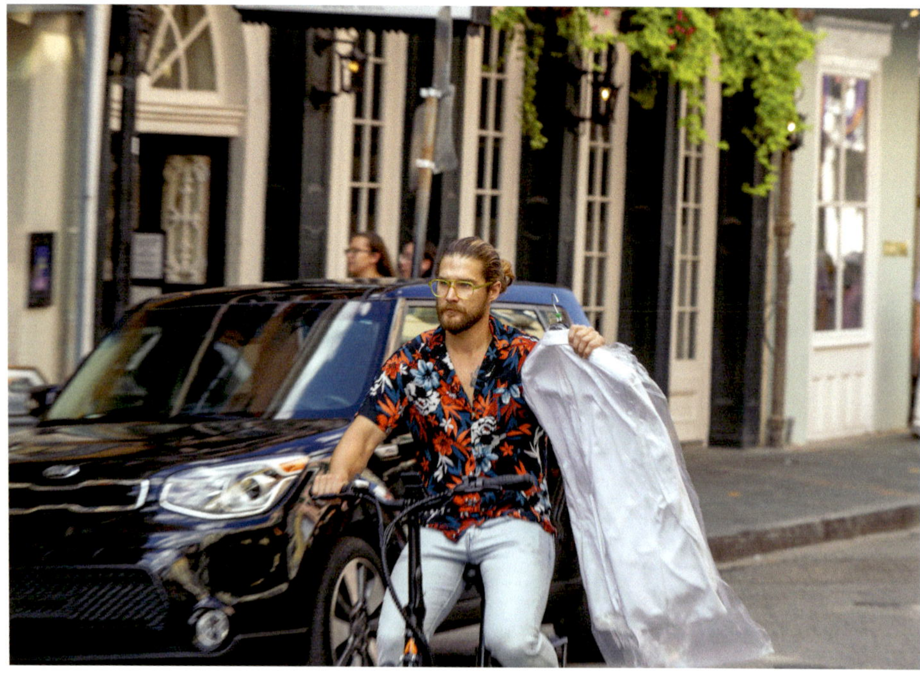

Pedaling through the French Quarter, he holds his dry cleaning aloft, the garments billowing like ghostly apparitions in the wind, a whimsical sight on two wheels.

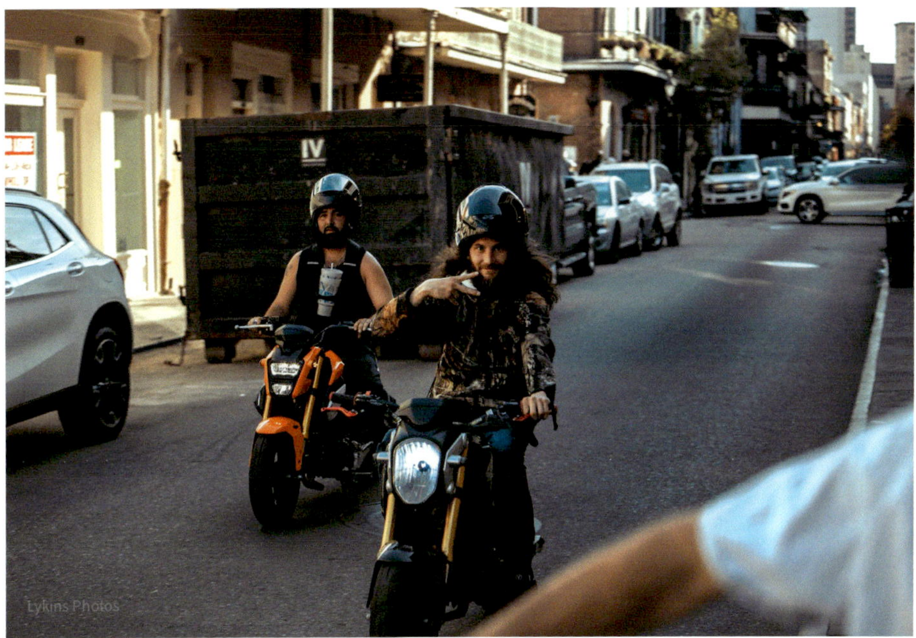

Two guys on minibikes zip through the French Quarter, their laughter blending with the hum of engines, adding a modern beat to the historic streets.

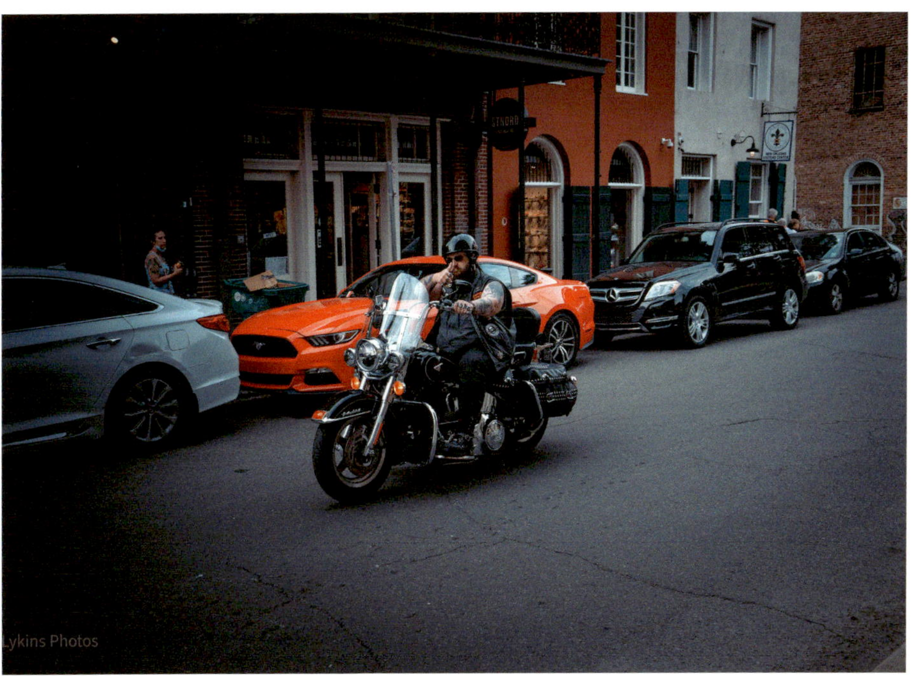

Caught in the moment, a burly biker flashes a thumbs-up, his expression as solemn as the open road, embodying the spirit of freedom on two wheels.

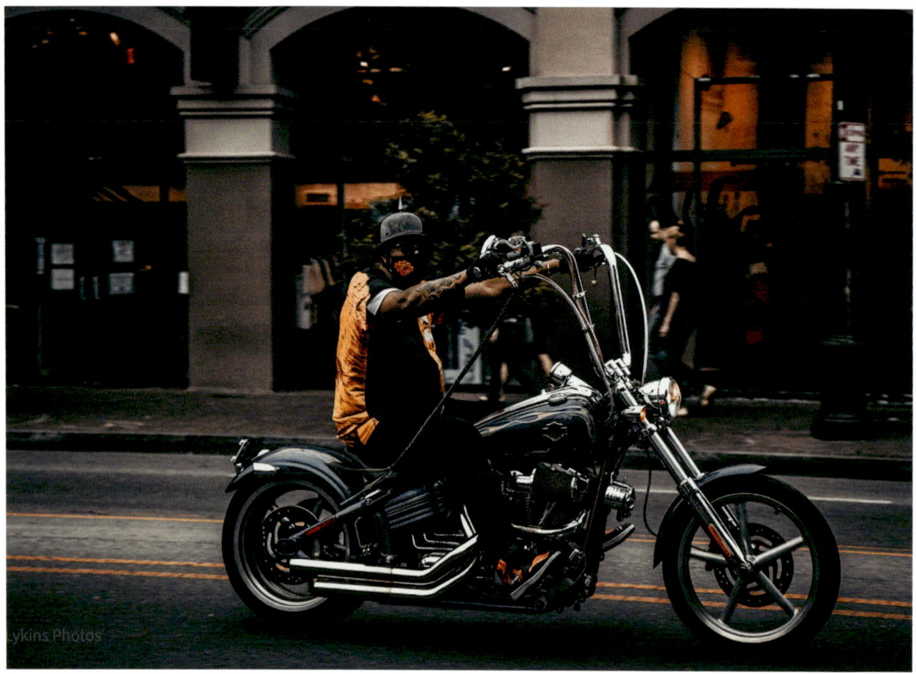

A biker with a bandana covering his nose and mouth, its pattern obscured by the shadow from his dark sunglasses. His eyes are hidden, adding an air of anonymity and cool mystery.

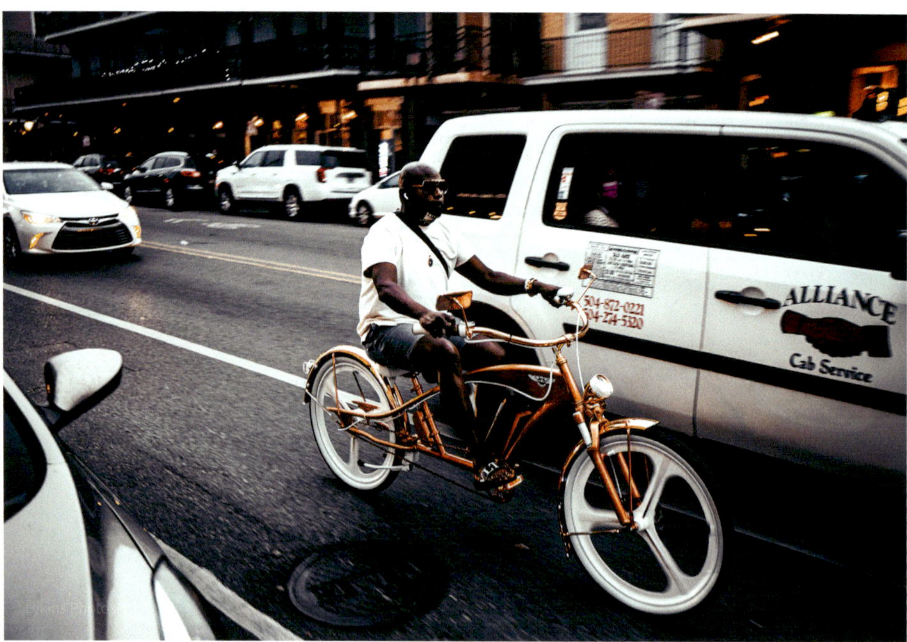

A guy on a sleek copper-colored bicycle expertly weaves through the bustling traffic of the Quarter, his figure a blur of motion amidst the vibrant urban backdrop.

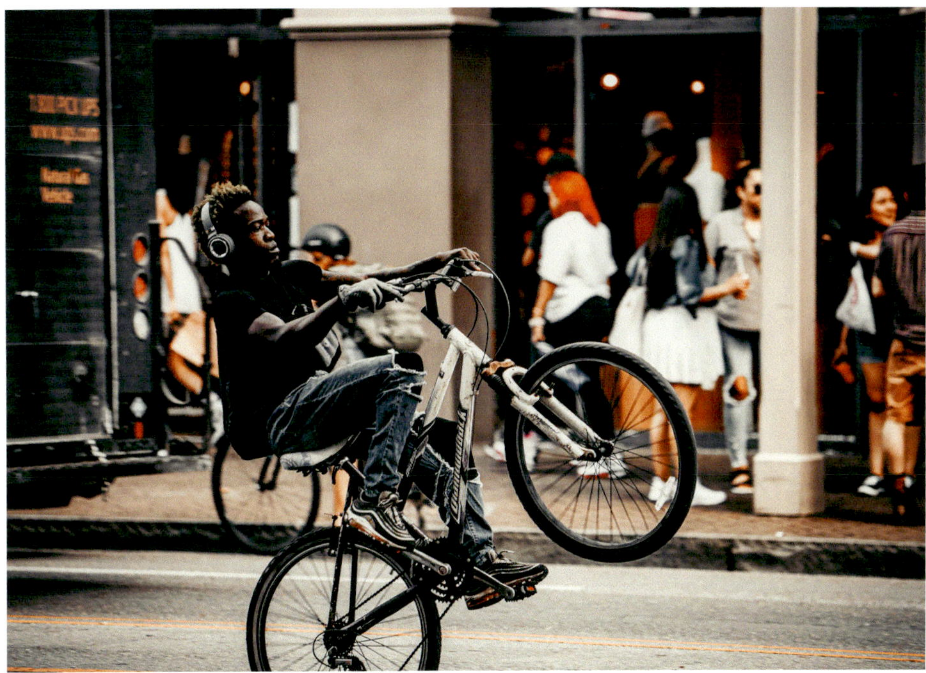

A bicyclist, lost in the rhythm of his music through headphones, effortlessly pops wheelies, his balance and joy evident in the motion.

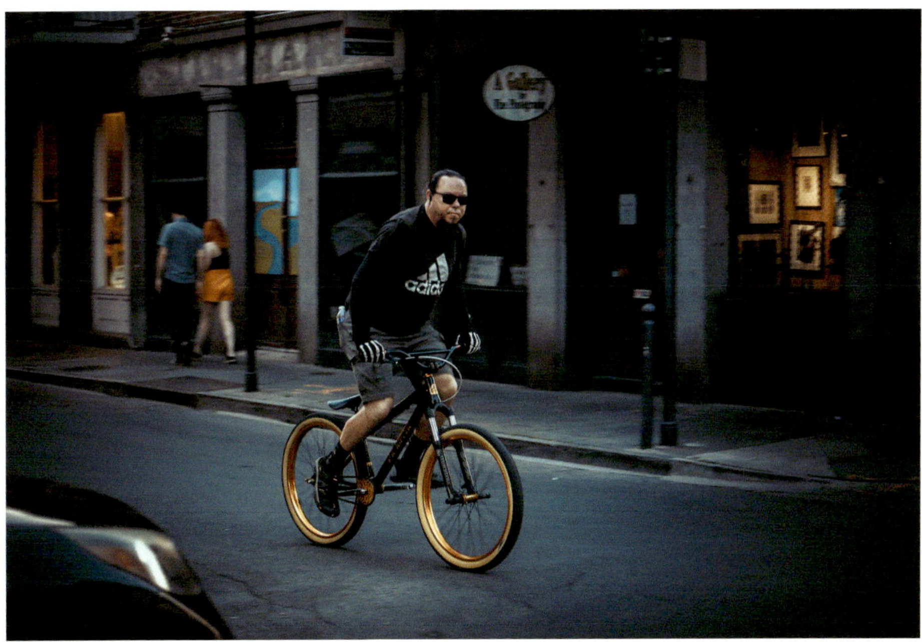

A cyclist on a bike with ornate, brass-framed wheels and gears reminiscent of the Steampunk-era glides silently through the mist of the early morning streets.

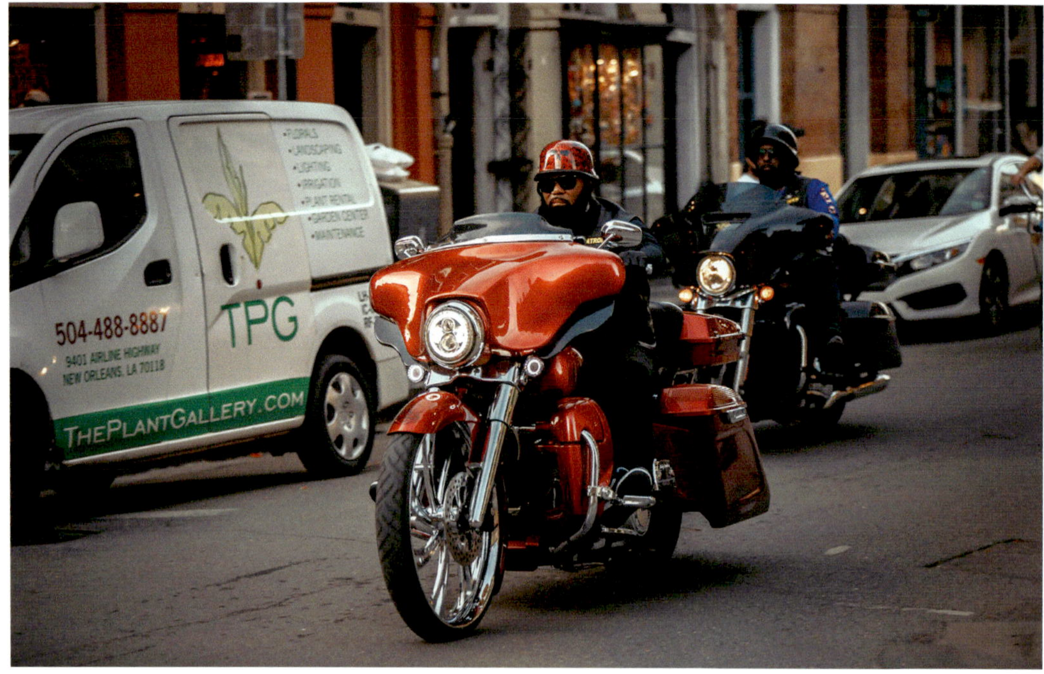

Ultimate biker, streets conquered, freedom on every turn.

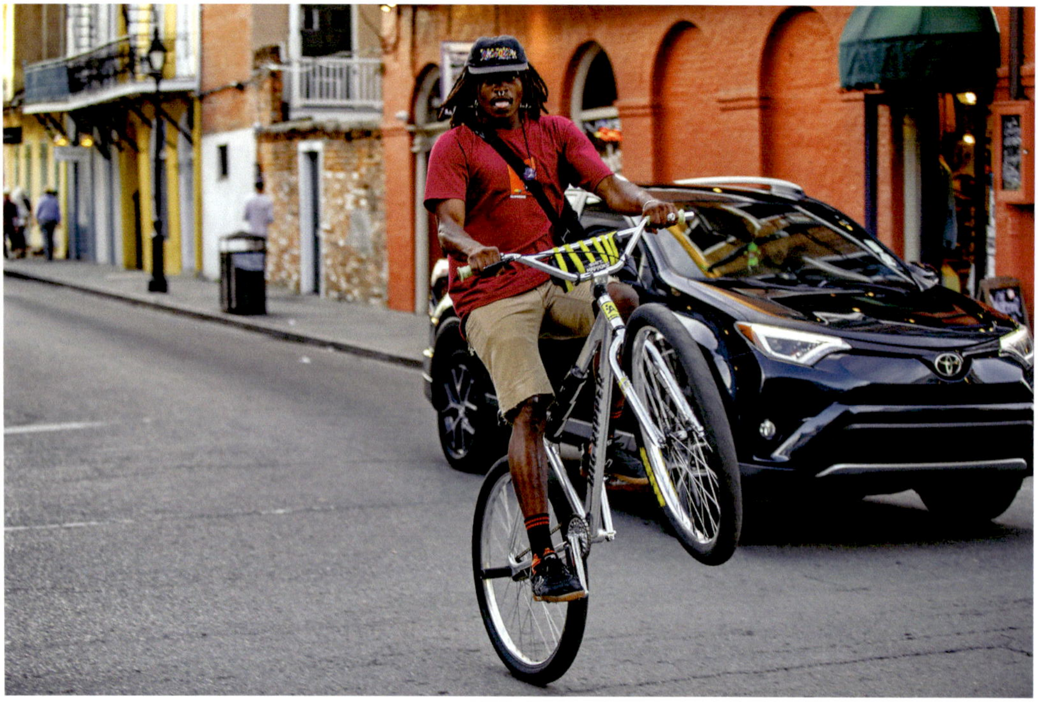

Caught in the act: Pierced cyclist flaunts his wheelie prowess for the camera.

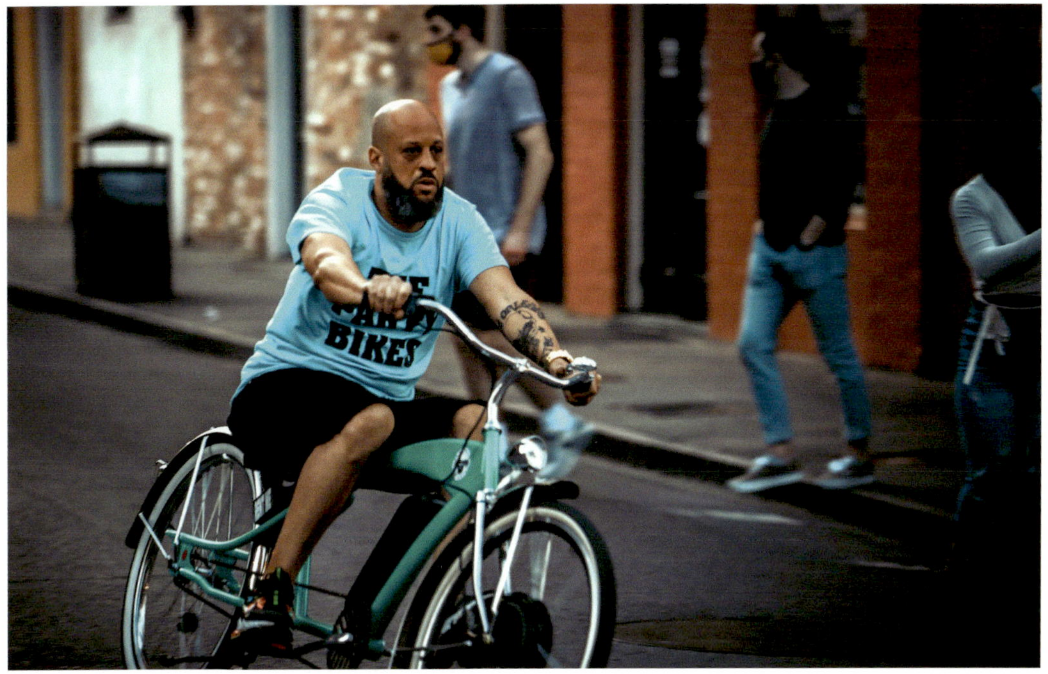

Street Blur: This cyclist's speed turns him into a fleeting urban shadow.

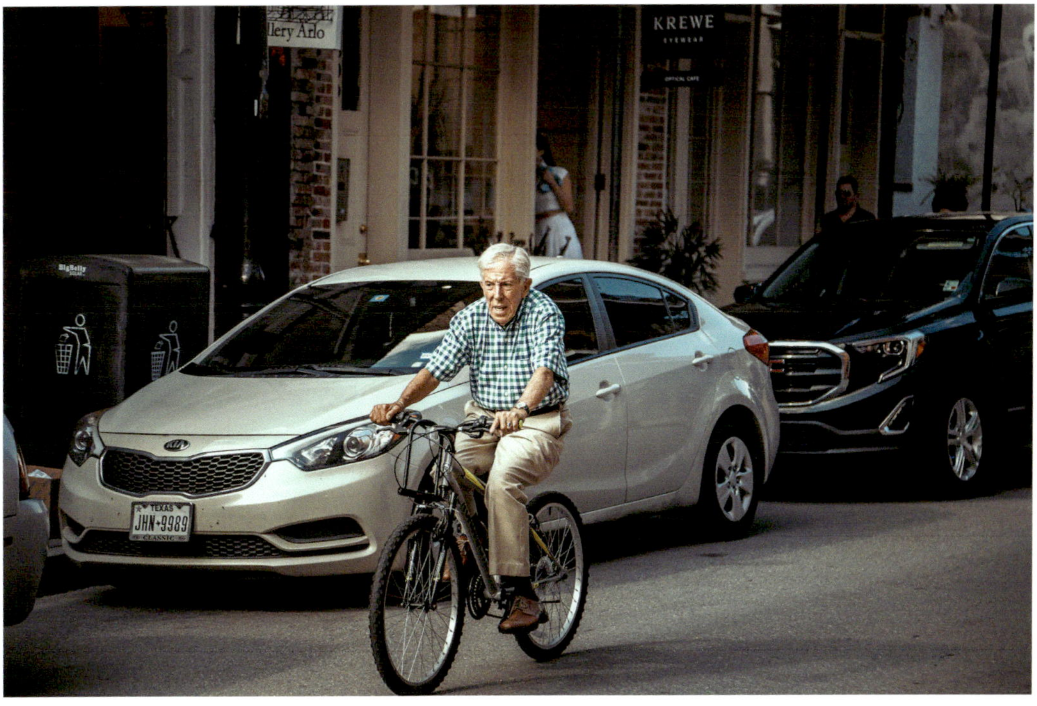

Pedaling Through Time: An elderly gentleman's joyful journey in the Quarter.

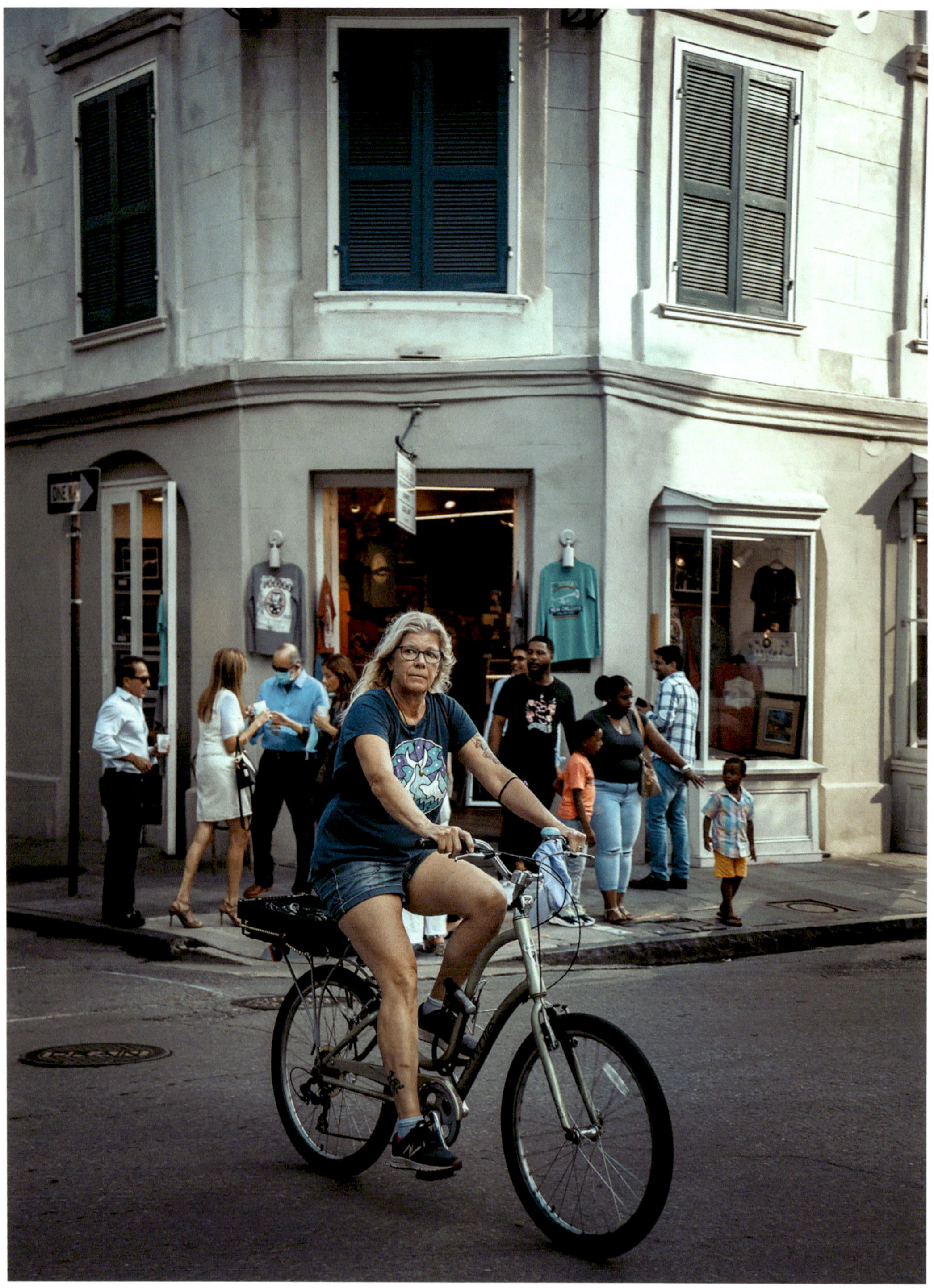

Captured a candid shot of a cyclist, though her expression suggests she might not have been thrilled about the photo.

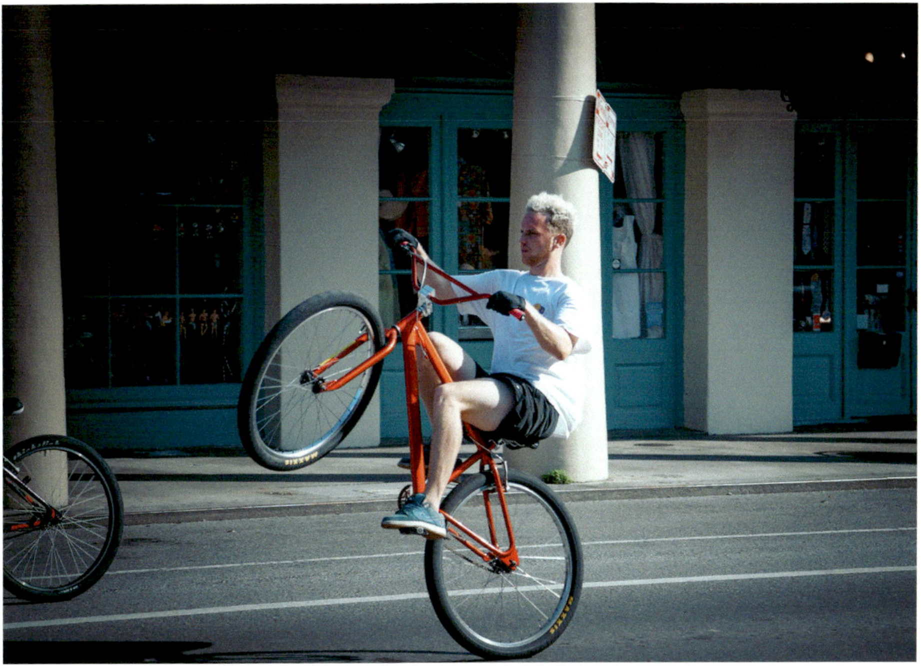

He popped a wheelie with the ease of a seasoned rider, effortlessly defying gravity.

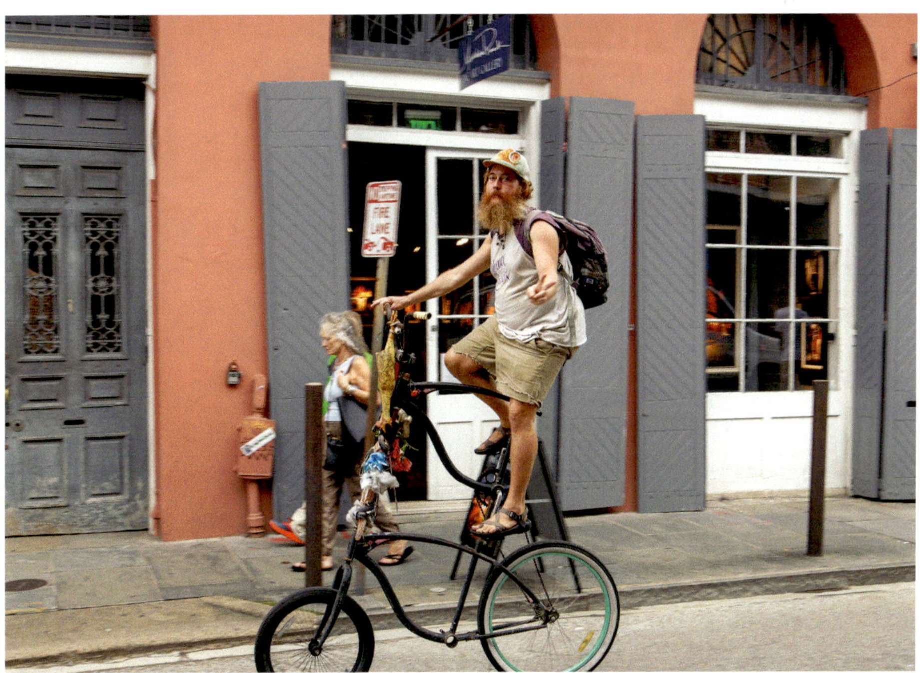

He was riding the bike of all bikes, a frame atop another, pointing down to the camera from the sky.

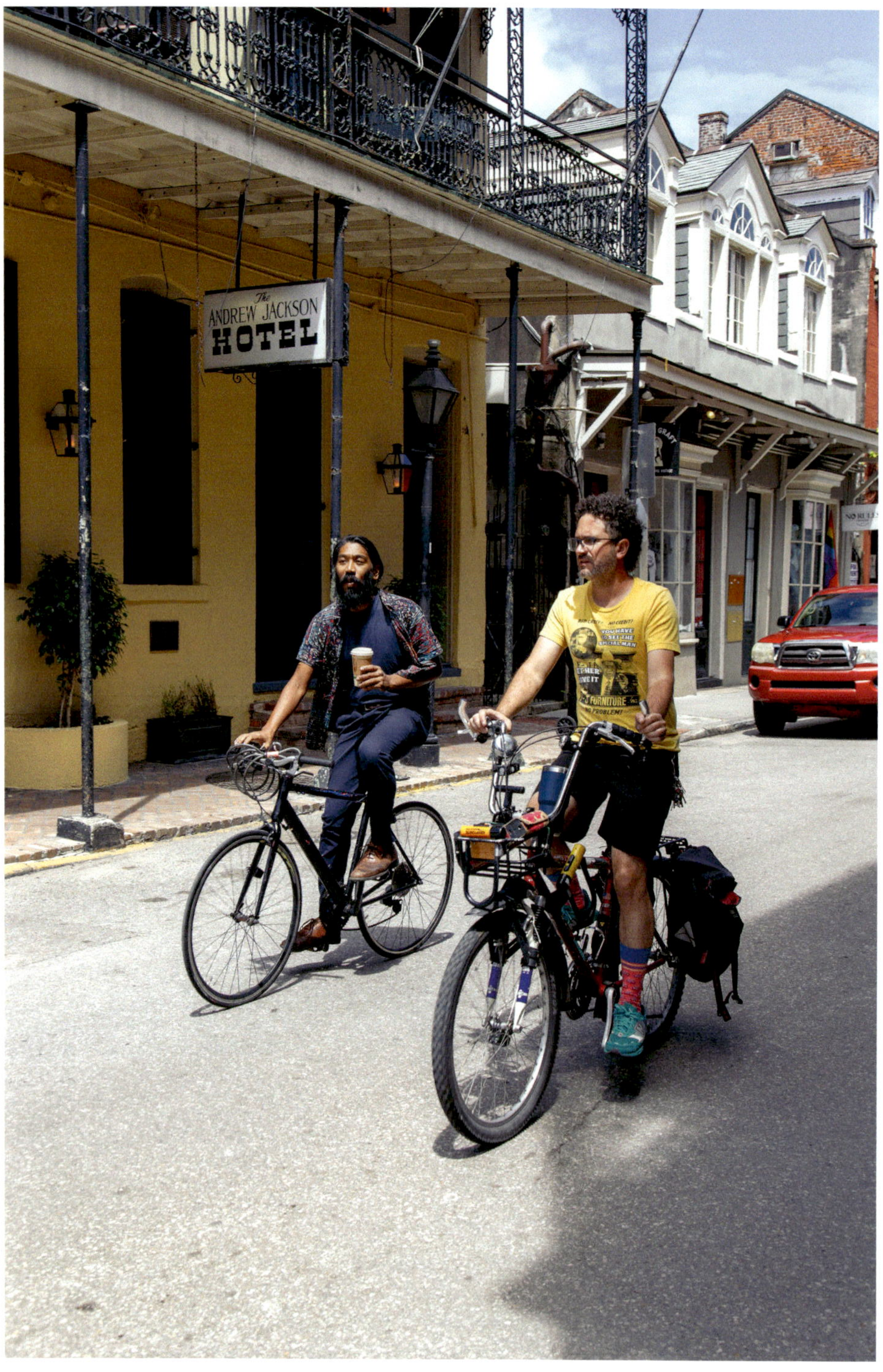

Two cyclists, worlds apart in their journey—one with a trek across the nation in his eyes, the other just a short ride to the end of the street.

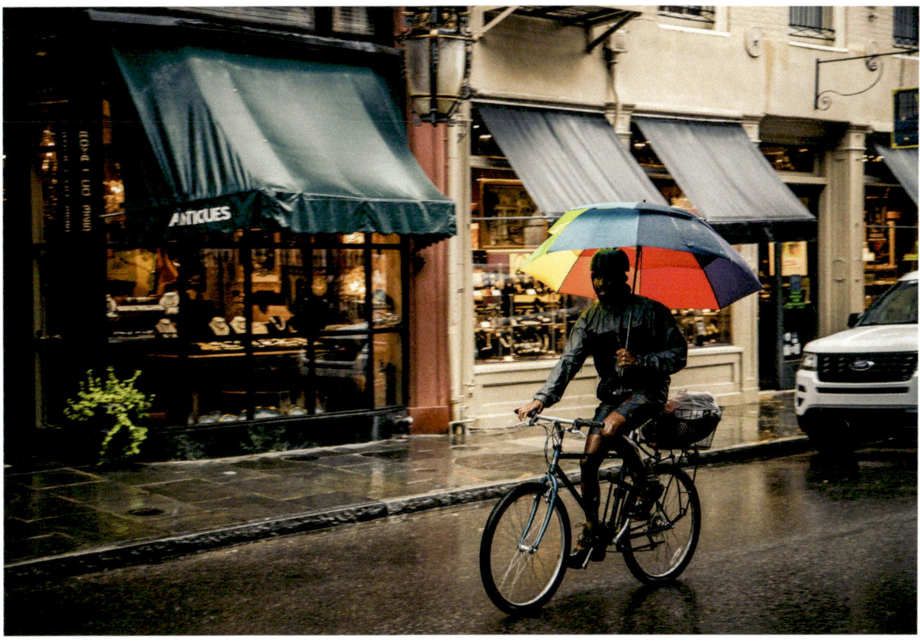

A lone cyclist braves the rain, one hand gripping the handlebars for balance, the other clutching an umbrella in a valiant effort to stay dry.

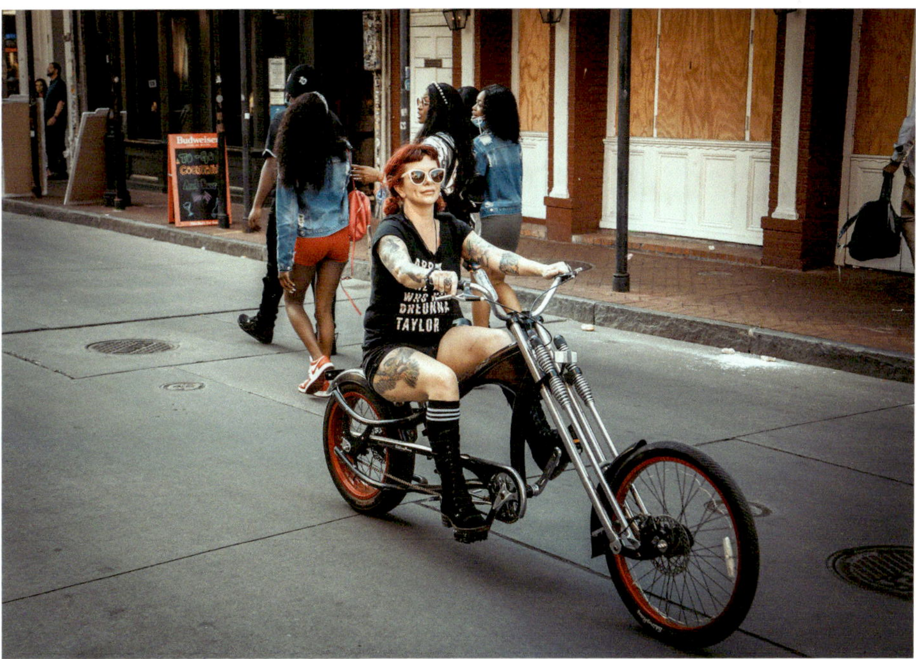

A stylish woman glides past on a chopper bike through the Quarter, her lips curving into what might be called a smirk, a mix of cool and playful acknowledgment.

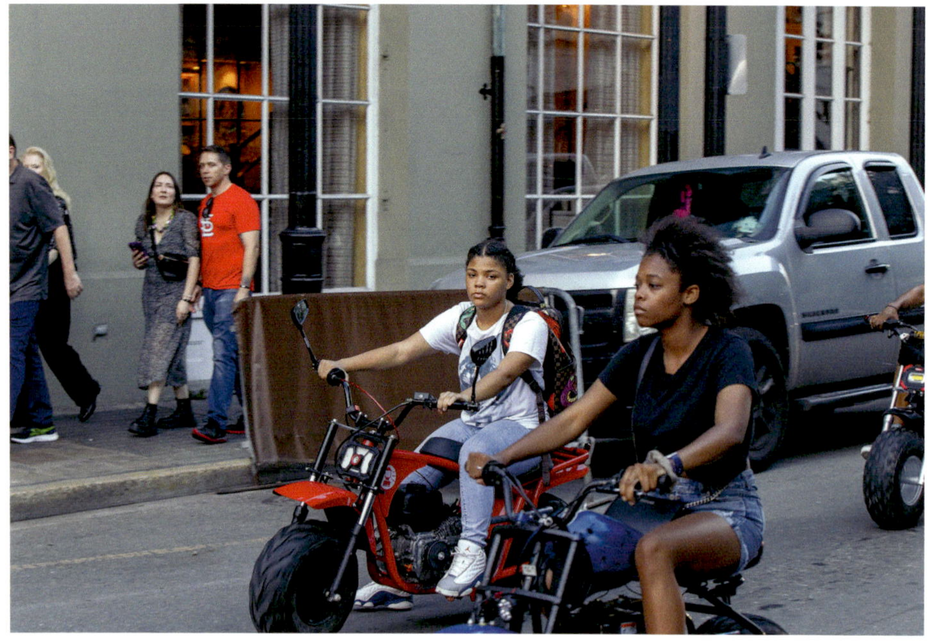

Two young girls, with serious, determined expressions, navigate their minibikes through the streets, their focus making them seem older than their years.

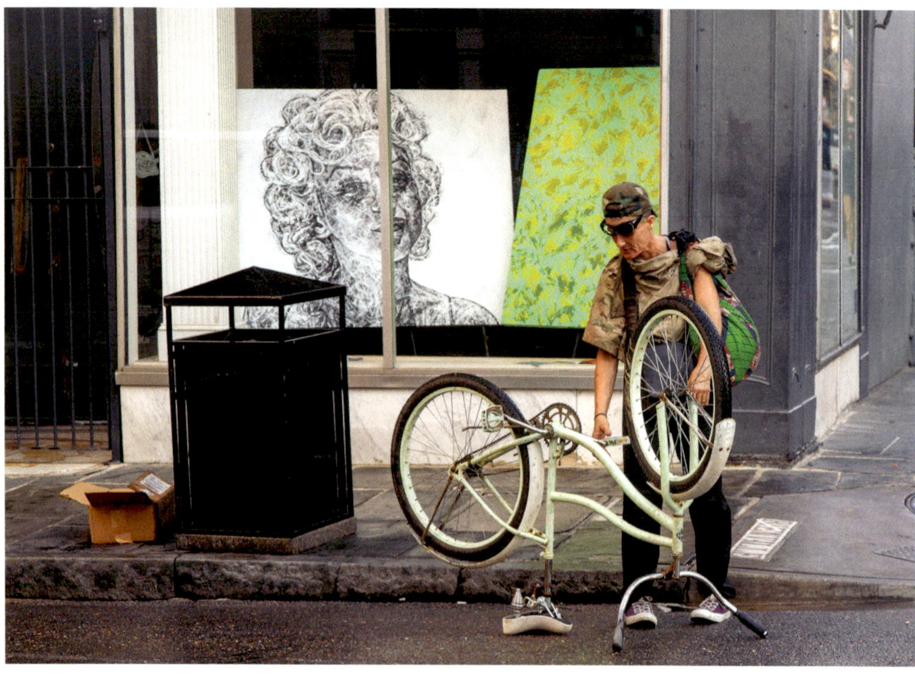

A man stands beside his overturned bike, his hands darkened with grease as he meticulously adjusts the chain, a scene familiar to anyone who's known the quirks of bicycle maintenance.

8

Echoes in Bronze and Stone

The French Quarter is not just a place of living history; it is also a gallery of statues that stand as silent sentinels, each telling a story of the past. This chapter explores these monuments, their significance, and the lessons they impart.

A Pantheon of Figures: From the heroic Joan of Arc, whose statue stands proudly at the Decatur and North Peters split, to the contemplative figure of Old Man River, these statues are more than mere decorations. They are embodiments of the city's history, culture, and the complex tapestry of human experience.

Founders and Explorers: Statues like that of Bienville, one of New Orleans' founders, remind us of the city's beginnings, the dreams, and the challenges faced by those who first settled this land.

Historical Figures: The statues also include revolutionaries and figures like Benito Juarez, whose presence in the Quarter sparks both admiration and controversy, reflecting the multifaceted nature of history.

Reminders of the Past: Each statue serves as a reminder, not just of glory but of the complexities of human history. They stand as:

Educational Tools: Teaching us about the struggles, achievements, and sometimes the mistakes of those who came before us.

Points of Reflection: They encourage us to reflect on our own times, considering how we might be remembered in the future.

Cultural Symbols: Representing not just individuals but the values, conflicts, and aspirations of their eras.

The Controversy and Conversation: The presence of these statues often sparks debate. Some argue for their removal due to the controversial actions of the figures they depict, while others believe they should remain as educational tools, reminders of both the good and the bad in our history.

A Living History Lesson: In this chapter, I have captured these statues not just as they stand but as they interact with the life around them. People pose with them, children climb on them, and tourists take selfies, all engaging with history in their own way. These interactions are as much a part of the Quarter's story as the statues themselves.

Through these photographs, I invite you to see these statues not just as static figures but as dynamic elements of the French Quarter's narrative. They challenge us to think, to learn, and to remember why we are here, in this place, at this time, shaped by the past but always moving forward.

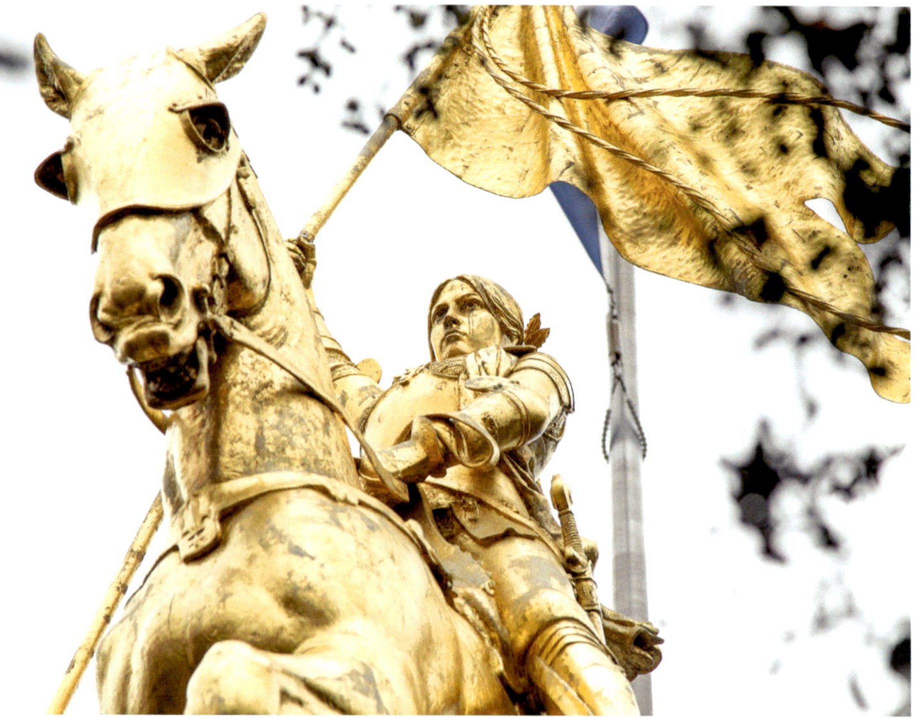

Joan of Arc, born *circa* 1412 in Domrémy, France, became a pivotal figure in the Hundred Years' War. Hearing divine voices, she led French forces to several victories against the English, famously aiding in the coronation of Charles VII. Captured by the Burgundians in 1430, she was sold to the English, tried for heresy, and burned at the stake in 1431. Rehabilitated posthumously, she remains an emblem of French nationalism and Catholic faith.

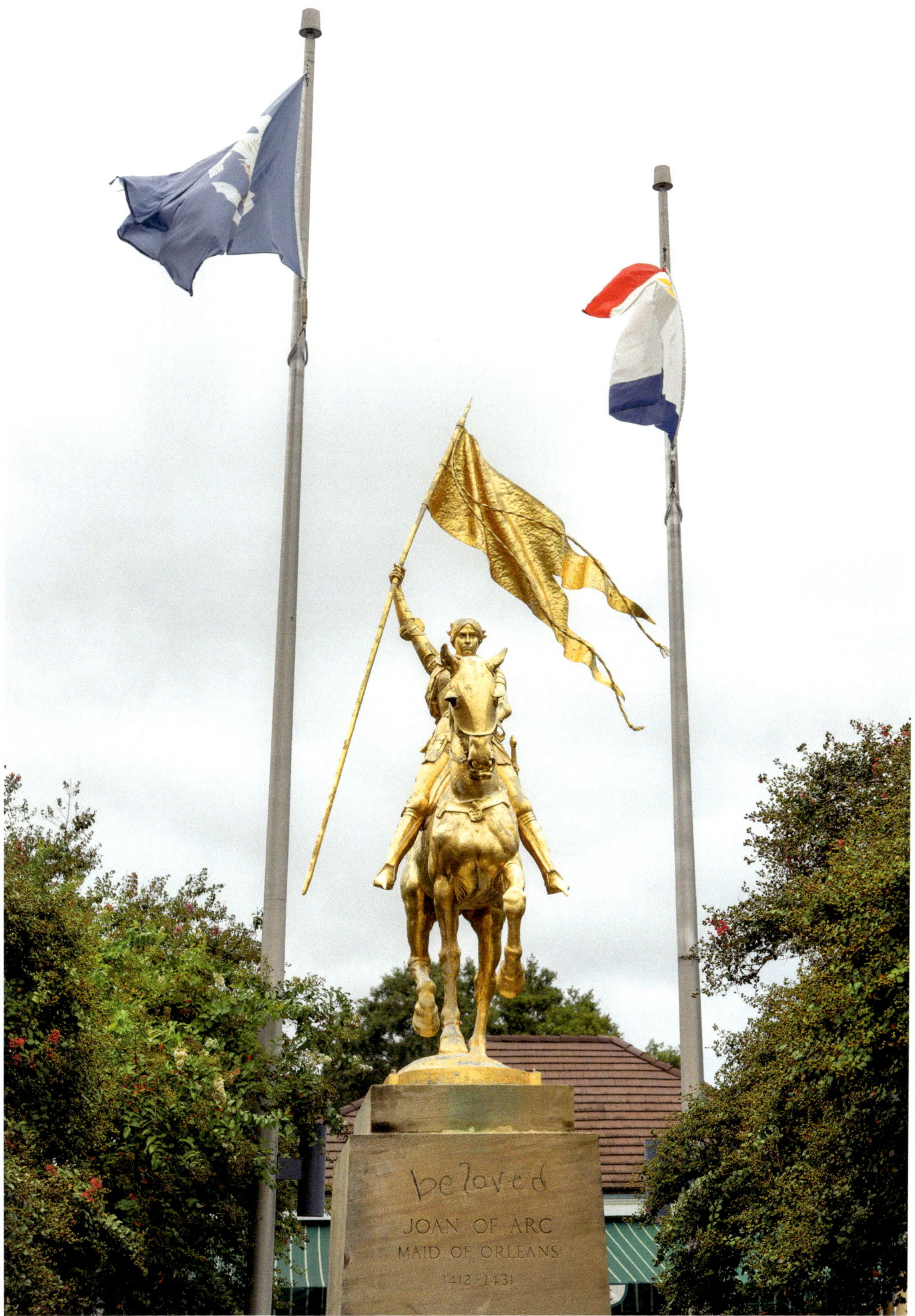
beloved
JOAN OF ARC
MAID OF ORLEANS
1412 - 1431

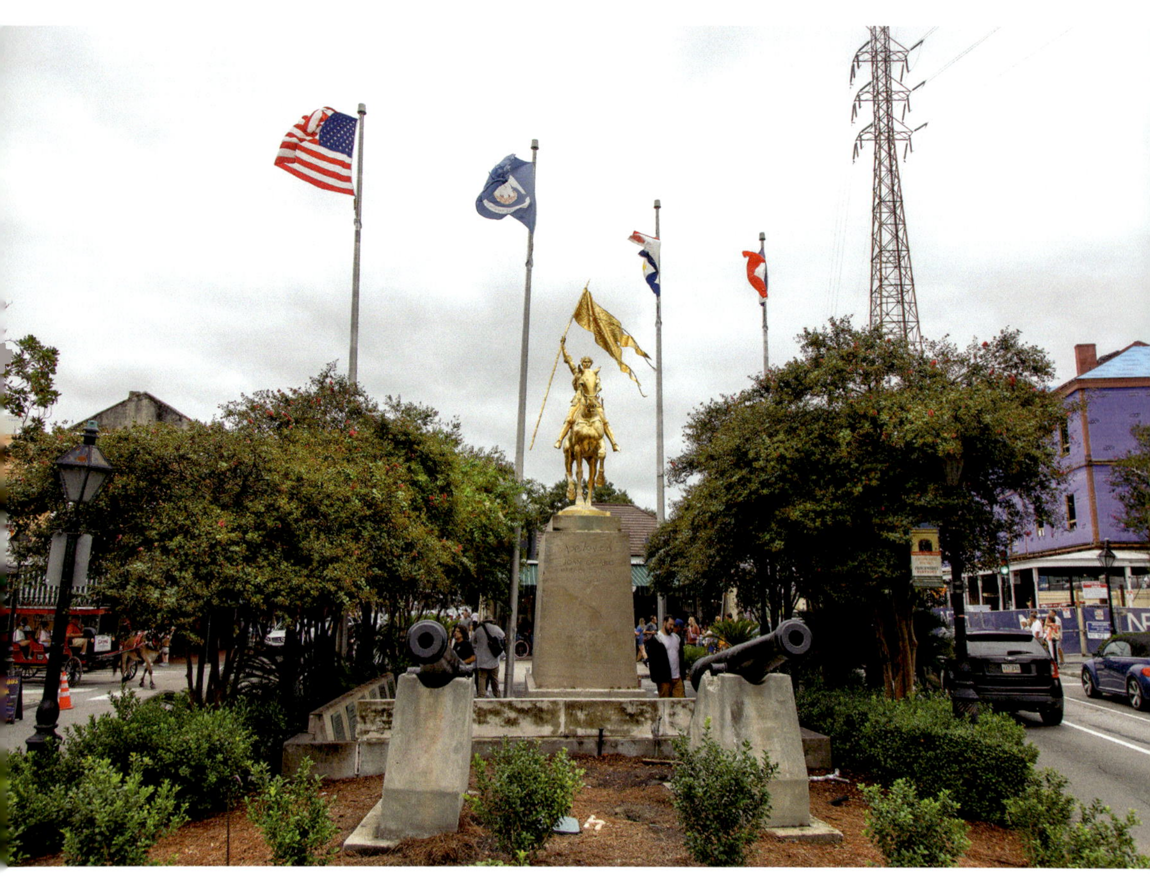

Opposite page: The French Quarter home boasts two balconies festooned with an array of statues. Each figure, from serene angels with outstretched wings to a sad giraffe, contributes to a gallery of stone and metal art. These sculptures, varying in size and style, watch over the street below, their expressions ranging from contemplative to playful, weaving a tapestry of history and culture into the home's facade.

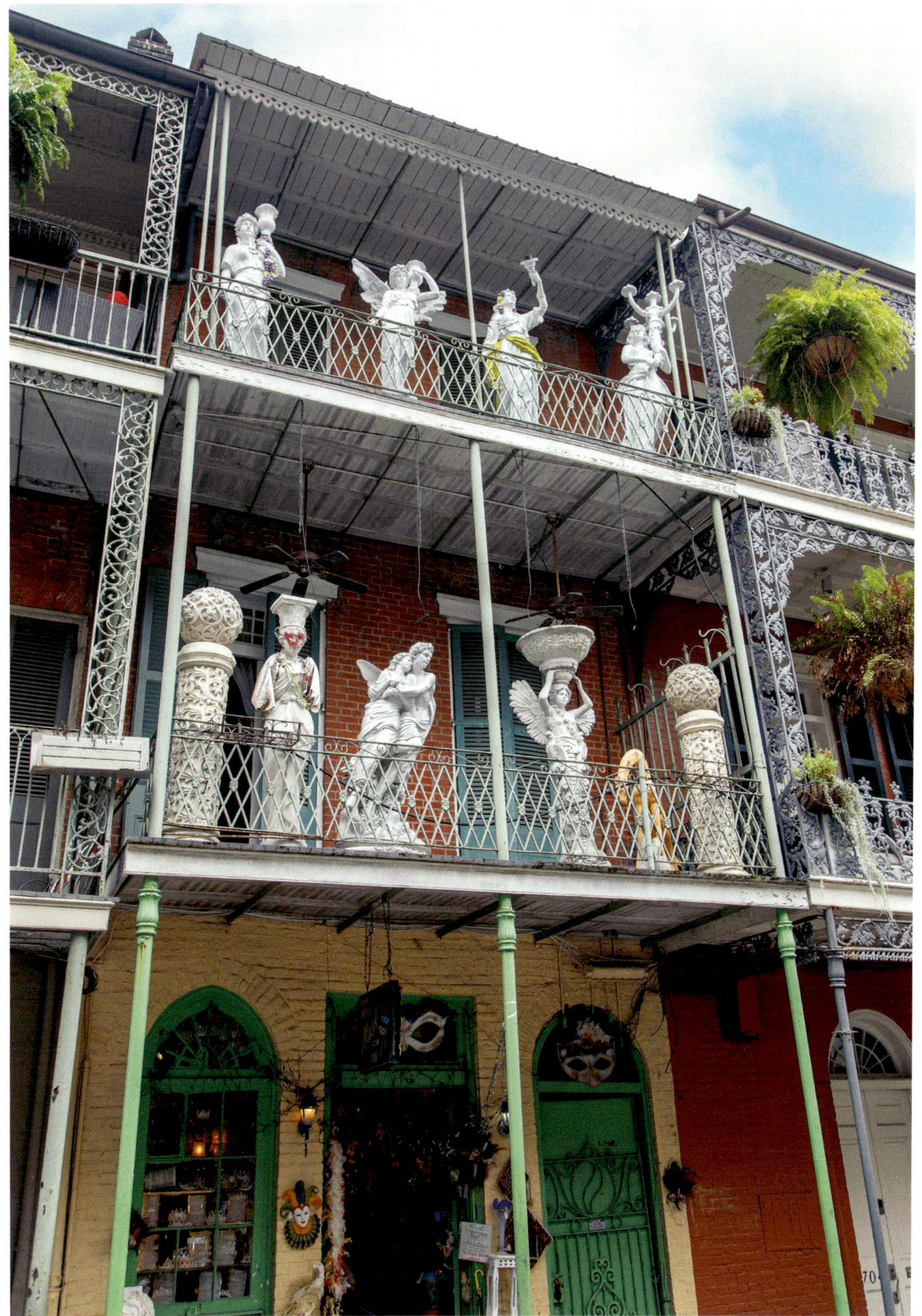

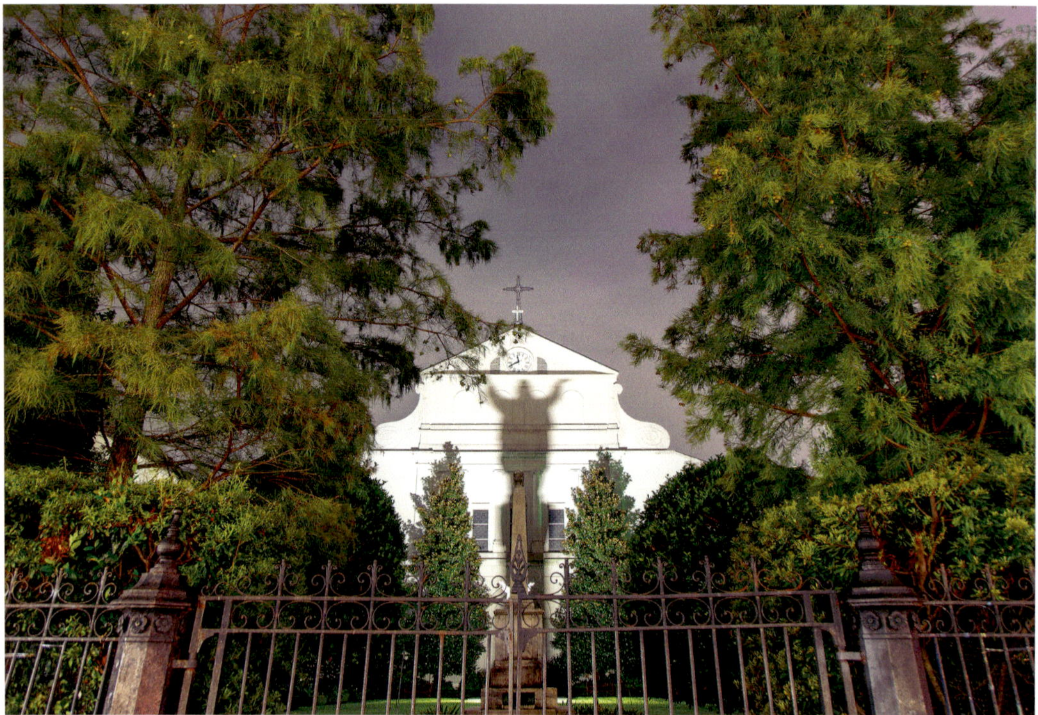

The shadow cast by the statue of Jesus with outstretched arms onto the cathedral's back wall is a dynamic interplay of light and darkness. It forms an ethereal silhouette, the elongated arms of the figure reaching towards the heavens, as if in a perpetual act of divine embrace or supplication. This shadow, soft at the edges, breathes life into the stone, suggesting movement and presence, altering the solemnity of the cathedral with its transient existence.

Opposite page: The Monument to the Immigrant in New Orleans, dedicated in 1995, commemorates the diverse immigrants who shaped the city. Located along the Mississippi River, it honors those escaping persecution and seeking new lives. Designed by Franco Alessandrini, it features a bronze plaque with the inscription in multiple languages, symbolizing unity and the contributions of immigrants to the vibrant cultural mosaic of New Orleans.

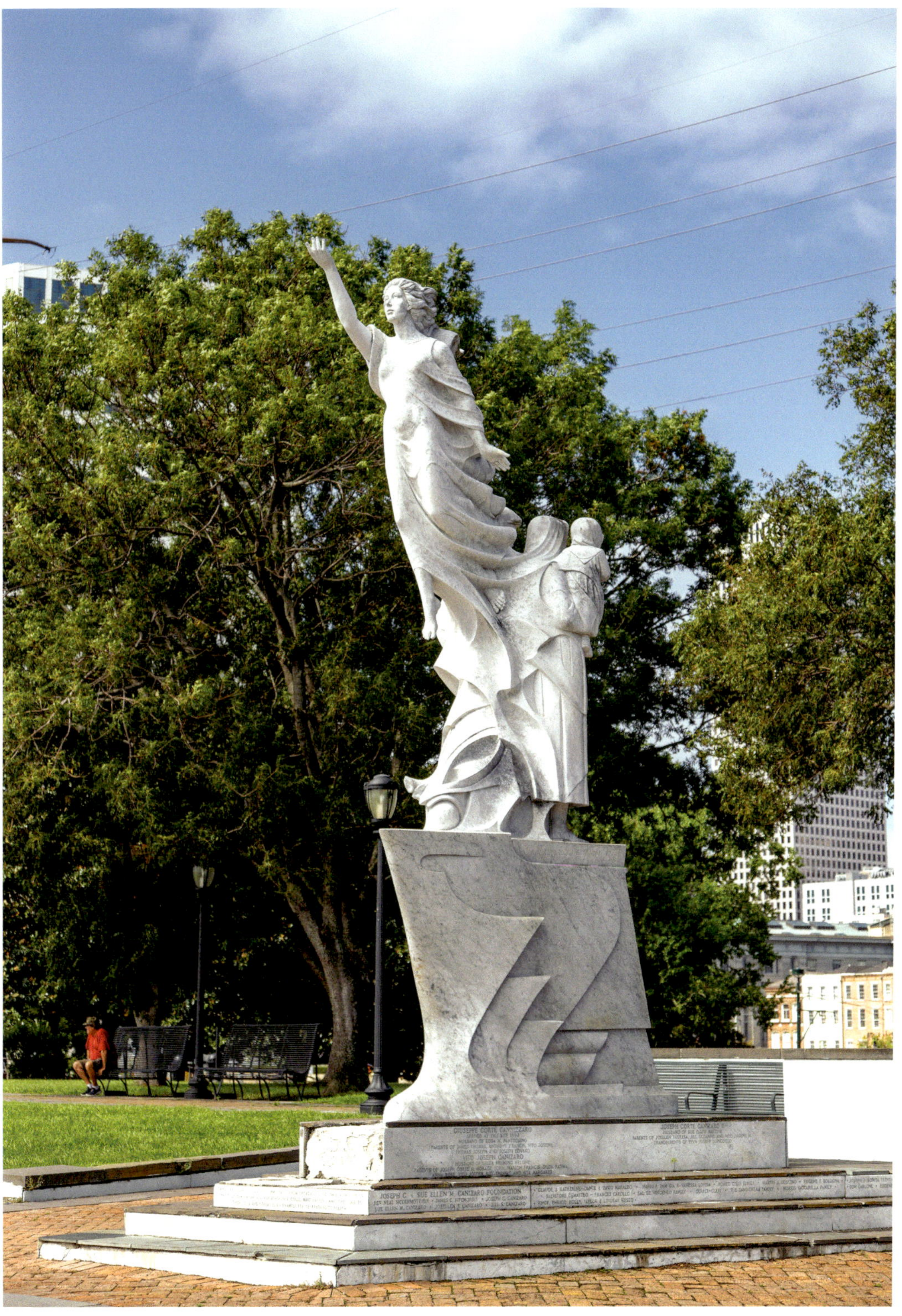
VITO JOSEPH CANIZARO
JOSEPH C. & SUE ELLEN M. CANIZARO FOUNDATION

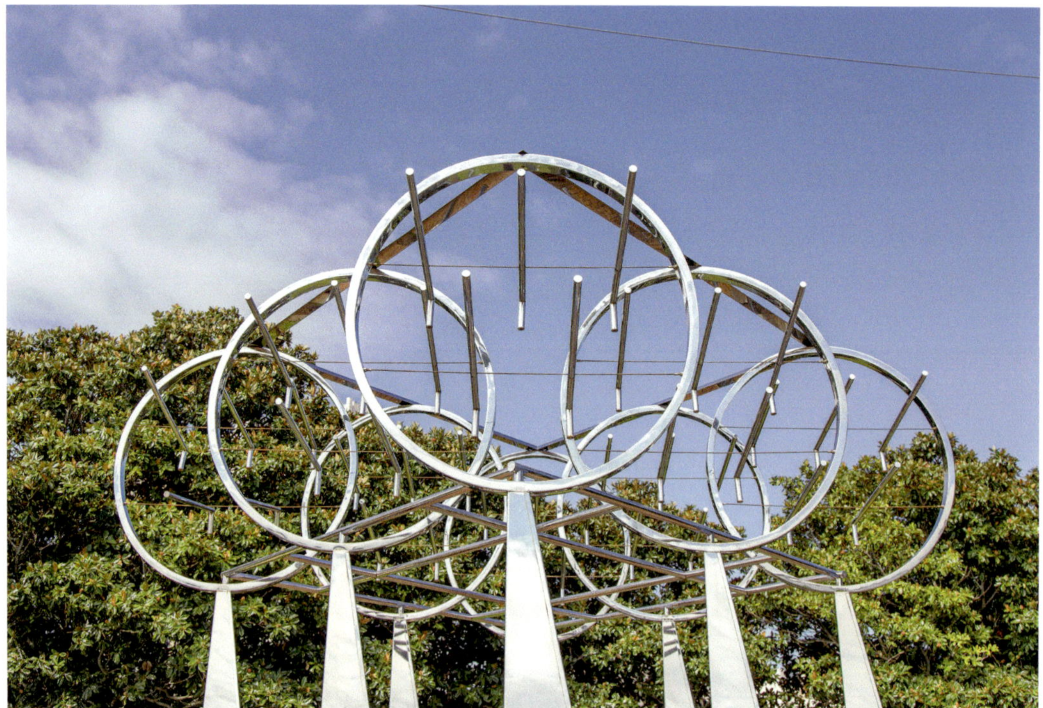

The "Ocean Song" sculpture in New Orleans, situated along the Mississippi River in the French Quarter, was created by artist Patrick Fagerberg. Installed in the late 1990s, this stainless-steel piece is notable for its fluid, wave-like design that reflects the river's movement, embodying the city's musical heritage and its connection to the waterway.

Opposite page: The statue of Jean-Baptiste Le Moyne, Sieur de Bienville, in New Orleans' French Quarter, was erected in 1955. Designed by sculptor Francisco Castro Leal, it stands in front of the Bienville Monument on Decatur Street. Bienville, the city's founder, is depicted in explorer's attire, symbolizing his role in establishing New Orleans in 1718. The monument honors his foundational contributions to the city, reflecting his vision for a French colonial settlement along the Mississippi River.

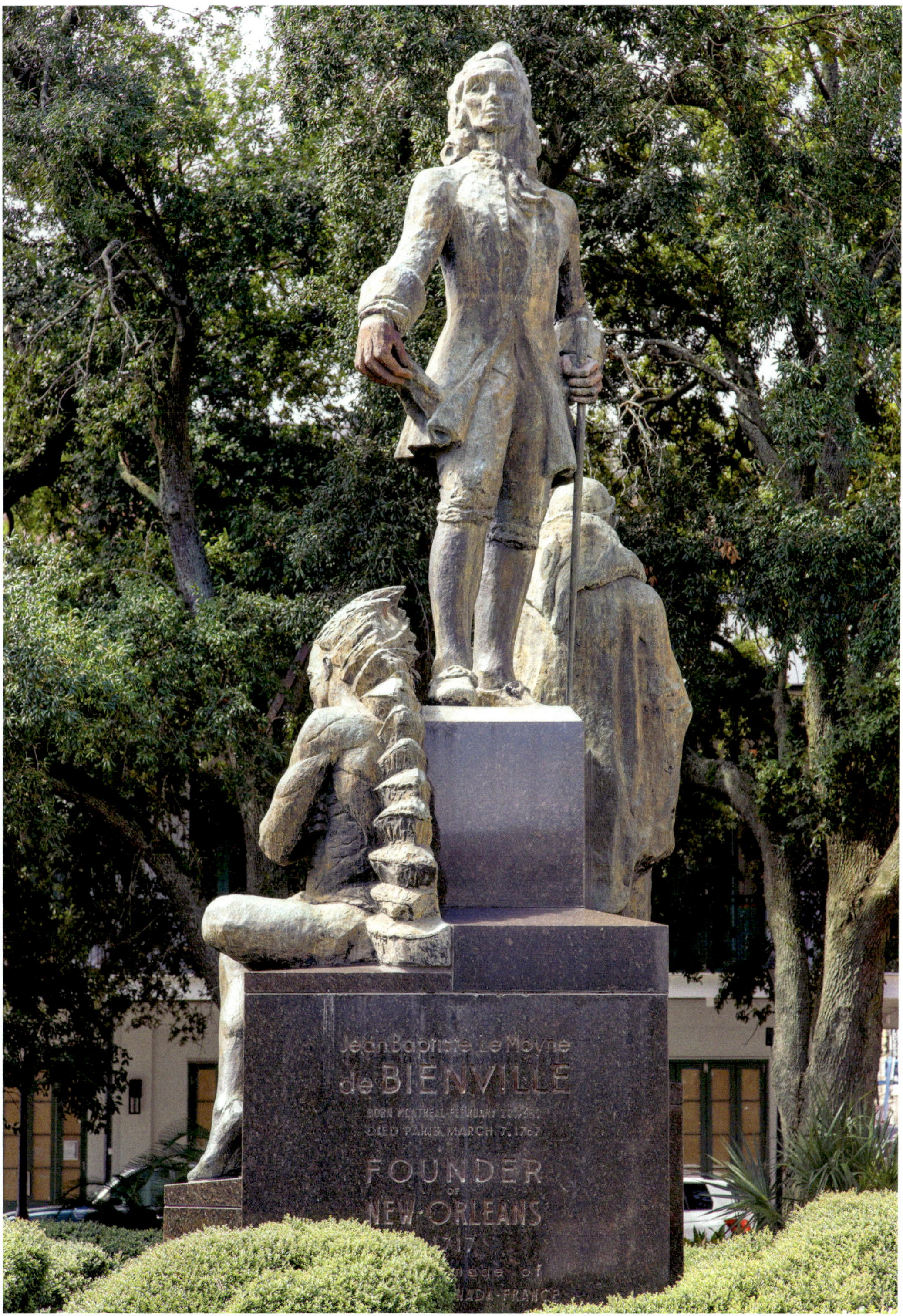
Jean Baptiste Le Moyne
de BIENVILLE
FOUNDER
OF
NEW·ORLEANS

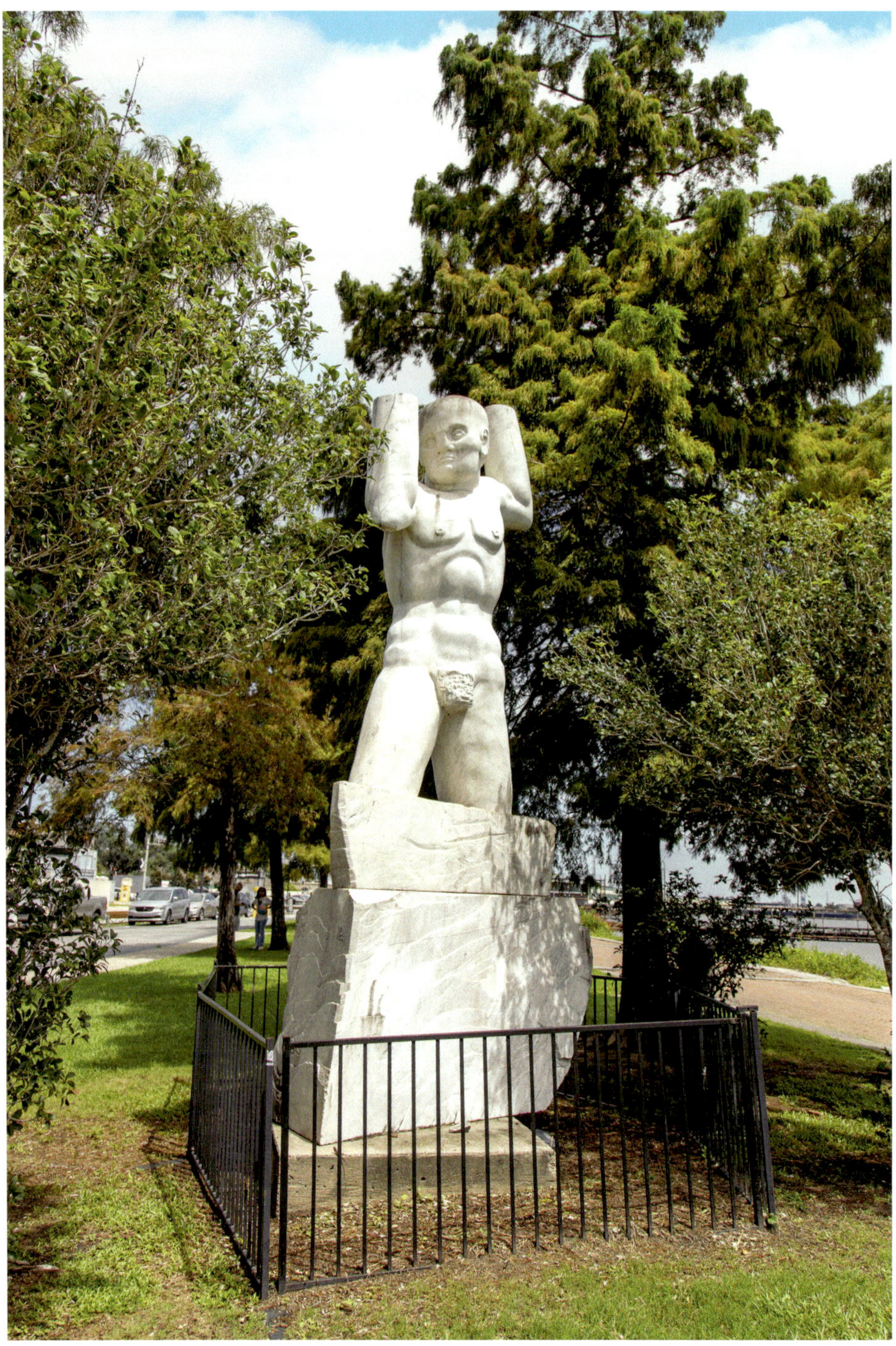

"Old Man River," also known as "The Riverman," located on the Moon Walk along the Mississippi River in the French Quarter. Created by Enrique Alférez in 1958, this white sculpture symbolizes the river's spirit, portraying an old man with a fish, representing the river's bounty and the city's deep connection to the waterway. The artwork has become an iconic symbol of New Orleans' relationship with the Mississippi.

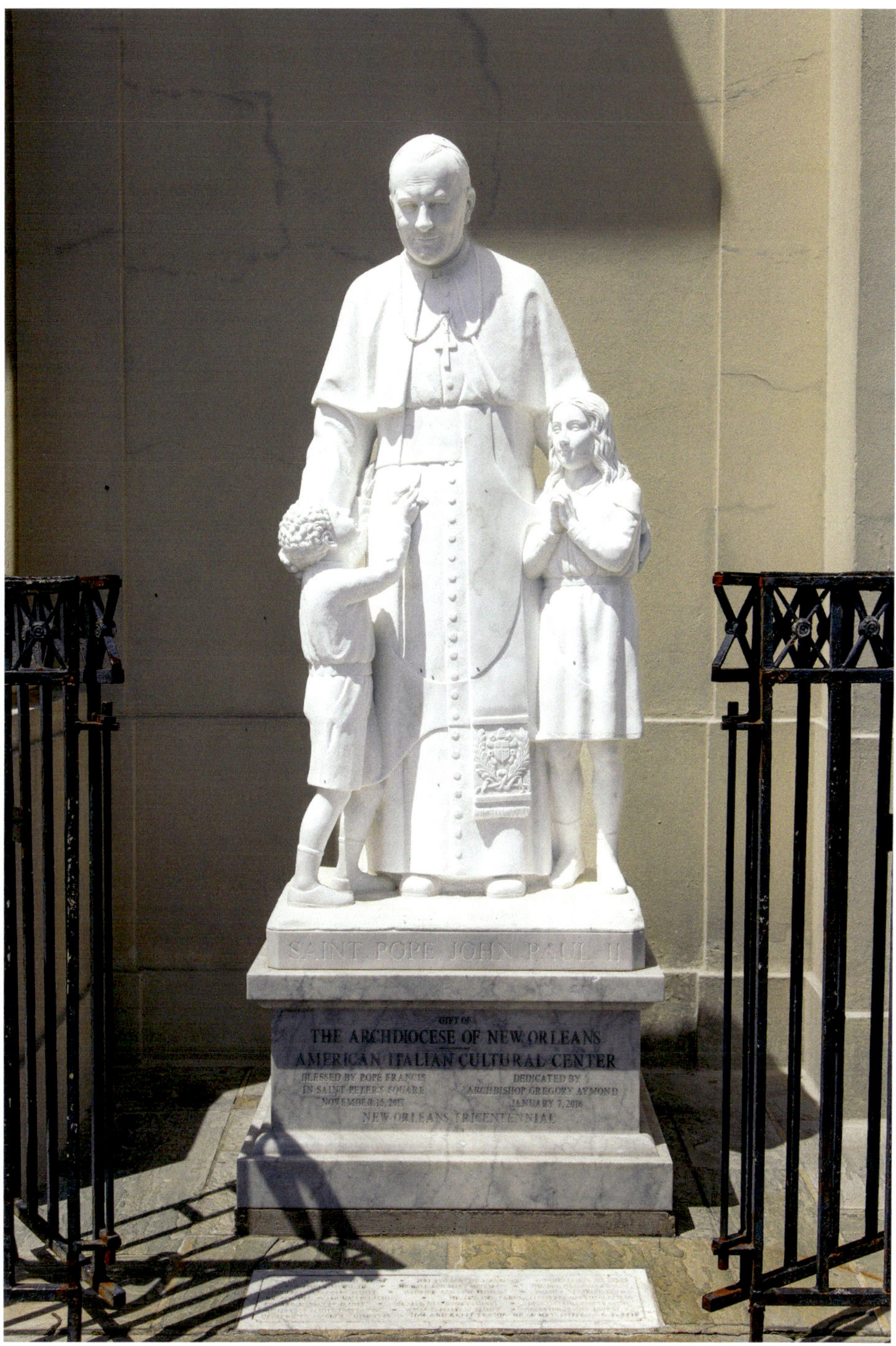

Saint Pope John Paul II.

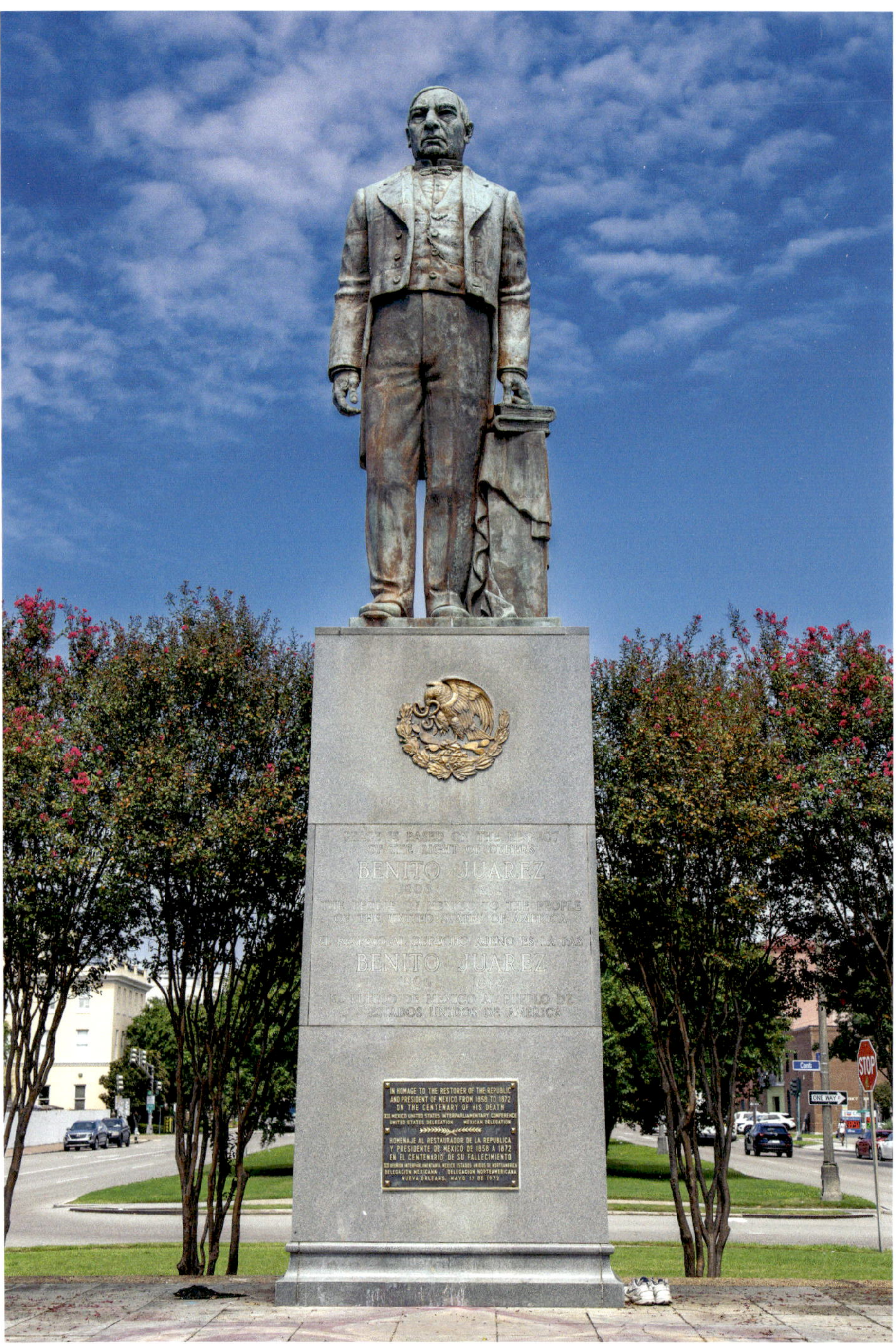

This bronze statue was donated by the Consulate General of Mexico to honor Juárez, a significant figure in Mexican history. Installed to celebrate Juárez's legacy, it serves as a cultural landmark, highlighting the contributions of Juárez to Mexican independence, reform, and his enduring impact on the relationship between Mexico and New Orleans.